THE

BARB OF TIME

The
Barb of Time

ON THE UNITY OF

EZRA POUND'S CANTOS

DANIEL D. PEARLMAN

New York · OXFORD UNIVERSITY PRESS · 1969

Copyright

Ezra Pound, *The Cantos*. Copyright 1924, 1937, 1940, 1948, 1956, © 1959 by Ezra Pound. Reprinted by permission of New Directions Publishing Corporation and Faber and Faber, Ltd. All previously unpublished and/or uncollected material, including letters, by Ezra Pound © 1969 by Ezra Pound. Used by permission of Dorothy Pound and New Directions Publishing Corporation. *ABC of Reading*. Copyright 1934, © 1963 by Ezra Pound. Reprinted by permission of New Directions Publishing Corporation and Faber and Faber, Ltd. *The Classic Noh Theatre in Japan*. © 1959 by New Directions Publishing Corporation. Reprinted by permission of New Directions Publishing Corporation and Faber and Faber, Ltd. *Literary Essays*. Copyright 1918, 1920, 1935 by Ezra Pound. Reprinted by permission of New Directions Publishing Corporation and Faber and Faber, Ltd. *Pavannes and Divagations*. Copyright © 1958 by Ezra Pound. Reprinted by permission of New Directions Publishing Corporation and Faber and Faber, Ltd. *Personae*. Copyright 1926 by Ezra Pound. Reprinted by permission of New Directions Publishing Corporation and Faber and Faber, Ltd. *Translations*. Copyright 1926, 1954, © 1957, 1958, 1960, 1962, 1963 by Ezra Pound. Reprinted by permission of New Directions Publishing Corporation and Faber and Faber, Ltd. *Confucius: The Great Digest & Unwobbling Pivot*. Copyright 1951 by New Directions Publishing Corporation. Reprinted by permission of New Directions Publishing Corporation and Faber and Faber, Ltd. *Gaudier-Brzeska, Guide to Kulchur, The Spirit of Romance, Polite Essays*: all rights reserved. Reprinted by permission of New Directions Publishing Corporation and Faber and Faber, Ltd. *Selected Poems*. Copyright 1926, 1934, 1937, 1940, 1948, 1949, © 1956, © 1957 by Ezra Pound. Reprinted by permission of New Directions Publishing Corporation and Faber and Faber, Ltd.

From *Understanding Media* by Marshall McLuhan. Copyright © 1964 by Marshall McLuhan. Used with permission of McGraw-Hill Book Company.

From *The Letters of Ezra Pound*, edited by D. D. Paige. Reprinted by permission of Harcourt, Brace & World, Inc.

FOR ALISON

Acknowledgments

MANY PEOPLE have assisted me in bringing this book to completion, but the following individuals and institutions have been especially helpful. I depended heavily for basic research materials on several libraries, especially those of Columbia University, Barnard College, and Brooklyn College. James H. Gibson, of Interlibrary Loans, Brooklyn College, secured items for me which I despaired of obtaining. Herbert Cahoon, Acting Director of the Morgan Library, allowed me to borrow his personal copy of the now rare *Pound Newsletter*. Professor Norman Holmes Pearson generously sent me one of his last two surviving copies of the series of Yale glosses on the *Cantos*, composed by students under his direction. I have also received generous assistance from various staff members of the Manuscript Division of the New York Public Library.

I owe a great deal to the insight and patience of Professor John Unterecker of Columbia University, who offered much good advice as well as timely slaps on the hand during the period when this book was first taking shape. Professor Hugh Kenner of the University of California at Santa Barbara, who seems to me unequalled among critics in his knowledge of Ezra Pound, was kind enough to read the completed manuscript with the most painstaking care. Not only did he point out my errors, but he generously provided me with information that he had had *viva voce* from Ezra Pound. The remaining blunders in this work are due rather to my afterthoughts than to his oversights.

I am deeply grateful to Princess Mary de Rachewiltz for a sympathetic and critical reading of my manuscript and for access to certain highly important source materials and other information that enables this book to contribute to the fund of basic scholarship on the *Cantos*. Mrs. Dorothy Pound and Mr. James Laughlin have kindly granted me permission to reproduce certain photographs of the "Source of the Seven Lakes Canto," and the photographs themselves were supplied by Mary de Rachewiltz. For the translation and scholarly annotation of this previously unavailable chief source of Canto 49, a unique manuscript of Chinese and Japanese poems (see Appendix B), I am completely indebted to Professor Sanehide Kodama of Doshisha Women's College, Kyoto, Japan. It is hoped that Professor Kodama's book on the oriental sources of Ezra Pound's poetry will not be too long in appearing.

I shall not soon forget the kindness of Mr. James Laughlin in facilitating my meeting with Ezra Pound in June, 1968, and it is through the good offices of Mr. Laughlin and Mrs. Dorothy Pound that I was granted permission to reproduce a series of excerpts from the unpublished letters of Ezra Pound to John Quinn concerning the formation of the early cantos (see Appendix A). My thanks, also, to another friend of Ezra Pound, the sculptress Joan Fitzgerald, who has graciously permitted me to reproduce her medallion of the poet made from the life (Venice, 1964) as jacket illustration.

To Olga Rudge, who read the entire manuscript of this book to Ezra Pound, and to Ezra Pound, who cared to listen, I express my deepest gratitude. All those delightful June days we spent in conversation together in Rapallo, Venice, and elsewhere in Italy, taught me much more than I could ever include in this or any other book.

My wife Paula shared with me the whole experience of making this book, and without her intimate involvement the pains would have been sharper and the joys less keen. Finally, I am grateful to the American Philosophical Society for a grant from the Penrose Fund which supported the completion of this project.

D.D.P.

Contents

THE

BARB OF TIME

Introduction

THE READER who enters upon a study of Ezra Pound's *Cantos* should prepare himself for the unpleasant discovery that even at this late date the poem consists almost entirely of vast tracts of *terra incognita*. Much good work by scholars and critics has, of course, been done, and the present study owes a considerable debt to it, but no present assessment of the *Cantos* can be truly valuable until the problem of the poem's meaning, as a whole and in its parts, has been satisfactorily dealt with. My own study concentrates on what I consider to be the crux of *Cantos* criticism, the question as to whether this physically enormous, sprawling poem has *major form*—an over-all design in which the parts are significantly related to the whole. Certain individual cantos and groups of cantos have already been shown to have more or less satisfactory form—in the sense that their materials appear to fall into coherent thematic patterns. Areas of *local* consistency, in other words, have been established. But the problem of the relation of all the parts of this vast poem to the gigantic whole remains unsolved. It is to this larger problem, which I call the problem of *major* form, that this study addresses itself, for I feel that no analysis of the structure and meaning of any individual part of the poem can ultimately satisfy if it fails to throw light on the structural role played by the fragment in the orchestration of the whole.

In determining major form, I feel that it is not enough to point out the fact that the *Cantos* exhibit thematic *coherence*. Demonstration of the coherence and internal self-consistency of

the poem's materials is, of course, essential. The existence of ir-
relevancies, whether for the space of a single canto or a whole
block of cantos, would seriously damage any claim that might
be made for the total unity of the *Cantos.* In addition to thematic unity, however, a poem, whether large or small, ought to
exhibit some sort of *development.* Dante's *Commedia* manifests an obvious sort of narrative development, a "plot" which
takes Dante on a journey from Hell to Paradise. This plot is the
skeletal structure on which a profounder process of *thematic*
development is made to depend, an inward, spiritual journey
which corresponds to the obvious, external journey.

The *Cantos* exhibits no "plot" structure, no narrative development, even though one unifying metaphor appears to be the
journey of Odysseus in quest of home. But if the poem can be
made to yield no thematic development, then its claim to serious consideration as a major epic poem is seriously weakened. If
Pound is introducing unrelated themes from one part of the
poem to the next, or is content with merely repeating the same
theme through a variety of different subject matters, then there
is no internal need for the poem to continue beyond the point
where Pound completes his initial statement of themes. If the
poem has major form, however, one should be able to demonstrate clearly a structure in which the individual parts cohere in
a pattern of cumulative thematic development. This development should tend toward the production of a total effect which
seems upon critical afterthought to have been inevitable.

Of the two or three extended attempts that have been made
to demonstrate the existence of major form in the *Cantos,* none
has achieved success. One of the difficulties has been Pound's
famed "ideogrammic" method, a procedure which dispenses
with grammatical logic as a means of connecting a string of
poetic images, depending, instead, upon a logic of association by
which juxtaposed images elucidate one another through patterns of similarity and contrast that are capable of a full range
of ironic and symbolic suggestiveness.

Perhaps the major stumbling block to criticism, however, has been the fact that the *Cantos* never seem to come to an end; they grind tormentingly on, in spite of all indications to the contrary, like Hamm and Clov in Beckett's *Endgame*. When their number passed one hundred, not a few Pound admirers and critics had to dispense with at least one illusion as to the way in which Dante's epic example affected Pound's poem. It had been expected as a matter of course that the not-too-clear parallel to the *Commedia* would be at least mechanically reinforced, if such a parallel were a major intention in the poem, by Pound's drawing a deliberate numerical parallel between his own cantos and Dante's. And yet as far back as the early 'twenties Pound had written of his "Having the crust to attempt a poem in 100 or *120* cantos" (italics mine).[1] As I shall attempt to show, the search for mechanical form in a poem as organically oriented as the *Cantos* is of necessity doomed to failure and succeeds only in setting up short-sighted formulas of a limited, often merely local applicability. Nevertheless, it is true that the continual appearance of new cantos is exasperating. They have been in the writing longer than many critics have lived. Indeed, if we are to believe Pound, he has been working on them for well over sixty years.[2] Now, however, the poem is drawing to a conclusion. After the latest volume of "drafts" and "fragments" (Cantos 110–117), Pound may very well publish several more, but at this date the critic can confidently proceed more or less normally with the task of analysis, fearing no great new surprises.

Pound himself has often been disturbed by the questions

1. Ezra Pound, *The Letters of Ezra Pound 1907–1941*, ed. D. D. Paige (New York, 1950), p. 180. The *Letters* may not have been available to Hugh Kenner when he wrote of Pound's "scheme of one hundred Cantos" in *The Poetry of Ezra Pound* (Norfolk, 1951), p. 300.

2. Pound declared some years ago, in an interview, " 'I began the Cantos about 1904, I suppose. I had various schemes, starting in 1904 or 1905.' " Quoted from *The Paris Review*, 28 (Summer-Fall 1962) by Donald Davie in *Ezra Pound: Poet as Sculptor* (New York, 1964), p. 30.

critics raise as to whether the *Cantos* possesses formal unity, a structure in which each part is clearly necessary to the elaboration of the whole and in which the whole is greater than the sum of the parts. In 1956, for example, he is said to have remarked to one of his visitors at St. Elizabeth's Hospital that "those who found no plan in the *Cantos* would be confounded when they were complete." [3] Perhaps one can forgive Pound the tone of Biblical prophecy if one realizes that the value of practically the whole life's work of a major poet is at stake in this issue.

When I first began to study the *Cantos,* I had no intention of ever entering the lists on either side in the hope of resolving so crucial a point. I soon became fascinated, however, by the theme of *time* in the *Cantos,* a theme which gradually revealed itself as all-pervasive. It emerged as the principal theme of the poem and as its very heart, from which all other recognized themes, both major and minor, branch out and to which they all return with heightened significance.

If such were really the case, and I had discovered the main theme of the poem, then it would logically follow that the existence or non-existence of major form in the *Cantos* should be discernible in the light of whatever changes or development, if any, took place in the theme of time. Such changes do indeed occur, and rather than marking the erratic and incoherent track of a madman or of an inferior poet, they serve to trace a course of progressive conceptual and spiritual development which no one but a poet of great architectonic genius and mental elasticity could have carved out over so many years, "Braving time." [4]

3. Quoted from Malcolm Bradbury, "A Visit to Ezra Pound," *Twentieth Century,* CLIX (June 1956), p. 605, in Max Halperen, "A Structural Reading of *The Cantos* of Ezra Pound" (Ph.D. dissertation: Florida State University, 1959), pp. 8–9.

4. Ezra Pound, "Envoi (1919)," *Personae* (New York, 1950), p. 197.

The position I take here, which I call "integrative," is an unpopular one. Almost all major Pound critics take the opposing, or "disintegrative," view, and this negative tendency in the criticism of the *Cantos* has grown prodigiously rather than subsided in recent years. The focus of attack is, of course, the apparent absence of major form in the poem. In an article entitled "Craft and Morals" A. Alvarez writes:

> The work has the hustle of artistic life, but not its inevitability. It is full of names, figures and actions; but the abiding central life of the artist judging and ordering the details, creating them in his own coherence, is not there.[5]

Noel Stock, a former Pound disciple, describes what he conceives to be the progressive breakdown of the *Cantos*:

> He begins to insert . . . lines which cannot bear the weight of meaning he intends . . . the meaning of the whole work becomes no clearer as he passes Canto 50, and then Canto 70, and actually begins to recede after he passes into the *Rock-Drill* section (Cantos 85–95). . . . the job of giving a major form to such a vast undertaking is beyond him, and when cracks begin to show he tries to fill them with hasty and inferior material.[6]

George P. Elliott sums up the critical consensus with perhaps a tincture of unnecessary enthusiasm:

> Do the *Cantos* have a true structure? . . . a stable, rational structure such as the highest excellence always builds and is always built upon? I think not; at least, I am not able rationally to grasp that order either from studying the poem or any of the exegeses of it—a disability I share with all those with

5. Noel Stock, ed., *Ezra Pound Perspectives: Essays in Honor of His Eightieth Birthday* (Chicago, 1965), p. 54.

6. Noel Stock, *Poet in Exile: Ezra Pound* (New York, 1964), p. 122

whom I have discussed the matter, including some whose critical assent only a madman would spurn.[7]

Elliott finds as root cause for the disunity of the *Cantos* that
"Pound is radically incoherent—not only the man-in-history
certified insane, but also the maker as you come to know him by
reading that large, occasionally splendid, disintegrating bundle
of poetry and mutter." [8] Despite the employment of *argu-
mentum ad hominem* supported by an after-blast of circular
reasoning, the opinion is typical rather than unique. Typical,
too, of the disintegrative approach is the logically inevitable conclusion Elliott draws, a damning of Pound with faint praise:
"My contention is that a brief collection of his best early lyrics
and of autonomous lyrical passages from the *Cantos* . . .
encompasses all his durable poetry.[9]

George Dekker, who has recently devoted an entire volume
to a very fine study of the *Cantos,* concurs in this view: "I see
little reason to suppose," he says, "that the final cantos [those to
come after Canto 109] will alter my present conviction that the
poem, as a poem, is a colossal failure.[10] "I am satisfied that certain cantos are a great deal better than others and that these
should be isolated for special attention." He considers it an important critical task "to isolate the cantos or parts of cantos
which are fairly complete poetic wholes: for the best of these
will survive; they are among the greatest poetic achievements of
this century." [11] "I think that if this kind of denial of the
poem's unity prevails, criticism will have reduced Pound from

7. George P. Elliott, "Poet of Many Voices," *Ezra Pound: A Collection of Critical Essays* (Twentieth Century Views), ed. Walter Sutton
(New Jersey, 1963), p. 161.

8. Ibid. p. 162.

9. Ibid. pp. 157–58.

10. *The Cantos of Ezra Pound: A Critical Study* (New York, 1963),
p. 202.

11. Ibid. p. 203.

consideration as a formidable major poet to the status of an occasionally brilliant but generally incoherent crank.

Unfortunately, the few integrative critics who do exist have done little to convince readers that the *Cantos* possesses major form. Clark Emery's excellent introductory book [12] contains a wealth of perceptive criticism and basic scholarship, a fine exposition of Pound's leading ideas, and a very good demonstration of some of the important thematic relationships that exist between the various sections of the poem. However, his attempt to display the unity of the poem restricts itself to consideration of its thematic coherence. He is not, if I read him correctly, concerned to reveal a pattern of thematic development that arises out of some inner necessity, or entelechy, which accounts for the elaboration of structure which he endeavors to describe.

Hugh Kenner, who writes brilliantly on many aspects of the *Cantos* and believes in the essential unity of the poem, conceives of the poem's structure in terms of "rhythms of recurrence":

> It was Pound's discovery that the logical end of conscientious rendering was an epic without (in the usual sense) a plot. . . . In the *Cantos* the place of a plot is taken by interlocking large-scale rhythms of recurrence.[13]

He goes on to make the unfortunate assumption, however, that because there is no conventional narrative structure there can be no other sort of development or progression that advances toward moments of climax:

> In the *Cantos* . . . while everything may be said to be as important as everything else, no action, single or multiple, is

12. *Ideas into Action: A Study of Ezra Pound's Cantos* (Coral Gables, 1958).

13. Hugh Kenner, *The Poetry of Ezra Pound* (Norfolk, 1951), p. 300.

being offered the reader for dramatic participation. . . . there is no sweep up to and away from a climactic moment or symbol.[14]

Discovering no line of structural or thematic development in the poem, he seems to accept the pattern of theme-repetition as alone sufficient to satisfy the requirements of structural unity:

> Whatever formulation [the reader] eventually comes to approve, he cannot but be made aware of the weighing of passage against passage as the poem's modus of structural unity.[15]

G. P. Elliott, the disintegrative critic quoted above, does an acceptable job of epitomizing Kenner's position while at the same time underscoring its insufficiency. Kenner, he says,

> devotes his energies to persuading you that the *Cantos* do have . . . a [rational] structure, the main principles of which seem to be "the rhythms of recurrence." It is not only a host of subjects, public and private, which recur, but also contrasting sets of imagery, for example those of mud and light. These subelements are composed into "ideograms" or "vortices," which, according to Kenner, are the structural units of the poem. . . . Granted that this statement means something, the recurrence of such elements cannot be called a structure . . . . behind recurrence there is the fundamental question: why the recurrence? . . . If the recurrences and juxtapositions of the Cantos are there for their own sake, the poem is elaborately trivial. Kenner fails to make clear what structurally valuable end these recurrences serve.[16]

Many critics note the repetitive pattern of pairs or triplets of themes, but they do not explain what necessary structure is being built by the repetitions.

There is no question that the device of repetition is essential to art and is basic to the *Cantos*. But equally important, or per-

14. Ibid. p. 277.
15. Ibid. p. 279.
16. G. P. Elliott, "Poet of Many Voices," p. 161.

haps more important (at least in those arts whose medium is language), is the need for recurrent themes to be given meaningful variation. Again, there is no question that the themes of the *Cantos* recur in continually varied contexts, but whether the variations contribute to any development of meaning is the crucial point for investigation.

The earliest recorded formulation of Pound's "main scheme" occurs in a letter to his father of April 11, 1927, in which it is described as

> . . . Rather like, or unlike subject and response and counter subject in fugue.
> A.A. Live man goes down into world of Dead
> C.B. The "repeat" in history
> B.C. The "magic moment" or moment of metamorphosis, bust thru from quotidien [sic] into "divine or permanent world." Gods, etc.[17]

In comparing his scheme to the organization of a fugue, Pound seems clearly to be limiting his discussion of structure to an explanation of his local technique, the varied juxtaposition and repetition of themes that will remain his consistent method of organizing image-complexes throughout the whole of the *Cantos*. He is making no conscious attempt here to display a "main scheme" in terms of the over-all plan of progressive development that would define the poem's major form. Indeed, if we take *Grove's Dictionary* as our guide, it appears that no idea of a poem's major form or over-all, longitudinal design is deducible from comparisons made to the "form" of the fugue:

> The main idea of a fugue is that of one voice contrasting with others; not, as in the first movement of a sonata, of one section contrasting longitudinally with other sections. Indeed the fugal "form", if there is such a thing at all, may be said to be "a question of texture rather than of design", and it has

17. *Letters of Ezra Pound*, p. 210.

even been suggested that the term "a fugue" is incorrect and that we should rather speak of a composition being written "in fugue", just as we speak of a poem being written in hexameters.[18]

If the *Cantos* does show thematic development out of some inner necessity that determines its over-all design and propels it toward an inevitable climax and resolution, then the fugal analogy does not help us determine that design: "Ideally a fugue has no point of termination. It could continue its contrapuntal involutions without ever coming to a logical point of rest." [19]

The next time we find Pound writing about the form of the *Cantos* is in a letter to John Drummond (February 18, 1932), in which he gives out another threefold schema for understanding the poem: "Best div. prob. the permanent, the recurrent, the casual." There are certain tendencies in these formulations we can now notice. Pound's unwillingness or inability to commit himself to any definite generalization as to the poem's structure is evident in the "like, or unlike" of the earlier letter and in the "prob." of the present one. Nevertheless, hindsight enables us to note the persistence through these two statements of the theme of time and the concentration, in the second statement, solely upon that abstract theme to the exclusion of reference to the more "concrete" motifs outlined in the letter to his father. One also notes Pound's fondness for ternary classification when he refers to the *Cantos* (a practice he follows in making other major formulations as well, such as his famous "three ways" of charging words with meaning: phanopoeia, melopoeia, and logopoeia). I hope to demonstrate, in the course of this investigation, that a three-in-one unity describes the line of development of the poem, the *three* representing three successive phases of development, the *one* representing the constant

18. Eric Blom, ed. *Grove's Dictionary of Music and Musicians*, fifth edition, Vol. III (New York, 1960), p. 513.

19. Murray Schafer, "Ezra Pound and Music," *Ezra Pound*, ed. Sutton, p. 141.

theme of time that becomes elaborated and transfigured through the three phases of the poem. The climax of the third phase, as I shall try to show, occurs in the *Pisan Cantos*, which in my opinion is the dramatic-poetic climax of the *Cantos*, after which the succeeding sections of the poem function as a sort of denouement. In this study, however, I shall proceed no further than the *Pisan Cantos*. I impose this limit on myself in the belief that the major development of the poem takes place between Cantos 1 and 84, and in the corollary belief that the evolution of major form in the poem can be demonstrated effectively through a study of the first eighty-four cantos.

Perhaps the most fascinating, and certainly the most misleading, statement Pound ever made on the form of the *Cantos* is the comparison of his own poem to Dante's great epic. In 1944 he wrote in Italian for a wartime Italian audience one of several "Money Pamphlets," [20] as they were called in English, entitled *An Introduction to the Economic Nature of the United States*. He starts out with a modest claim to being a poet rather than an economic historian, and says,

> For forty years I have schooled myself, not to write the economic history of the U.S. or any other country, but to write an epic poem which begins "In the Dark Forest," crosses the Purgatory of human error, and ends in the light, "fra i maestri di color che sanno." [21]

If one is already aware of the profound influence of Dante on the *Cantos*, it becomes all the easier now to imagine that the

20. "Money Pamphlets" were published in English translation by Peter Russell in London. *An Introduction* appeared in English in 1950. Three of these pamphlets, including the above, were reprinted in significantly bowdlerized form, omitting some of Pound's hysterically fascist pronouncements, in *Impact: Essays on Ignorance and the Decline of American Civilization*, edited and with Introduction by Noel Stock (Chicago, 1960).

21. Ezra Pound, *Impact*, p. 15.

poem will exhibit a tripartite development comparable to that in the *Commedia,* which begins with an *Inferno,* passes to a *Purgatorio,* and ends with a *Paradiso.* So far, however, no one has been able to demonstrate the existence of such a "plot" in the *Cantos.* Just as in the *Commedia,* images representing these three spiritual states are intermingled throughout Pound's poem, but if the *Cantos* clearly borrows this unifying imagistic structure from Dante, there is no corresponding certainty that Pound has in any way appropriated Dante's plot structure. I believe that the major form of the *Cantos* is, finally, perceptible as a line of development in three stages—from an *inferno,* through a *purgatorio,* and into a *paradiso*—but the three-stage journey that Pound undertakes is by no means a slavish imitation of the narrative structure of the *Commedia.*

Perhaps one ought to take Pound's statement in its temporal context and suspect that he was simply trying to impress his Italian readers. Could he gain authority for himself in any better way than to suggest that as poet he was following in the footsteps of Dante? Pound himself nevertheless permits this oversimplification to be perpetuated in bookjacket blurbs, as in the one for *Thrones: 96–109 de los cantares:* "Critics have long recognized a structural parallel between Pound's *Cantos* and *The Divine Comedy.*" As a matter of fact, critics have long ceased imagining any structural parallel of the sort, just as, for the most part, they have ceased believing that any rationally discernible structure obtains in the poem at all.

I have pointed out that statements, double-edged in their suggestiveness, made by Ezra Pound himself on the form of the *Cantos,* are not to be trusted implicitly. I do not mean to give the impression, however, that Pound offers such clues irresponsibly. On the contrary, as the light of his intellect strikes his subject matter at different angles at different times in his career, the contour of his work seems to shift and change. "It is futile to argue about the 'right' plan," says Hugh Kenner, "or to imply that Pound doesn't know his own mind. . . . Ten thousand different-looking cross-sections, all equally 'correct,' can be taken of any complex organism. A slight change in the angle of cut will reveal a wholly new surface." [22]

Pound did not start out, as Dante did, with a definite over-view as to the physical dimensions and conceptual scope of his poem. In a letter of July 1922, he reveals his tentative approach to the problem of major form, a clear idea of which he does not seem to have as yet worked out:

> The first 11 cantos are preparation of the palette. I *have to* get down all the colours or elements I want for the poem. Some perhaps too enigmatically and abbreviatedly. I hope, heaven help me, to bring them into some sort of design and architecture later.

More than a year was to pass after he wrote this letter before Pound even knew how he wanted his poem to begin. It was not until August or September of 1923 that Pound "entirely revised the beginning of the poem," [23] eliminating most of what had appeared in 1917, in *Poetry* magazine, as the first three cantos. He has continued to be so tentative about the final form of the poem that he has never bothered to change the title of the first thirty cantos, which even in the latest editions of the poem still reads "A Draft of XXX Cantos."

It seems to me that the poem has developed somehow like a tree, taking form from a hidden, predetermining center that Pound has never been able adequately to verbalize. In a

22. Kenner, *The Poetry of Ezra Pound*, p. 314. The "cross-sections" Kenner speaks of are two-dimensional views of the poem, and it seems to me that two-dimensional views, reflections of Pound's immediate thematic or structural concerns, are precisely what Pound gives us in his occasional pronouncements on the form of the *Cantos*. It is the critic's concern to give as full a *three*-dimensional view of a complex poem as he can, and to reveal, ultimately, the underlying anatomy that organizes the complexity of such "complex organisms."

23. Myles Slatin, "A History of Pound's Cantos I–XVI, 1915–1925," *American Literature* 35 (May 1963), p. 191.

"Credo" published in 1911, Pound made the following definition of form:

> *Form.*—I think there is a "fluid" as well as a "solid" con-
> tent, that some poems may have form as a tree has form, some
> as water poured into a vase. That most symmetrical forms have
> certain uses. That a vast number of subjects cannot be precisely,
> and therefore not properly rendered in symmetrical forms.[24]

He is contrasting, in this statement, organic with mechanical
form, form which grows from within and appears asymmetrical
(the tree) with symmetrical form imposed from without (the
shape taken by water in a vase), and the last sentence shows
him to be defending the validity of organic form.

I believe that the *Cantos* has consistently grown from
within, assimilating whatever materials the environment has
afforded but never permitting its course of development to be
determined by those materials. The metaphor is an organic one,
but so too is the major metaphor of the *Cantos*, the Odyssean
voyage, which implies the working out of an entelechy, an intuited personal destiny that unfolds itself in time but cannot in
its essence be changed by time. The winds of fortune might
blow (and for Pound they have often raged furiously enough)
but the poet's job would be to steer home toward Ithaca,
which, like the voyager himself, would upon his arrival look the
same as ever and yet look remarkably different, transformed by
a sea-change into something more rich than strange. The motif
of the Odyssean voyage with which the poem begins, suggests
also that the itinerary and final destination will not be clear to
the reader at the start, but that in time the shore of the poet-
voyager's homeland ought to reveal itself with ever-increasing
definition as his destiny works itself out in the successive phases
of the poem. In this view of the *Cantos* I am in accord with

24. *The Literary Essays of Ezra Pound*, ed. T. S. Eliot (Norfolk,
1954), p. 9.

Hugh Kenner, one of the few integrative critics, who expresses it in relation to the growth of Pound's concept of usury:

> If sixteen years after writing Canto XLV Pound has only now made a definition of Usura . . . the moral is not that he was bluffing in 1937, but that he could identify Usura and see where it fitted in long before he could enclose it in his mind and say exactly what it was.
>
> That is why the meaning of the Cantos is cumulative, and why Pound was able to embark on his long poem without having thought out a rigorous scheme.[25]

The theme suggested by the poem's opening motif of a voyage in quest of knowledge is *the unfolding of the human spirit in the medium of time.* Spirit and Time are, as I shall attempt to show, the basic metaphysical pair into which all the welter of images, themes, persons, and ideas in the *Cantos* polarize themselves. Spirit and Time are the great protagonist and antagonist, in all their varying guises, in this essentially dramatic rather than static poem. If the poem is truly dramatic, then the protagonist, Spirit, in its successive encounters with Time, ought to undergo progressive stages of awareness—a process of metaphysical deepening—and there ought to be a grand resolution of these "mighty opposites" as the poem draws to a close. The outline of development I propose here should theoretically, in its neat and logical symmetry (by which I do not imply that the poem is itself divisible into mechanically symmetrical parts, like Dante's *Commedia*), answer to the requirements of major form, and I maintain that such a development does in fact take place.

A kind of Hegelian progression of *thesis* challenged by an *antithesis*, both of which are transcended in a *synthesis*, characterizes the three major phases of the *Cantos*. Such a design is never anywhere consciously expressed by Pound as the ultimate

25. *Gnomon: Essays on Contemporary Literature* (New York, 1958), p. 134.

method behind his apparent madness, but the idea of a Hegelian progression can perhaps be read into the description he gives of his fundamental technique as fugal. In the already quoted letter to his father he indicates the method of his poem to be "Rather like, or unlike subject and response and counter subject in fugue." According to *Grove's Dictionary*, the "subject" of a fugue is "the theme on which the whole work hangs," and that "must be clearly and unequivocally presented at the outset." For the moment, we may regard this as the Hegelian thesis. The "response" in fugue "is what its name implies, a *reply*. The subject alone is a 'broken arc'; it requires the answer to complete the 'perfect round.' " [26] If we assume that the Hegelian thesis implies a complementary antithesis, then the fugal response would correspond to the antithesis. The "counter-subject" of a fugue answers perfectly to the idea of a synthesis resulting from the interaction of the thesis and antithesis. The counter-subject arises as follows:

> While the second voice announces the answer ["response"], the first voice [which originally announces the "subject"] goes on its way in counterpoint with it. Sometimes this counterpoint takes the shape of a definite theme of which further use is made in the course of the fugue; it is then called a "counter-subject." [27]

Thus, the interaction of subject and response produces a third entity which may be regarded as a synthesis. In that same letter Pound then lists three items which, if read in order of their presentation as subject [thesis], response [antithesis], and counter-subject [synthesis], appear to correspond with my own formulation of the basic conflict and thematic development of the *Cantos*. Thus, "Live man goes down into world of Dead" is the thesis, or Spirit, as I have mentioned above. The "repeat in history" I take to mean the varied embodiments in time of

26. Blom, ed., *Grove's Dictionary*, Vol. III, p. 514 f.
27. Ibid. p. 517.

timeless myths: Malatesta's defeats and triumphs as a Renaissance Odyssey, Chinese history as an incarnation of Confucian
principles, etc. The "repeat in history" may thus be regarded as
Time, the antithesis or complement of myth and the medium
in which Spirit must operate. "The 'magic moment' or moment
of metamorphosis, bust thru from quotidien into 'divine or permanent world.' Gods, etc." is the synthesis resulting from the
interaction of the human spirit with time.

Pound's fundamental imagistic structure, his local procedure, thus appears to anticipate in miniature what I believe he
does on the grand scale in three successive phases. The correspondence between small and large is like the correspondence
between the seed and the plant, or between microscopic and
macroscopic crystal structure, and supports my sense that the
Cantos is an organic continuum ordered from within.

This fundamental poetic device of the *Cantos*, the juxtaposition of thesis and antithesis, may have resulted from Pound's
close attention to the method of Joyce. Pound's first three
cantos, as originally published, evidently failed to satisfy him
soon after their publication, for their talky, Browningesque style
was immediately superseded in Cantos 4 through 7 (printed in
Poems 1918–21) by the final, characteristically compressed
style of the *Cantos* as we know them. In May 1918, at a time
when he was still composing this second group of cantos and
radically altering the poem's style, he has this to say of the texture of Joyce's prose:

> On almost every page of Joyce you will find just such swift al-
> ternation of subjective beauty and external shabbiness, squalor,
> and sordidness. It is the bass and treble of his method.[28]

The "swift alternation of subjective beauty and external shabbi-
ness," Spirit versus Time, thesis and antithesis, is equally the
"bass and treble" of Pound's own method in the *Cantos*. Just as

28. "Joyce," *Literary Essays*, p. 412.

Pound may have learned something from Joyce about patterning his images, he may equally well have been influenced by
Joyce in his consideration of a major form for the *Cantos*. As
we can see from a subsequent article of his on Joyce, Pound
studied *Ulysses* very attentively: for the obvious reason that he
himself was doing something analogous in epic dimension and
in the selection of a fundamental myth, and for the less obvious
reason that he admired its imagistic technique. But he was also
concerned with the way Joyce solved the problem of major
form. In the article just alluded to, Pound gives attention to the
over-all structure of *Ulysses*:

> Qu'est-ce que l'*Ulysses* de James Joyce? Ce roman appartient
> à la grande classe de romans en forme de sonate, c'est-à-dire,
> dans la forme: thème, contrethème, rencontre, développement,
> finale.[29]

The metaphor of the sonata with its rounded, complete form
involving *development* and a *finale* must have represented for
Pound, in relation to the *Cantos*, a spur to the consideration of
over-all design.

Pound's main effort in the *Cantos*, as I hope to demonstrate, is to organize his materials with respect to certain major
time concepts in order to criticize radically the whole cultural
environment of modern Western society. He performs this cri-
tique more and more constructively as he gains deeper and
deeper insight into the enduring values of our culture. The pro-
gram he outlined for himself as early as 1912 he has never abandoned:

> One wants to find out what sort of things endure, and what
> sort of things are transient; what sort of things recur; . . . to

29. "James Joyce et Pecuchet" [June 1922], *Polite Essays* (Norfolk,
1940), p. 89. "What is James Joyce's *Ulysses*? This novel belongs to the
great class of novels in sonata form, that is, in the form: Theme, counter-
theme, confrontation, development, finale."

learn upon what the forces, constructive and dispersive, of social order, move.[30]

Pound was setting himself the considerable task of discovering the first principles behind human social behavior. If, in working toward this goal, he felt with greater and greater urgency the need to determine the nature of time, it is probable that he felt it to be a question of fundamental importance, not only to the poet but to humanity at large. "What, if anything," asks Hans Meyerhoff, "endures throughout the constantly changing stream of consciousness of the individual? The question, what is man, therefore invariably refers to the question of what is time." [31] The *Cantos*, as I read the poem, is precisely an elaboration of this thesis—that the central problems in all spheres of human involvement must be referred ultimately to a consideration of the nature of time. All of the poem's sub-themes, whether metaphysical, political, social, moral, economic, or aesthetic, interrelate and reveal their full significance in the light only of the single unifying major theme of time.

There are basically two concepts of time which determine the dramatic interplay of images, persons, and themes in the *Cantos*: linear time and cyclical time. The definitions I shall offer of these concepts are not intended to have scientific precision, but rather to summarize in abstract terms the meaning of these concepts as I have come to understand Pound's use of them in the poem itself. Linear time, for Pound, is that constant succession of moments, presumed to be irreversible and infinitely extensible in a single direction, which common sense perceives as the unalterable temporal order of past, present, and future, and which can be measured by mechanical instruments as a series of discrete intervals of uniform length, each exactly the same as the next. Cyclical time, as Pound presents it, is that

30. *Patria Mia* (Chicago, 1950), p. 68. This essay was originally written in 1912.

31. Hans Meyerhoff, *Time in Literature* (Berkeley, 1955), p. 2.

time-system exhibited in the seasonal and cosmic rhythms of nature, which are characterized by perpetual recurrence, the cycle of birth, death, and rebirth in organic nature. It is this time-scheme that gives archaic or primitive man freedom from any sense of history as a series of unique and unrepeatable events and allows him to live in an unceasing present.[32]

Another way of presenting the contrast between these two types of time is to view them as mechanical time versus organic time. Mechanical time is clock-measured and ticks off its seconds without regard to the flow of human experience, whereas organic time, as Pound employs it, is the sense of duration as subjectively experienced. Its moments are qualitatively distinguished, exhibit no necessary uniform rate of flow nor single, irreversible direction of flow. On the contrary, it is characterized by "dynamic fusion, or interpenetration, of the causal order in experience and memory," [33] so that its flow does not correspond to the measure of clock or calendar time. Organic time as subjectively experienced becomes identified, in the *Cantos*, with cyclical time as manifest in the cosmic and seasonal cycles. The common feature which they display is *recurrence*, the recapturability of the past. In this they are distinguished from mechanical time, which is unidirectional and irreversible.

Pound sets the forces and representatives of mechanical time in conflict with those of organic time. When the clock, with its uniform beat, is imposed ruthlessly upon organic processes, with their variable beat, the result is a derangement in the healthy functioning of living things. In *Time and Western Man* (1927), a polemical condemnation of the prevailing anti-

32. See Mircea Eliade, *Cosmos and History: The Myth of the Eternal Return*, trans. Willard R. Trask (New York, 1959), p. 86. Eliade's conception of primitive man's relation to time furnishes an extraordinary parallel to my own conception of Pound's relation to organic time, as this is discoverable in the *Cantos*.

33. Meyerhoff, *Time in Literature*, p. 85. The author's characterization of subjectively experienced time, as it appears in literature, corresponds at many points with what I have called "organic time" in the *Cantos*.

intellectual time-philosophy which the author saw almost everywhere in twentieth-century arts and letters, Wyndham Lewis expressed the incompatibility of mechanical and organic time much as Pound might have done:

> Life in the rough, or on the average, should be there in its natural grace, chaos and beauty; not cut down and arranged into a machine-made system. Its natural gait and movement it derives from its cosmic existence; and where too obsessing a human law—or time, or beat—gets imposed upon it, the life and beauty depart from it.[34]

The major dramatic conflict that is developed in the *Cantos* derives from just this presumed incompatibility of time-systems. It is often impossible to prove a direct "influence," but since Pound undoubtedly read, and read closely, this book, which placed him in the contemporary "time-school" and called him, among other things, a "revolutionary simpleton," it is quite possible that Lewis's formulations about time-systems helped clarify or reinforce Pound's own time conceptions, which in essential ways ran parallel to Lewis's.[35]

34. Wyndham Lewis, *Time and Western Man* (Boston, 1957), p. 26. The book was first published in 1927 in London.

35. Lewis defined the revolutionary simpleton as, "in one word, a romantic." (p. 27.) He went on to say: "Pound is—that is my belief—a genuine *naïf*. He is a sort of revolutionary simpleton!" (p. 38.) Lewis's talent for turning compliments is illustrated in the following: "Pound is, I believe, only pretending to be alive for form's sake. His effective work seems finished." (p. 41.)

Late in 1928 Pound indirectly answered Lewis, revealing an ambivalence towards him which seems never to have changed: "In parenthesis I am FOR Mr. Lewis, even when he is wrong, and I am against the abominable public and race amongst which he lives, whether they are cursing him for his merits or praising him for irrelevant reasons.

"I believe that all large mammals shd. be preserved." (*The Exile,* No. 4 [Autumn 1928], p. 106.)

In 1938, Pound makes direct acknowledgment of Lewis's accusation, which appears to have rankled in the poet for over a decade: "Mr. W.

Pound's distrust of the forces of mechanical time is not to be confused with any simplistic aversion to the machine as such. He is not against the machine-world and for the primitive, uncomplicated life of nature, but is opposed rather to the machine mentality, which is characterized by an utter lack of respect for the rhythms of natural processes in its attempts to tinker with living organisms. In general, what Pound comes to explore and condemn in the *Cantos* is the effect of *artificial systems of measurement* when they do not take into account the "natural gait," the natural productive and reproductive rhythms of living things.

Pound's conception of the nature of history and his treatment of the subject matter of history in the *Cantos* is at bottom determined by his distrust of linear mechanical time and his reverence for cyclical organic time. For Pound, the meaning of an historical event is not determined by its immediate temporal context, its relative position in a unidirectional, linear sequence of events; an event gains significance only insofar as it substantively imitates a pre-established archetype or myth, which

---

Lewis, calling me in one place a revolutionary simpleton, makes honorable amend, calling himself a chronological idiot in another." (*Guide to Kulchur* [London, 1938], p. 234n.)

Lewis described the current time-philosophy, to which he considered Pound addicted, as follows: "The analysis of the contemporary time-philosophy which Bergson exemplifies is so fanatically directed to disintegrate and to banish the bogey of 'concreteness' that it would be impossible not to receive the impression of a peculiar hostility to 'the concrete,' in its most inclusive sense, in favour of something abstract and mental.

". . . the problem of the 'abstract' versus the 'concrete' [is] at the base of the various world-pictures to be discussed. For what I have called the time-school, time and change are the ultimate reality. They are *the abstract school*, it could be said.

". . . the position we are attacking is the *abstract* one, as against the *concrete* of, say, such an 'idealism' as that of Berkeley, Bradley or Bosanquet." (*Time and Western Man*, pp. 164–65.) As this study will emphasize, Pound, too, was antagonistic to any mode of abstract thought which ignored the primacy of concrete reality.

in Pound's view expresses "a sort of permanent basis in humanity"—man's "kinship to the vital universe" [36]—and is therefore independent of chronological time. History, wherever meaningful, is marked by recurrence rather than novelty. He thinks, for example, that by studying Chinese history "we might acquire some balance in NOT mistaking recurrence for innovation." [37] "Nothing is new, and all good is renewal," he wrote in the late 'thirties.[38] If we regard the Western conception of history as that of a chronologically ordered, causally linked *chain of events*, we must then define Pound's mind as fundamentally *ahistorical*. He shares the cyclical time-consciousness of archaic man, of primitive, traditional societies in "their revolt against concrete, historical time, their nostalgia for a periodical return to the mythical time of the beginning of things, to the 'Great Time.'" [39] The main difference between archaic man and modern, Judaeo-Christian man is that

> the former feels himself indissolubly connected with the Cosmos and the cosmic rhythms, whereas the latter insists that he is connected only with History. (Eliade, p. vii)

For archaic man, History as we understand it is unreal. Any object or event, according to Eliade, "becomes real only insofar as it imitates or repeats an archetype," and "everything which lacks an exemplary model is 'meaningless,' i.e. it lacks reality." (p. 34) In the *Cantos*, a great majority of the events of

36. Ezra Pound, *The Spirit of Romance* (New York, 1952), p. 92. The original edition was published in 1910.

37. Ezra Pound, *Guide to Kulchur* (Norfolk, 1952), p. 274. This is a reprint, with minor additions, of the original 1938 edition, published under the same title in England and, more staidly, as *Culture* in the United States.

38. "D'Artagnan Twenty Years After," *The Criterion*, XVI (July 1937), p. 607, cited in Halperen, "A Structural Reading of *The Cantos*," p. 36.

39. Eliade, *Cosmos and History*, p. xi.

Western history are presented as a meaningless chaos because they result from a loss of vital contact with the myths that give life form, meaning, and value. Increasingly metaphysical, Pound develops the idea of the *unreality* of so much of Western history only at a late stage of the poem, in the *Pisan Cantos*.

As to what constitutes the reality of the "Self" Pound is never in doubt. For archaic man, Self becomes truly *real* only insofar as one identifies himself with the timeless archetype.[40] Similarly, for Pound, fullness of being is enjoyed in creative activity, which is a process of cultural renewal, of "making it new," to use a favorite Confucian phrase of his. For Pound, creation is restoration. If the Self has the capacity to negate the historical chain of events by cultural renewal, by revival of the "Great Time" or mythical moment of original creation, then it is obvious that in Pound's view self-identity has nothing essentially to do with time as history. On the contrary, for Pound as poet living in the modern world, engulfed by all the moral and material consequences of its prevailingly historical, linear time-consciousness, historical time is the fundamental enemy of the Self or Spirit.

In the *Cantos*, contrasting pairs of themes are associated with the historical, linear time-consciousness on the one hand, and with the ahistorical, cyclical time-consciousness on the other. Associated with linear time as inimical to the spirit are false abstraction, usury, bad art, all forms of social tyranny and disorder. Associated with cyclical time are precise terminology, economic justice, good art, individual freedom, and social order. Ultimately, all the poem's themes relate to this fundamental conflict of time-systems.

We may also note that the conflict of Pound's own spirit with historical time was the basic motivation behind his writing the poem in the first place. His sensibility could not bear to suffer "the whips and scorns of time" because he could in no way satisfactorily rationalize them and thereby render them

40. Ibid.

tolerable. Like archaic man, he, too, regards "history," or events which do not conform to desirable archetypal patterns, as equivalent to suffering.[41] Archaic man regards suffering "as a consequence of a deviation in respect to the 'norm.'"[42] A poetic sensibility which feels itself trapped and suffering in a norm*less*, chaotic time-world has no choice but to come to grips with that time-world and to fight for survival.

The *Cantos* is a record of that struggle against history, a conflict which governs the development of major form in the poem. Pound's strategy in pitting his spirit against time-as-history is not unusual: first get to know your antagonist as well as you can; then discover the means of foiling him; then fully engage and—if you can—conquer him. This three-step strategy corresponds to the three major phases of the *Cantos*. The present work divides itself accordingly into three Parts, each of which will study one of the major sections, or "phases," of the poem. (I prefer to use *phases* to avoid any connotation that there are exact structural breakoff points between the successive stages of development of the poem's major form.)

Part One is entitled "*Inferno:* Time as Disorder." Part Two is labeled "*Purgatorio:* Time as Order." Part Three is the "*Paradiso:* Time as Love." No exact parallel is intended to the three divisions of the *Commedia*, for Pound's value-system and whole way of thinking are quite different from Dante's. But there is perfect appropriateness in such suggestive labeling if one regards the three phases of Pound's epic as corresponding to Despair, Hope, and Triumph. In the first phase of the poem, which persists up through Canto 46[43] the time-embattled human spirit struggles against overwhelming odds to achieve

41. Ibid. p. 97n.

42. Ibid. p. 98.

43. For the sake of uniformity I shall use Pound's later, Arabic numbering system exclusively rather than the earlier Roman system (e.g., Canto XXXIX)—except, of course, in citing the published titles of sections of the poem.

order in spite of surrounding chaos. Time and the clock emerge
as the crucial symbol of *negation,* of moral disorder, in these
cantos. Western history is portrayed by and large in a state of
progressive confusion and decay. The prevailing historical pes-
simism of these cantos is memorably captured in Canto 11: "In
the gloom, the gold gathers the light against it."

Time in these early cantos emerges as synonymous with history, especially Western history in its negative manifestations as
a record of *violations of natural order.* Nature, in the eyes of
those who represent the forces of negation, is fraught with danger and must be suppressed. For the constructive, poetic consciousness in these cantos, however, nature is value-neutral, a
chaos of destructive and creative potencies which it is man's
task to order and control. The concept of order elaborated
through this first phase in counterpoint and counterpoise to the
chaos reigning in the objective world is that of subjective, psychological order: "order within," the only force capable of creative resistance to the different kinds of chaos represented by
nature and history.

Part Two, "*Purgatorio:* Time as Order," traces through
phase two of the poem Pound's deepened awareness of the *basis*
of order within. External nature, which in phase one remained
value-neutral, is now regarded by Pound as the standard for
order within and, by extension, for social order in general. Nature as chaos gives way completely to the Confucian vision of
nature as the great model and example to human beings for
proper self-regulation and for the ordering of society. Pound
now presents nature as the objective evidence that rational law,
and not chaos, governs the external universe; for nature's mode
of operation is organic time, the cosmic and seasonal cycles by
which healthy societies regulate their behavior in all spheres of
activity. From Cantos 31 through 71 Pound uses segments of
history, largely American and Chinese, to show that only those
men and societies governed by a reverence for organic time have
the inner strength to resist the destructive efforts of those who
live by mechanical time. Examples of the Confucian ethical

principle of *acting in due season,* or "timeliness," begin to assert
themselves from Canto 31 onward, as Pound transfers his attention from the attainment of order within to the practical
methods by which such inner harmony can be made to spread
outward into society at large. Economics is stressed in these
cantos because nature will yield up her abundance to the en-
richment of a whole society only if there is no artificial economic obstruction keeping the producer from his raw materials
and the product from the consumer. Thus economics must be
brought into harmony with the seasons, with the productive
rhythms and capacities of chthonic nature and human nature
both. Nature itself as the paradigm of social order is not, for
Pound, the dream of an impractical idealist, but rather the
principle by which actual societies have flourished in the past.
Pound regards the possibility of implementing that paradigm in
the present as the real hope for re-establishing the "Great
Time" or earthly paradise that forever remains possible but is
not always realized. And therefore I regard this section as a
Purgatorio: the emphasis is on hope rather than on suffering.

Cantos 74 through 84 constitute what I examine in Part
Three as the *"Paradiso:* Time as Love." If, indeed, as T. S.
Eliot says, it is only *through* time that time is conquered, then
the second phase of the *Cantos* was absolutely necessary for the
triumph of the spirit in the third. The poet, beleaguered by the
forces of mechanical time now as never before, must either conquer or die in this highly dramatic test of his first principles. He
conquers by undergoing a profound mystical experience which
reveals to him the illusory nature of historical time and place,
and consequently even of his own ego. He is visited by the revelation of immanent Love in the universe, and in the very pit of
hell is capable finally of the paradoxical utterance: "out of all
this beauty something must come." [44]

44. *The Pisan Cantos,* Canto 84, p. 117. The edition of the *Cantos*
used throughout is *The Cantos of Ezra Pound* (New York, 1948), which
contains Cantos 1–84 (except for the as yet unpublished Cantos 72 and
73)

In his direct, subjective contact with the abundant goodness of the cosmos, Everyman-Pound experiences on his pulses the metaphysical *essence* of the earthly paradise of all his poetical and polemical visions. What he experiences concretely can be more or less formulated abstractly as follows: Pound sees organic time, envisaged in phase two as the rational form of nature, to be the universal expression of suprarational benevolent love. This is not to imply that Pound gives up his more mundane aspirations toward an earthly paradise yet to be established through socio-political reform, but rather that he now feels the political "translation" of his mystical certainty to be inevitable ("something must come"). Having attained through heightened awareness, or cosmic consciousness, a "Paradise Within," he can look forward with absolute faith to an eventual political paradise on earth.

I do not undertake the study of those sequences of cantos published after the *Pisans;* nevertheless, I would like to state my general impression of their relation to the rest of the poem. I believe that in the cantos following the Pisan sequence Pound reworks old material and introduces new in the light of his deepened insight. It seems to me that in *Rock-Drill* and *Thrones* Pound's Pisan vision of organic time as the palpable form of Love is given greater and greater philosophical formulation and clarification, and I am further convinced that the general direction of all of Pound's efforts in the *Cantos* is that of philosophical rumination succeeding upon great moments of vision.

By way of summarizing the scheme offered above, I note two parallel developments. The concept of nature in the *Cantos* undergoes three stages of definition: (1) nature equals chaos; (2) nature equals reason; (3) nature equals love. The concept of time also undergoes triple development: (1) spirit in conflict with time-as-history; (2) spirit in harmony with time-as-nature; (3) spirit in communion with time, i.e. spirit and time-as-nature are *one* in the reconciling synthesis of love.

I believe that what I outline here as the major form of the *Cantos* is a rational, harmonious structure that strikes one with a sense of its inevitability. Perhaps a work of art does not absolutely need major form in order to achieve greatness, but such a possibility strikes me as, at the very least, highly debatable. *Moby Dick* may be a good example of the critics' confusion on this point, since its plotlessness and shifting narrative point of view indicate to some critics its lack of major form, whereas its subtle symbolic structure is, for other critics, evidence of a great, informing design. At one time Pound himself seems to have deprecated the need for major form, perhaps in order to justify, in his own mind, the lack of immediately perceptible major form in the *Cantos*. In an essay of 1928 on William Carlos Williams, he said, "It can do us no harm to . . . consider the number of very important chunks of world-literature in which form, major form, is remarkable mainly for absence." [45] He goes on, in the next paragraph, to give as examples the *Iliad*, the *Prometheus* of Aeschylus, the works of Montaigne and Rabelais, and the unfinished *Bouvard and Pécuchet* (and the absence of major form in some of these works is, to say the least, arguable), then makes the following point: "The component of these great works and *the* indispensable component is texture." Later in the essay it appears, however, that what Pound means by major form is "clever" or "accomplished" form, something as artificial as "plot," which he considers bad not in itself but only when it does not arise out of "some inner need." "The best pages of Williams," he says,

> . . . are those where he has made the least effort to fit anything into either story, book, or (*In the American Grain*) into an essay. I would almost move from that isolated instance to the generalization that plot, major form, or outline should be left to authors who feel some inner need for the same . . . and to books where the said form, plot, etc., springs naturally from the matter treated.

45. Ezra Pound, *Polite Essays* (Norfolk, 1940), p. 75.

Although Pound was not interested in major form in the sense of "plot," he was undoubtedly interested in achieving some sort of over-all design that could be rationally demonstrated, as he indicates in a letter of 1939:

> As to the *form* of *The Cantos:* All I can say or pray is: *wait* till it's there. I mean wait till I get 'em written and then if it don't show, I will start exegesis. I haven't an Aquinas-map; Aquinas *not* valid now.[46]

Pound denies that any "Aquinas-map," any pre-existent system of thought like that which was available to Dante, will be found to elucidate the *Cantos,* but it is clear that he felt the need for more than "texture" (one doesn't have to "wait" for evidence of texture) to justify the unity of his poem. There is no doubt that many passages in the *Cantos* have great individual intensity, or richness of poetic texture, but they would emerge as even greater if seen as elements in a grand design which endues each part with more than local significance.

The existence of stretches of "boredom" in the *Cantos,* undeniable but hardly as extensive as some critics would make out, does not invalidate any claim the poem may have to greatness. Milton and Dante are liable to the same charge and yet have managed to survive the onslaughts of time. As to the frequent charge of "obscurity" leveled against the poem, I believe that critics have done enough admirable work in past decades to refute most such allegations, which are often the mask for complaints against the poem's difficulty—and of its difficulty there can be no question.

It is universally admitted that the *Cantos* contains many passages of great poetry, but because of overwhelming doubts on the question of major form, only a few critics venture to call it a great *poem.* The obvious general *purpose* of the *Cantos* has never been a mystery, but the whole question of the difference

46. *Letters*, p. 418.

between the intention and the result, the problem of the poetic implementation of the leading "ideas," still baffles criticism. As a recent critic says:

> The general theme of the work is clear enough: the quest for civilization and the descent into corruption of a number of societies and times, classical, Renaissance, Chinese, American, contemporary. But that is so large that it brings the reader no nearer than to be told that in *Finnegans Wake* a man is born, lives, copulates, dies.[47]

I have said before that the statements made by Pound himself on the form of the *Cantos* are not necessarily very helpful, because they tend to be either very limited, vague, or ambiguous, and sound as cryptic as anything in the poem itself. Critics themselves have concentrated on the analysis of individual passages or the tracing out of specific themes rather than devoting much attention to the problem of over-all form. The results of such labors have been very fruitful, and no critic could presume to tackle the larger problems unless he had learned a great deal from his predecessors. Nevertheless, in regard to the later cantos especially, there is still a great dearth of criticism and even of fundamental scholarship. The lack of scholarship is always the greater impediment, it seems to me; but the exception to this rule occurs in much of the criticism, published and unpublished, of Cantos 1–71: here the student often finds the text of the poem buried under mounds of scholarship whose relevance is frequently questionable and whose very presence sets up the most formidable of barriers between Pound and the would-be reader. The game of source-hunting has been going on for a long time and is not yet over. Yet a discriminating method must be worked out whereby what is truly *relevant* in the source-material is emphasized to the exclusion of the distracting and misleading contexts.

47. A. Alvarez, "Craft and Morals," *Ezra Pound Perspectives*, ed. Noel Stock, pp. 53–54.

Such a task is the critic's. My own will be to rely on what the text alone suggests, and to use parallels and sources to amplify only what I believe deducible from the bare poem itself. I am convinced that where such a method is not adhered to, anarchy must ensue, and that in the name of scholarship the greatest disservice is rendered the poem: the denial of its autonomy.

One word more as to the form of this study: Very little in life is more tedious than reading through discussions of the *Cantos* constructed on the mechanical principle of canto-by-canto explication. By their lack of selectivity, by their devotion of approximately equal attention to every canto (and frequently, therefore, of relatively scant attention to highly important cantos), such studies unconsciously confess to the absence of any perception of over-all structure in the *Cantos*—a failure to see the wood for the trees. My own study will necessarily encounter the opposite sort of criticism. The exercise of selectivity is open to the objection that too much is being avoided or bypassed which, if met head on, might unanswerably contradict the thesis being developed. I shall attempt to minimize such objections by giving at least a general appreciation of the structure and significance of the stretches of material to which I do not give detailed attention. My usual method, however, will be to explicate only those passages which I deem to be *nodal points* in the articulation of the poem's major form. Such passages will necessarily concern the theme of time, and I hope that most of them will be of such intrinsic poetic value that the many pages of explication devoted to them will seem justified.

PART ONE

Inferno

TIME AS DISORDER

CHAPTER 1

Canto 1 as Microcosm

THROUGH the symbolic use of Greek myth, the first canto suggests not only the major themes to be elaborated in the poem, but foreshadows, like a microcosm, the total structural development of the *Cantos*. Except for the last seven lines, Canto 1 consists of Pound's abbreviated English translation of Andreas Divus's Renaissance Latin translation of the opening lines of the eleventh book of the *Odyssey*. Book XI is called the "Book of the Dead" or "Nekuia," because it concerns Odysseus' visit to Hades.[1] The blood-sacrifice Odysseus makes to Tiresias, who gives the voyager prophetic counsel on how to return to Ithaca, announces the *Cantos*' all-embracing theme of the need for cultural renewal—man's need to re-establish contact with whatever has been vital in his cultural heritage so that he may know what meaningful course to pursue in the future.

Pound begins his epic in the midst of chronological or narrative time, *in medias res*. But in another and deeper sense he begins outside this "profane" flow of time, for the Nekuia and the ritual act of sacrifice abolish chronological time and place Odysseus in the timeless realm of unchanging myth. The historical chain of events, the concatenation of cause and effect, is

1. E. M. Glenn, *The Analyst*, No. VIII (Department of English, Northwestern University, n.d.), p. 3. (*The Analyst*, in mimeographed form, appears irregularly under the general editorship of Robert Mayo. The intention of the publication with regard to the *Cantos* has been mainly to provide scholarly background rather than critical interpretation.) My own debt to *The Analyst* is considerable, for it is one of the chief scholarly sources for the first eleven cantos.

broken and will no longer determine the fate of Pound's Odysseus until such time as he disregards Tiresias' wisdom and deviates from the pattern of behavior prescribed by the myth. Just as Odysseus' act of blood-sacrifice puts him in touch with the living past and contradicts the irreversible flow of historical time, so too Pound's reverent act of *translation* denies meaning to historical time by showing Homer still to be alive in the so-called present. This translation of a translation of Homer collapses time and makes co-eval not three, but actually five different layers of civilization. Not only is there a continuity of creative impulse between Homeric Greece, Renaissance Italy, and the present, but the Anglo-Saxon rhythms of Pound's English suggest another period whose vital spark has been recaptured; and the Renaissance Latin of Andreas Divus evidences the living continuity of the classical Latin tongue as a literary vehicle.

In the original version of the present canto, then entitled "Canto III," Divus's translation is introduced by the following comment, which quotes Burckhardt: "More than the Roman city, the Roman speech"/(Holds fast its part among the ever-living)." Pound wants us to understand especially that Divus has dealt fittingly with Homer, has "Caught up his cadence, word and syllable." [2] When Pound, in line 68 of Canto 1 as it now stands, says, "Lie quiet Divus," this is indeed a critical moment in the canto, but the command is not as cryptic as *The Analyst* would suppose. It is simply that Pound has propitiated Divus's ghost by the sacrificial offering of vital translation, just as Odysseus has satisfied Tiresias' ghost by giving it new life through a blood transfusion. In the same way, Divus might have said, "Lie quiet Homer," after successfully translating him into Latin. Whatever was truly alive in the past, Pound is saying through all this, is always capable of rebirth; and the dead weight of historical time can always be abolished.

There is no conscious intimation here of the theme of or-

2. Ezra Pound, "Canto III," *Poetry* X (August 1917), p. 250.

ganic time, which Pound will set in opposition to mechanical time in the middle phase of the *Cantos*. And yet the Nekuia of Canto 1, which suggests the need to renew vital contact with the cultural tradition, stands as prototype for the later Nekuia passage of Canto 47, which mythically represents man's need for vital contact with chthonic nature and the cosmic and seasonal cycles, a contact which must serve as the basis of cultural renewal. The myths, symbols, and structure of Canto 1 foreshadow the major developments of theme and structure in the poem as a whole.

Time in the first canto is Odysseus' antagonist. It is broadly symbolized by the rough, inimical sea, "spiteful Neptune," as Tiresias calls it, which Odysseus will overcome but at the loss of "all companions." It is historical time which Pound's Odysseus must conquer, and the souls of its victims rise up "out of Erebus"—"souls stained with recent tears," men "mauled with bronze lance heads"—crowding about Odysseus and crying out to him and to Pound for more blood sacrifices, which I read as a symbolic cry for vindication against the brutality of history. The sea symbolizes not only history, but even more obviously nature, both of which the will must learn to cope with if it is creatively to transform the environment. And Odysseus *polumetis*, the man of many counsels or wiles, dramatizes the creative will capable of effective resistance to the destructive countercurrents of historical time.

The Odyssean voyager-poet of the *Cantos* stands in marked contrast to the Odyssean poet-hero of the *Hugh Selwyn Mauberley* sequences, which Pound wrote while putting the finishing touches on the early cantos. Mauberley is a type of the ineffectual aesthete of the 'nineties. In the first poem of the sequence, which sums up his failure to make an impression on his environment, Mauberley is presented as an Odysseus "out of key with his time" who has "Observed the elegance of Circe's hair" without having gained the wisdom needed to bridge the gap between his poetic self and the world. The result, in the second sequence, is Pound's vision of a Mauberley seen passively *drifting*, not actively steering, in the suspiciously calm waters of an utterly psychotic withdrawal from reality. Announcing his end, he writes on an oar "Here drifted/ an hedonist," [3] and the suggestion is of the fate of drunken Elpenor in the *Odyssey* and in Pound's first canto. *Mauberley* depicts the downhill journey of a comparatively narrow, will-less aesthete, quite unlike the Odysseus of Canto 1, who is heroically many-minded and active in gaining wisdom for the effective exertion of his will upon the environment.

If *Mauberley* presents Pound's conception of the poet as decadent, the *Cantos* presents Pound's conception of the poet as hero, whose ideal role is actively to exert a determining influence on the social environment. Odysseus is the archetype for all those later "heroes" of active, creative will who crop up in the *Cantos:* Malatesta, Confucius, Thomas Jefferson, Mussolini, and others. Odysseus against the sea, the initial image of the poem, establishes in symbolic form the basic polarity or conflict of forces which will reappear in many guises throughout the *Cantos* but can always be reduced to the formulation of will versus nature or will versus history. The polarity which I have suggested earlier to be all-encompassing remains that of *spirit* and *time* (for the concept of time ultimately includes both nature and history).

The second part of Canto 1, consisting of the last seven lines only, is a flash preview of the spiritual adventures in store for the poet-hero of the *Cantos*. As opposed to the rational narrative style of the Nekuia passage, the method here is elliptical, discontinuous, and the tone is oracular or *prophetic*, for reasons which I will soon make clear. The brevity of the passage makes it worth quoting in full:

> And he sailed, by Sirens and thence outward and away
> And unto Circe.
>> Venerandam,

3. *Personae* (New York, 1950), p. 203.

In the Cretan's phrase, with the golden crown, Aphrodite,
Cypri munimenta sortita est, mirthful, oricalchi, with golden
Girdles and breast bands, thou with dark eyelids
Bearing the golden bough of Argicida. So that:

The first two lines reverse the actual sequence of events in
Book XII of the *Odyssey*, where, after leaving the underworld,
Odysseus first rejoins Circe and later encounters the Sirens. The
apparent justification for the reversal is that Pound is presenting
images of the feminine in ascending order of desirability. We
shall meet the Sirens, Circe, and Aphrodite later on, always in
significant contexts, throughout the *Cantos*. First mentioned in
the passage quoted are the Sirens, whose beauty promises only
disaster. The ambiguous Circe is next, the goddess who can
turn men to swine or, if dominated by an Odysseus, provide
physical love and practical guidance. Aphrodite is the "crown"
of feminine beauty, and because she is "venerandam," worthy
of reverence, she symbolizes equally the spiritual dimensions of
such beauty.

The same sea of nature, the same life-force, throws up these
three possibilities of experience for Odysseus, which range from
physical danger to the most exalted vision of beauty. It is worth
noting that Pound, unlike T. S. Eliot, rejects dualism and does
not regard material and spiritual reality as essentially at odds. In
an early essay he speaks favorably of Remy de Gourmont, who
"does not grant the duality of body and soul, or at least suggests
that this medieval duality is unsatisfactory; there is an interpenetration, an osmosis of body and soul, at least for hypothesis." [4]
Pound goes on to praise Gourmont's "conception of love, passion, emotion as an intellectual instigation," and throughout
the *Cantos* we shall see that Aphrodite, goddess of love, stands
for both physical passion and for the highest and most enduring
kind of beauty that the spirit of man motivated by love can cre-

4. Ezra Pound, "Rémy de Gourmont," in *Literary Essays*, ed. T. S.
Eliot (Norfolk, 1954), p. 341.

ate. In one way or another all the villains of the poem attempt to deny, repress, or abuse sex, nature, the life-force in any and all of its forms; the heroes try to enter into creative harmony with nature.

Pound's non-dualistic view of nature as a physical-spiritual continuum is so important to the *Cantos* that it is worth giving it a name. I find the term *holism*, as defined by Jan Smuts in *Holism and Evolution*, the most fitting one available. Holism, says Smuts,

> represents the organic order as arising from and inside the inorganic or physical order without in any way derogating from it. If in the end it erects on the physical a superstructure which is more and more ideal and spiritual, that does not mean a denial of the physical. The idealism of Holism does not deny matter, but affirms and welcomes and affectionately embraces it.[5]

The pagan, and the archaic man in general, have tended to regard the world holistically, at least in the sense of a physical-spiritual continuum. Odysseus' communication with Tiresias through the blood of a sacrificed sheep symbolizes, in Canto 1, Pound's belief that the world of spirit and the world of nature are interdependent aspects of the same underlying *Ding an sich* that manifests itself temporally in the form of polarity. One of the most important metaphysical principles of Confucianism, the philosophy which informs the *Cantos* from beginning to end (as we shall see), is just this holistic principle expressed by the sage and rendered thus in Pound's translation:

> The celestial and earthly process can be defined in a single phrase; its actions and its creations have no duality.[6]

5. Jan Christiaan Smuts, *Holism and Evolution* (New York, 1961), p. 329. (Originally published in 1926.) I might mention here that Pound has told me he did not read Smuts.

6. Ezra Pound, trans., *Confucius: The Great Digest & Unwobbling Pivot* (New York, 1951), p. 183.

When the last seven lines of Canto 1 are examined in the light of the holistic principle, Aphrodite and the Sirens are seen as the two polar extremes of the *Ding and sich* which is nature. Circe, as a mediating center between the destructive and creative extremes, will come to represent that harmony with nature which Odysseus-Pound must attain before he can be vouchsafed the vision of Aphrodite. The point is that nature will be for man no more than what he wills it to be, its creative or destructive effects on him depending entirely on the quality of his will —or, better, the direction of his will. This concept of the direction of the will is the foundation of Pound's ethical world-view. Whether it be the creation of an enduring work of art or of a lasting social order, neither comes about by chance. It is "a matter of WILL," says Pound. "It is also a matter of the DIRECTION OF THE WILL," and "this phrase," he says, "brings us ultimately both to Confucius and Dante." [7] It was in Dante's *De vulgari eloquentia* "that Pound . . . discovered the term *directio voluntatis,* link between Confucius and the best of medieval Europe." [8] Pound takes the Confucian ideogram 志 as "The will, the direction of the will, . . . the officer standing over the heart." [9] The ideogram can thus represent the harmonious conjunction of Odysseus and the sea, the will and nature, or Kung (Confucius) and Eleusis. In the *Cantos* Kung stands for the principle of order, the force of reason, intelligence, and human-heartedness, whereas Eleusis stands for Dionysian energy, the life-force itself. Civilizations rise because of Eleusinian energy, but they are maintained in health and stability by Kung, the principle of order.

If the proper direction of the will is the result of an educative process, then it seems to me clear that the three necessary stages in the development of the will are appropriately repre-

7. Ezra Pound, *Jefferson and/or Mussolini: L'idea statale: Fascism as I Have Seen It* (New York, 1935), p. 16.
8. Noel Stock, "Introduction," *Impact,* p. xiii.
9. *Confucius,* p. 22.

sented in the sequence Sirens-Circe-Aphrodite. Lacking knowledge of the self and knowledge of the world, the will is incapable of proper direction and acts destructively. The Sirens symbolize the danger of self-annihilation encountered not only by individuals but by entire civilizations whose wills are misdirected. Circe represents that crucial middle stage of development, the attainment of self-knowledge and harmony with nature which individuals must have if they are to create enduring works, and which societies must possess if they are to maintain themselves for long against the forces of chaos and dissolution. In Canto 39 Odysseus achieves harmony with Circe, whose power bestializes the other members of his crew, because Odysseus alone is capable of a balanced reaction to the lure of sex and can assign it a proper place in his psychic economy. The third stage of the development of the will, the vision of Aphrodite, is the fruitful result of the achievement of inner harmony: cultural rebirth in general, enduring creations in art and the kind of social order that promotes the fullest realization of human potential. For Pound, the Highest Good is based upon the balanced functioning of *all* the human faculties *in due proportion*. He quotes with favor a translator of Aristotle who criticizes that philosopher's

> tendency to think of the End not as the sum of the Goods, but as one Good which is the Best. Man's welfare thus is ultimately found to consist not in the employment of all his faculties in due proportion, but only in the activity of the highest faculty, the "theoretic" intellect,[10]

and Pound adds, "That leads you plumb bang down to the 'split man.'" For Pound, as a Confucian, the proper direction of the will hinges as much upon "the sense of proportion" [11] as upon the sense of "timeliness" which I dwelt upon in the introduction.

10. Ezra Pound, *Guide to Kulchur* (Norfolk, 1952), pp. 342–43.
11. Ezra Pound, *Impact*, p. 134.

Earlier I expressed the feeling that these last lines of Canto 1 were "prophetic." The evidence seems unequivocal that Pound had no clear, conscious conception when beginning the *Cantos* of the over-all design the apparent fragments would fall into; yet I find in the sequence Sirens-Circe-Aphrodite an extraordinarily accurate outline of what I conceive to be the ultimate major form. The Sirens seem to represent what I describe as the first phase of the poem, the spirit's encounter with time: Nature and history will overwhelmingly come to mean chaos and destruction for the embattled spirit of Odysseus-Pound in this phase of the poem. (For Pound's villains and life-deniers, nature appears unqualifiedly destructive.) Circe, literally the major female figure in the second phase of the poem, could very well symbolize nature as order. In this phase of the poem, hope is seen for man if he adjusts the rhythms of his life to those of organic time. Aphrodite seems to represent the final phase of the poem, the attainment of the earthly paradise, "*Paradiso:* Time as Love." [12]

If my conception of the major form of the *Cantos* is defensible, then Canto 1 foreshadows in microcosm not only the major themes to be developed, but the over-all design of the poem as well. A profound intuition, I believe, gave Pound a sense of the whole from the very start. His use of myth rather than abstract statement enabled him to express much more than he could have "known." "The mythological exposition," Pound says, ". . . permits an expression of intuition without denting the edges or shaving off the nose and ears of a verity.[13]

12. A partial parallel to the Sirens-Circe-Aphrodite trio is afforded in Canto 1 of the *Commedia*, where Dante encounters three mysterious beasts, leopard, lion, and she-wolf, which critics variously interpret as representative of the three major regions of the damned which the poet is to pass through in the *Inferno*.

13. *Guide to Kulchur*, p. 127.

CHAPTER II

The Barb of Time

THE READING of Cantos 1 through 30 becomes most satisfying if one can discern some sort of thematic development or progression in them. The natural question is, after all, "What is Pound driving at by means of all these mythical, historical, and autobiographical shenanigans?" The answer seems quite clearly to be that Pound is portraying the decay of Western civilization, both moral and spiritual, from its vital, legendary beginnings in ancient myth to the sapless chaos of modern times. The method of "narration" is not chronological, but resembles rather the stream-of-consciousness technique of a Joyce or a Faulkner—especially the technique of Faulkner in *Absalom! Absalom!*, in which certain images are briefly and obscurely introduced at the beginning, then picked up again and expanded, and later retrieved and elaborated ever more explicitly until there is a final merging of the separate strands into coherence. The method is anticipatory and can be graphically represented as an ever-widening spiral which corresponds to the cyclical order of human memory, where the past, the present, and the future "are not serially, progressively, and uniformly ordered but are always inextricably and dynamically associated and mixed up with each other." The logic of the stream-of-consciousness technique is the subjective logic of images whose sequence "is causally determined by *significant associations* rather than by objective causal connections in the outside world." [1]

Pound's technique involved the initial "planting" of certain

1. Hans Meyerhoff, *Time in Literature* (Berkeley 1955), pp. 23 f.

myths of passion which are then to be elaborated in various ways through the progressive introduction of new materials—mythic, literary, historical, autobiographical. The new materials are intended to have *significant associations* with the initial myths; flashes of history, for example, reveal the timeless verity of the truths shadowed forth in myth. Cantos 2–7, as one critic points out, "deal with passion myths, modes of love and violence in metamorphosis." [2] In the myths Pound chooses, the theme of metamorphosis is obvious not only in the sense of "bodies changed/ To different forms" [3] by the gods, but also, more generally, in the Platonic sense which implies the recurrence of eternal "ideas," in different forms according to the accidental differences of time and place in which they emerge. The idea of eternal beauty, for example, embodies itself in various goddesses like Aphrodite and Diana, and in various mortal women like Helen of Troy and Eleanor of Aquitaine. One has to distinguish, however, between two distinct kinds of metamorphosis, positive and negative. Positive metamorphosis is characterized by the persistence within change of the untrammeled manifestations of forces such as Love, Beauty, Wisdom: Tiresias recurs as Confucius, for example, to re-embody Wisdom in its undiluted glory. Negative metamorphosis is Pound's major technique of irony in the *Cantos*, by which we see in various historical events or characters a garbled or debased version of the mythic archetype. To take just one instance, Baldy Bacon in Canto 12 is a debased modern version of many-minded Odysseus and functions as a commentary on modern times.

I shall limit my focus in this chapter to Cantos 2 through 5, developing especially an analysis of Canto 5, the first of Pound's

2. Christine Brooke-Rose, "Piers Plowman in the Modern Wasteland," in *Ezra Pound Perspectives*, ed. Noel Stock (Chicago, 1965), p. 172.

3. Ovid, *Metamorphoses*, trans. Rolfe Humphries (Bloomington, 1960), p. 3.

obviously intended "time" cantos. A distant view of Cantos 2 through 5 discovers a broad alternating movement: two succeeding pairs of cantos in which the first of each pair presents passion myths and the second concentrates on the ravages of time. Within the broad movement of alternation there is also a thematic progression, an intensification of the conflict between the irrepressible urgency of the natural passions and man's misdirected attempts to harness his passional self.

Canto 2 has been treated critically many times, and *The Analyst* (No. XVIII) devotes a twenty-five page issue to it alone. It is true, of course, that Canto 2 is Pound's first experiment in the poem with the Ovidian theme of metamorphosis, but it seems to me that much of the scholarship has dwelt upon matters of secondary importance and that the *formal* significance of the canto, that is, its relationship to the *Cantos* as a whole, has not received adequate attention. The canto develops at length only three myths, which appear successively to the mind's eye of Odysseus-Pound, the voyager, as visions taking form in the sea.

The first vision is from an episode in the third book of the *Iliad*, in which the Trojan elders, admiring the divine beauty of Helen, nevertheless counsel Priam to ship her back whence she came, "Back among Grecian faces," out of fear of the danger she represents to the city. The second vision, occupying most of the canto, is from the third book of Ovid's *Metamorphoses*. Greedy sailors, in defiance of their captain, Acoetes, attempt to kidnap the young god Dionysus "for a little slave money," unaware of the true identity of the drunken lad. The result is their transformation into fish. Acoetes is recounting the story to King Pentheus in obvious warning to the king to respect the power of the god. (In Ovid, not in Pound, Pentheus attempts to repress the rites of Dionysus and is in turn torn limb from limb by the female devotees of the god.)

The third vision, which has no classical source but is paralleled by Pound to the myth of Daphne and Apollo, concerns the transformation of the sea-nymph Ileuthyeria into coral. Her metamorphosis saves her from rape by a "band of tritons," lured to her by her great beauty. It is interesting to note that the attempted "rape" of Dionysus results in the punitive metamorphosis of the greed-inspired, would-be rapists, whereas the attempted rape of the nymph brings down no vindictive metamorphosis upon the would-be rapists; it results rather in the transformation of the nymph herself—into the rich permanence of coral. Where love is the motivating force, the transformation appears to be a positive one. The subordinate myth of Tyro, raped by Poseidon, appears immediately after that of the sea-nymph, as though to affirm the divine nature of natural passion and its ultimate creativity.

All three visions, not only the last two, involve metamorphoses. Helen, feared as a destroyer, brings on the destruction of Troy. Dionysus, object of the sailors' greed, turns the irreverent seamen into fish. The nymph, object of the tritons' passion, is transformed by the divine power of love into a coral-tree, which has the permanence and beauty of a work of art. The initial point I have to make in summarizing these myths is that *fear*, *greed*, and *love*, in that order, are suggested by Pound to be the motivating forces of the respective transformations. The major point I have to make is that these myths are an intentional elaboration, in precise order, of the sequence of possible attitudes of the will to the life-force given in Canto 1 as Sirens-Circe-Aphrodite.

The Sirens are a projection of the will's fear of nature and consequent rejection and repression of her. The Sirens symbolize nature regarded by man as a power for destruction only. And so the myth of the Sirens is metamorphosed by Pound in Canto 2 into the myth of Helen feared by the Trojan elders as a force for destruction. Circe represents the possibility of the will's achieving harmony with nature. Acoetes, in the Dionysus myth, achieves a proper relationship to the god, whereas the sailors' greed provokes them to "rape" the god and they are transformed as Circe transforms lust-ridden men into animals. The sailors' love of money is a perversion of natural love, of reverence for nature, and prefigures the usury theme of the *Cantos*. Lastly, the vision of a beautiful sea goddess in the beauty of a coral formation develops the theme of Aphrodite, the form which love takes when man's will is directed toward the creation of order and beauty out of the welter of nature. The mood of the lines describing the sea-nymph is lyrical and imitates the movement of waves:

> If you will lean over the rock,
> > the coral face under wave-tinge,
> Rose-paleness under water-shift,
> > Ileuthyeria, fair Dafne of sea-bords . . .

"Aphrodite we glimpse," says Hugh Kenner, "whenever the work breaks through into lyric, or forms half-congeal in the waves, or eyes pierce the mist, or some flux of events locks into an intelligible pattern." [4]

I think that what these myths suggest, fundamentally, is that nature cannot be repressed or perverted for long without serious consequences being visited upon her violators. One is reminded of Emerson's idea of "Compensation," but more pertinent are the Greek concepts of Hubris and Nemesis. The irreverent call down a Nemesis upon themselves for their Hubris in acting contrary to the will of the gods. The inexorable consequence of a denial of the life-force is not only the outrage perpetrated against others but a spiritual impoverishment, a diminution of being, in the wrong-doer himself. The punishment is expressed trenchantly in the fate of the "obstructors of knowledge" in Canto 14, where Episcopus is shown "waving a condom full of black-beetles."

Perhaps the profoundest anticipation of Phase Two of the

---

4. "Under the Larches of Paradise," *Gnomon: Essays on Contemporary Literature* (New York, 1958), p. 286.

Cantos is discoverable in these concepts of Hubris and Nemesis. It is well enough known that Confucianism is the philosophical underpinning of the *Cantos* as a whole, but Confucianism is itself based on the older Chinese myth of the Yang and Yin. The Confucian document *Li Ki*, or *Book of Rites*, a portion of which Pound translates in Canto 52 as introduction to the Chinese history cantos, is thoroughly permeated with the Yin-Yang philosophy. The Greek concept of Hubris and Nemesis finds its Chinese equivalent in the ethical implications of Yin-Yang thought. Professor Yu-Lan states that

> *yang* originally meant . . . sunshine and light; . . . *yin* meant . . . shadow or darkness. In later development, the Yang and Yin came to be regarded as two cosmic principles or forces, respectively representing masculinity, activity . . . for the Yang, and femininity, passivity . . . for the Yin.

Everything in the universe arises from the interaction of these two cosmic principles, and if either is repressed, "then there are earthquakes." [5] When violence is done to nature, nature reacts violently in reprisal. In Chinese thought, a kind of poetic justice inheres in the universe, to which the Greek Nemesis corresponds. The myths Pound employs in the *Cantos*, then, seem to have the further function of revealing the *moral* nature of things, intuited by the archaic consciousness but more and more to be ignored, forgotten, and repressed as Western civilization advances, rudderless, into chaos.

Canto 3 is the first portrait in the poem of the "drear waste" of Western history. Two images of the baffled will, locked out of "home," are developed at length. In an autobiographical passage at the beginning, Pound describes himself as the penniless young poet he was in 1908, sitting on the steps of the gondola platform beside the Venetian customshouse (he lived nearby in

5. Fung Yu-Lan. *A Short History of Chinese Philosophy* (New York, 1948), p. 138.

a room in San Trovaso). He portrays himself in ironic contrast
to Browning, who in the third Canto of *Sordello* sits on Venetian palace steps in a much more romantic setting. Pound
stresses his unromantic inability to afford a gondola, apparently
the one that still crosses the Grand Canal to St. Mark's Square:
to reach San Marco by foot from the Dogana is, of course, possible, but would require a rather long roundabout walk. If "the
gondolas cost too much, that year," the poet may not simply be
saying that he couldn't afford one, but that the price was in any
case unjust. He is economically frustrated from freely moving
about the city he loves, the city which is depicted in Canto 17
as a type of the earthly paradise. In contrast to his present circumstances, the poet, looking across the Grand Canal, has a
vision of the timeless beauty of Tuscany, of the gods floating
"in the azure air" in the unspoiled time before time began,
"back before dew was shed." The theme of time is thus beginning to be explored, although it will not become explicit until
Canto 5.

    We see another type of the baffled will in the Cid, an Odys-
sean hero who is literally exiled from home. One strongly suspects a subject-rhyme, an intended comparison and contrast,
between the young Pound and El Cid. Unjustly deprived of
home, money, possessions, El Cid needs "pay for his menie" to
break "his way to Valencia." Rather than passively sitting on
steps, however, the Cid is shown as resourcefully acting to re-
lieve his distress by tricking the money-lenders Raquel and
Vidas into provisioning himself and his entourage so that he
may gain the means to improve his condition. Perhaps Pound is
intentionally contrasting the will of modern Western man,
stymied by economic injustice, with the creative will of the
European Middle Ages, which did not allow a perverse economic system to frustrate its creativity. The Cid is an heroic
model for modern man to follow.

    The cultural decay intervening between the Middle Ages
and modern times strikes us in a few brief flashes at the end of

the canto. What happened to the constructive will of the Middle Ages before it became baffled in modern times is evidently its perversion to destructive ends: "Ignez da Castro murdered" introduces the Renaissance theme which is to gather resonance in the cantos to come. The Renaissance, for Pound, is generally a time of violent disorder and decay in the spheres of religion, morality, politics, and art. The treacherous political murder of beautiful Ignez de Castro, described in Camoens's *Lusiads*, reappears in Canto 30.[6] The decay of the Renaissance is most powerfully suggested in the final line of the canto, "Silk tatters, 'Nec Spe Nec Metu,' " in which the stoic motto of the Este family, "With neither hope nor fear," is contrasted with the decay that supervened when the Estes fell away from this noble precept. The decay of the Estes is one of the major historical subjects treated in the first thirty cantos.

In the first thirty cantos, the theme of man exiled from the city that he loves, of natural feeling thwarted by social tyranny, whether political or economic, reaches climactic development in Pound's lengthy treatment of the rise and fall of Venice. This "city" theme, presented in a muted and undramatic way at the beginning of Canto 3, is introduced in Cantos 4 and 5 with an ominous suggestiveness. The beginning of Canto 4 parallels that of Canto 3. The narrator in Canto 4 again looks at a city— now the smoking ruins of Troy—and contrasts it with his paradisal vision of a "Choros nympharum," a vision of Dionysian ecstasies. It is obvious that something has gone wrong, and the myths of violent passion that follow serve to "explain" what has gone wrong. In these myths, the male will is seen as incapable of controlling sexual passion, and the result is tragic violence for

6. Pound's instinctive "anticipations" of subjects developed later can occasionally be very artful *afterthoughts* rather than true anticipations. Recently, when Pound allowed me to examine his copy of the first sixteen cantos, I noticed that no reference to Ignez de Castro appeared in that early version of Canto 3. He had obviously added it much later after writing or planning Canto 30.

the innocent and guilty alike. The muted theme of ideal har-
mony of the will with nature is expressed in allusions to Catul-
lus's epithalamion praising the bride Aurunculeia, "Hymen, Io
Hymenæe!" But the theme of disharmony emerges pointedly in
Pound's rendering of "Fu-Fu" ("Wind Song," or "Ode to the
Wind"), which he found in the Fenollosa manuscripts.[7]

> And So-Gioku, saying:
> "This wind, sire, is the king's wind,
>   This wind is wind of the palace,
>
>   .   .   .
>
> And Ran-ti, opening his collar:
> "This wind roars in the earth's bag,
>   it lays the water with rushes;
> No wind is the king's wind.

The relation of the will to the passions, or of the ruler to his
subjects, is in dispute in these lines. The irreverent delusion
that a man can have absolute sway over the forces of nature is
what Ran-ti attempts to puncture.

The theme expressed by Ran-ti, and the materials with
which it combines in the opening lines of the next stanza, serve
as a kind of bridge giving direct access to Canto 5. This transitional passage is worth close examination, for a proper explanation of the lines will clarify the time-theme of the following
canto:

> The camel drivers sit in the turn of the stairs,
>   Look down on Ecbatan of plotted streets,
> "Danaë! Danaë!
>   What wind is the king's?"

---

7. This source was recently discovered by Professor Sanehide Kodama.
The normally indispensable *Annotated Index to the Cantos of Ezra Pound*,
by John Hamilton Edwards and William W. Vasse (Berkeley, 1959),
erroneously assumes the Arthur Waley translation of this poem by So-
Gioku to be Pound's source.

The myth of Danaë is treated less cryptically fourteen lines later, where it is once again associated with the city of Ecbatan: "Ecbatan, upon the gilded tower in Ecbatan/ Lay the god's bride, lay ever, waiting the golden rain." Danaë was imprisoned in a brazen tower by her father Acrisius, King of Argos, who feared an oracle predicting that she would bear a son who would kill him. Eventually Zeus visited Danaë in the form of a "golden rain" and she became the mother of Perseus, who grew up and ultimately killed Acrisius by accident with a discus.

Ecbatan (or Agbatana), the great fortress-city of the Medes, was built by King Deioces in the sixth century B.C. in the form of concentric circles of walls. "There are seven circles in all," says Herodotus; "within the innermost circle are the king's dwellings and the treasuries." Each of the walls is of a different color, "and the battlements of the last two circles are coated, these with silver and those with gold." [8] In the first of the *Pisan Cantos* Pound refers to Ecbatan as "the city of Dioce," an image for the earthly paradise. Deioces was chosen by the Medes to be their king because of his reputation for justice. Once enthroned, he established law and order among his people. But the association in Canto 4 of the cruel Acrisius with the just Deioces is contradictory. As a matter of fact, the Ecbatan of Cantos 4 and 5 is a city of *injustice* rather than of justice. The most obvious clue is the line "What wind is the king's?" which implies criticism of Acrisius for his arrogance against nature and the gods in trying to suppress his daughter's sexuality. Less obvious is the disdain of the camel drivers, who "Look down on Ecbatan of plotted streets." The original version of Canto 4 reads "Look down *to* Ecbatan of plotted streets" [9] (my italics), so that the later change implies a change in meaning from neutral observation to observation with supe-

8. *Herodotus*, Book I, §98. [*Herodotus*, with an English translation by A. D. Godley (The Loeb Classical Library), Vol. I.]

9. Ezra Pound, *Poems 1918–21* (New York, 1921), p. 76. The volume includes the original versions of Cantos 4 through 7.

rior, detached *disapproval* of the "plotted streets," the *artificial order* that government achieves at the cost of violence to nature, irreverence to man and the gods.[10] The myth of Danaë, in which the oracle speaks the truth in spite of all appearances, suggests that Hubris has encountered Nemesis and that those who attempt to achieve order at the cost of life do so finally at the cost of their own lives as well.

What remains unaccounted for is Pound's association of Ecbatan, presumably the city of Deioces, with the unjust Acrisius' Argos. The explanation emerges, however, upon a further reading of Herodotus. Ecbatan, the capital of Media, had *four* kings, the first of whom was the founder, Deioces, then Phraortes, Cyaxares, and Astyages. It is the Ecbatan that represents the Median kingdom in its last stage of decline, the Ecbatan of Astyages, that Pound couples with the Argos of Acrisius. For Astyages was dethroned by *his* grandson Cyrus the Elder, founder of the Persian empire, in the same mythical manner by which Acrisius met his nemesis in his grandson Perseus. Astyages had a dream which seemed to portend that his grandson would become ruler of all Asia. To eliminate that possibility, he kept his pregnant daughter Mandane well guarded and upon the birth of Cyrus delivered him to his faithful servant Harpagus with orders to kill the child. In the manner of such legends, the child escaped death, grew up, and led the Persians in battle against Astyages, whom Cyrus defeated and imprisoned. The supremacy of the Medes thereby passed to the

10. My view of Ecbatan as a city of injustice, of "plotted streets" like the "Charter'd streets" of Blake's London, is just the opposite to the view developed in Walter Baumann's monograph, *The Rose in the Steel Dust* (Francke Verlag, Bern, 1967). Baumann considers Ecbatan to be Pound's consistent image of the Ideal City in this Canto as well as in the *Pisan Cantos* (where it is unquestionably the Ideal City). In spite of my disagreement with him on this point, which is essential to my development of the time-theme in Canto 5, Baumann's study of Canto 4 is in many respects illuminating, and is the most extensive yet made (comprising pp. 17–53 of his book).

Persians.[11] Pound is setting up the general thesis that the achievement of order at the expense of Eleusinian energy is the sure sign that a civilization is dying.

Canto 5 begins in the same manner I have described for the two previous cantos. First the narrator presents his composite vision of an evil, unnatural city; then he gives us paradisal images of perfect order in terms of Neoplatonic light imagery. Neoplatonic philosophers have a significant but frequently un-differentiated role to play in the *Cantos*. In the poem, the most important of these philosophers is Plotinus, who serves as Pound's guide through the Hell of Canto 15 and out into the sunlight. Pound employs the light imagery used by a number of Neoplatonists, or philosophers influenced by Neoplatonism (late-classical, non-Christian figures such as Plotinus and his disciple Iamblichus, as well as medieval Christian thinkers such as Scotus Erigena or the humanist Gemistus Plethon) to stand generally for a state of divine ecstasy including total illumina-tion of the mind. In his *Guide to Kulchur* he speaks of "Iam-blichus on the fire of the gods [the "Iamblichus' light," ap-parently, of Canto 5] . . . which comes down into a man and produces superior ecstasies, feelings of regained youth, super-youth and so forth." Of the "two mystic states" that "can be dissociated," Iamblichus, and the Neoplatonists in general (the chapter title is "Neo-Platonicks, Etc.") incline toward "the ecstatic-beneficent-and-benevolent, contemplation of the divine love, the divine splendour with goodwill toward others." The other mysticism Pound characterizes as "the bestial, namely the fanatical, the man on fire with God and anxious to stick his snotty nose into other men's business." [12] Pound feels that the Platonists have always made men aware of transcendent Mind, which he associates with light:

> Plato periodically caused enthusiasm among his disciples. And the Platonists after him have caused man after man to be sud-

11. *Herodotus*, Book I, §107 ff.
12. *Guide to Kulchur*, p. 223.

denly conscious of the reality of the *nous*, of mind, apart from any man's individual mind, of the sea crystalline and enduring, of the bright as it were molten glass that envelops us, full of light.[13]

Platonists, in Pound's generalizing view, have tended to affirm the life-force:

Plato has repeatedly stirred men to a sort of enthusiasm productive of action, and . . . one cannot completely discount this value as life force.[14]

Canto 5 is constructed on an interesting directional metaphor, movement upward contending with movement downward in physical, aesthetic, and moral terms. The first twelve lines begin with an image of stasis that develops into a quick downward tumble into history and time. The first lines carry over the Danaë-Ecbatan theme from Canto 4:

> Great bulk, huge mass, thesaurus;
> Ecbatan, the clock ticks and fades out[,] [15]
>
> The bride awaiting the god's touch; Ecbatan,
> City of patterned streets; again the vision:

The thesaurus or treasury of Ecbatan, which parallels the central citadel in which Danaë-Mandane, the life-force, Aphrodite herself is locked away, is presented unbeautifully as a meaningless and sterile mass of matter corresponding to the static, un-

13. Ibid. p. 44.
14. Ibid. p. 347.
15. The New Directions edition of the *Cantos* omits punctuation here, but the English edition supplies a comma, which seems to me necessary to avoid a needless ambiguity. Perhaps the wisest choice of punctuation is found in the early version in *Poems 1918–21* (p. 78), where the line in dispute ends with a *semicolon* and makes more grammatical sense in supporting the parallel disjointedness of the first four lines of the canto.

impregnated body of the waiting "bride" of Zeus. Ecbatan is, as
we have seen before, an image of *sterile order*, and Pound introduces the theme of clock time, mechanical time, as a symbol
of *order* without time-abrogating *significance*, the mere marking
of time, the empty succession of equally dead intervals. The
clock becomes the symbol, then, of the unhealthy, misdirected
will as it manifests itself in social injustice. Clock-time characterizes also the passive "feminine" consciousness of the poet
when unimpregnated by the "god's touch" of inspiration or
"the vision." This theme will shortly emerge more openly, so
that clock-time will have multiple reference to the state of the
arts as well as to that of government and of individual moral
action. The alternation of clock-tick and vision marks the di-
lemma of the poet as well as of society, and the two are for
Pound intimately related.

The following lines reveal the pattern of downward movement that results necessarily from spiritual stasis:

> Down in the viae stradae, toga'd the crowd, [and arm'd,
> Rushing on populous business,] [16]
> and from parapet looked down
> and North was Egypt,
>   the celestial Nile, blue deep,
>   cutting low barren land,
> Old men and camels
>   working the water-wheels;

The allusion is again to Herodotus, now to the invasion of
Egypt by Cyrus' son Cambyses. If we recall that Cyrus was the
nemesis of his grandfather Astyages, whose Ecbatan is the one
logically alluded to in this and the previous canto, then we find
Pound continuing to relate a family history of disaster. Cambyses, dreaming that his brother Smerdis would replace him as

16. The bracketed phrases are deleted in the Faber and Faber edition,
but I believe that at least the phrase "and arm'd" is necessary to the sense
of the passage.

king, proceeded to have his brother killed. Later, however, a pseudo-Smerdis usurped the throne in Ecbatan, and Cambyses, marching back from Egypt to quell the revolution at home, died of an accidentally self-inflicted wound in the genitals, "in the same part where he himself had once smitten the Egyptian god Apis." [17] Although the theme of fratricide is not alluded to by Pound in connection with Cambyses, it crops up later in the canto in the murder of Giovanni Borgia, presumably by his own brother Cesare. Cambyses was not only fratricidal, but incestuous as well, so that he, too, like Acrisius and Astyages, meets an appropriate nemesis for violating nature, in the sense of violating the moral order established by the gods and conceived of as "natural" for man.

Pound alludes only to Cambyses' march against Egypt and emphasizes the *downward* moral and spiritual direction of his activities with the repetition of "down" and the sense of reaching bottom in the "low barren land" along the Nile. The "Old men and camels/ working the water-wheels" again symbolize the empty repetition of mechanical time (the Egyptians measured time with water-wheels). It is ironic that Ecbatan, the clock, and the water-wheel are superficially images of circular order but represent, in their barren futility, linear time.

The Neoplatonic imagery of the next lines draws us sharply *upward* in direction:

> [Measureless seas and stars,][18]
> Iamblichus' light,
>> the souls ascending,
> Sparks like a partridge covey,
>> Like the "ciocco", brand struck in the game.

Integrative ascent of souls toward unity in the One (Plotinus' Absolute) contrasts with the previous imagery of descent into the multiplicity of the togaed "crowd" bent on destruction.

17. *Herodotus*, Book III, §64.
18. The bracketed line is deleted from the Faber text.

Pound draws on Dante's description of the sphere of Jupiter, which is the sphere of justice and world order in the *Paradiso*, for the images of bird and burning brand used for souls arising. In Dante the souls fly up *"come augelli surti di rivera"* (as birds risen from a river-bank) and as innumerable sparks rising *"nel percuoter de' ciocchi arsi"* (when burning logs are struck).[19] These rising souls are lights which form the phrase DILIGITE JUSTITIAM QUI IUDICATIS TERRAM (Love justice, ye that judge the earth), the final group of souls forming "the head and neck of the Roman eagle, the divine augury and promise . . . of the world's final order and peace." [20] The merging of a *togaed* crowd with the previous Cambyses material suggests that Pound intends a contrast between Rome in decline, due to injustice, and Rome in its full glory as a symbol of order and justice.

In the following lines the theme of time emerges again, but in relation now to the theme of artistic creativity rather than to the theme of social injustice with which it was connected at the opening of the canto:

> Topaz I manage, and three sorts of blue;
> > but on the barb of time.
> The fire? always, and the vision always,
> Ear dull, perhaps, with the vision, flitting
> And fading at will. Weaving with points of gold,
> Gold-yellow, saffron . . .

Topaz belongs in the range of yellow and golden colors classically associated with Aphrodite. In *The Analyst* (No. III), John J. Espey identifies "three sorts of blue" as an allusion to Pound's own early poem "Blandula, Tenulla, Vagula," in which the poet addresses his soul and speaks of meeting it, after physical death, in an earthly, sensuous paradise: "Will not our cult

19. Dante, *Paradiso*, XVIII, 11. 73, 100. The English translation in parenthesis is from John D. Sinclair's *The Divine Comedy of Dante Alighieri: III Paradiso* (New York, 1961).

20. Ibid. p. 267.

be founded on the waves/ Clear sapphire, cobalt, cyanine,/ On triune azures, the impalpable/ Mirrors unstill of the eternal change?" Blue, however, has in any case become associated in previous cantos with the changing colors of sea and sky, so that it is self-sufficient as a symbol of natural beauty. The relative permanence of the topaz as a gem and its golden color suggest that it is the poet's "philosopher's stone" of Love, by which he is enabled to transmute the ever-changing beauty of nature, the flux, into the permanence of poetic form just as the alchemist ideally can change baser metals into gold. "Weaving with points of gold," which represents poetic creation, carries forward this muted alchemical image of turning crude experience into golden art. *The barb of time* is the antithesis to the permanence of topaz and is the intruder which from time to time disrupts the poet's creative accord with nature. This intrusion is nothing else than *time as social evil,* the point of the opening lines of the canto. It would be extremely misleading to give time here the stereotyped meaning of "the flux of experience," which lumps together the flux of nature and the flux of history as if they were much the same thing. I have, I believe, already indicated that Pound's attitudes toward nature and toward history are diametrically opposed, and it is this fundamental distinction which is indispensable to an understanding of the theme of time and thereby of the *Cantos* as a whole.

The three lines beginning with "The fire? always, and the vision always" are a restatement of the topaz-time antithesis. The fire of passion and the light of vision are permanent possessions of the poet in the potential sense, but "the barb of time" occasionally dulls the melopoeic or music-making ear just as it dulls the phanopoeic or image-making vision. The result is an art that bears witness to this struggle against chaos. The poet pictures himself as "weaving" a tapestry of various hues of gold, culling his golden threads from the poetry of Catullus, Propertius, and Sappho, in that order; but "time" punctures the vision and the music; the "Titter of sound about me, always" makes classical perfection extremely difficult to achieve. The result is art as only partially ordered chaos, which Pound considers an effect as satisfactory as that of classical perfection. He said, in an essay of 1928:

> Art very possibly *ought* to be the supreme achievement, the "accomplished"; but there is the other satisfactory effect, that of a man hurling himself at an indomitable chaos, and yanking and hauling as much of it as possible into some sort of order (or beauty), aware of it both as chaos and as potential.[21]

In addition to representing different types of poetic gold, the series "gold/ Gold-yellow, saffron" seems also to have the general function of announcing the theme of love dealt with in the classical poems that are then alluded to. Topaz, gold, and other yellows are associated with Aphrodite, goddess of love, and the color saffron now reintroduces the bride Aurunculeia from Canto 4 ("Saffron sandal so petals the narrow foot").

In the web of allusions to classical poems which follows, Pound gives us images of three types of love shown in a sequence of descent from perfect hymeneal harmony to the barren frustration of unrequited love. First, according to this pattern, is Catullus' epithalamium to Aurunculeia (Carmen 61) which represents the ideal union of lovers in marriage. Secondly, the phrase "here Sextus had seen her" suggests the adulterous love relationship, unfaithful on the male's part, between Sextus Propertius and Cynthia.[22] The "Titter of sound" constantly breaking in upon the harmony of the poet's vision suggests the cynicism, skepticism, and faithlessness that undermine the harmony of pure love. Thirdly, Pound presents a kind of montage of Sappho's poems to Atthis, the young girl who deserted the poetess for another woman, Andromeda. The theme of infertility is stressed with the mournful repetition of "the vinestocks lie untended" in association with the phrase "Atthis,

21. *Polite Essays*, p. 77.
22. See "Homage to Sextus Propertius," *Personae*, pp. 224–25.

unfruitful." Sappho's love is the vinestock blasted by Atthis's betrayal, and perhaps the literal fruitlessness of Lesbian love is also suggested. "Fades the light from the sea," Pound writes in paraphrasing the grief of Sappho. Pound has been weaving a tapestry of types of poetic gold, and at the same time a tapestry of types of love, from ecstatic to mournful.

This downward movement in the spectrum of love seems now to be counterbalanced by a thematic upswing, a movement towards reintegration suggested by two love legends from the troubadour biographies. The first tale ends as mournfully as Sappho's, but on a note of reunion of a sort. (After "Fades the light from the sea," the pathetic fallacy accompanying the Sappho montage, the light seems now dimly to return in the Poicebot episode, which is marked near the end by the parenthetical "Sea change, a grey in the water.") Poicebot, irresponsibly abandoning his wife, succumbs to wanderlust. Sometime after she had been abandoned, his wife is made pregnant by a knight "out of England"[23] who has "put glamour upon her." Poicebot, returning from Spain, footloose and lusty, seeks out a prostitute and finds one—his wife, "changed and familiar face." The "moral" seems to be that the laws of nature, as we saw in Danaë's case, do not suspend themselves for the convenience of men. The second motif, the tale of Pieire de Maensac, suggests that love obeys a law higher than the laws of men, that in the ideal society the laws of the heart are acknowledged as superior to the laws of men, which are frequently short-sighted and tyrannically abusive of the nature of things. The troubadour Pieire de Maensac ran off with the wife of Bernart de Tierci (who was obviously a failure as a lover) to the castle of the Dauphin of Auvergne. Tierci tried to gain her back by force but could prevail neither against love nor the Dauphin, who "stood with de Maensac." The Dauphin's defense of de Maensac is the

23. See Pound's account in "Troubadours—Their Sorts and Conditions," *The Literary Essays of Ezra Pound*, ed. T. S. Eliot (Norfolk, 1954), pp. 95–96. The tale of Pieire de Maensac follows on pp. 96–97.

peak of the last upward movement in the canto; it represents the ideal of social order, a united front of love (nature), poetry (the arts), and politics. (Tierci reappears significantly in Canto 23 in connection with the theme of Christian fanaticism that is developed in the latter portion of the first thirty cantos.)

At this point the metaphor of *descent* takes sudden hold and dominates the canto to the end:

> John Borgia is bathed at last. (Clock-tick pierces the vision)
> Tiber, dark with the cloak, wet cat gleaming in patches.
> Click of the hooves, through garbage,
> Clutching the greasy stone.

The first line of this passage is spaced more effectively as two lines in the first printed version (*Dial*, August 1921, p. 199), where the theme of time is given central—and centered— prominence as follows:

> John Borgia is bathed at last.
> (Clock-tick pierces the vision)

Giovanni Borgia, presumed to have been murdered (in 1497) at the instigation of his brother Cesare, recalls us to the theme of unnatural violence against kindred suggested in the legends of Acrisius, Astyages, and Cambyses. The clock-tick, like the sword that pierced the body of Borgia, is the "barb" of time that pierces the vision of perfect harmony the poet has just enjoyed. Mechanical time is the symbol of moral disorder, the violation of nature, the perversion of natural feeling that reaches a maximum in an act such as fratricide. The clock-tick reverberates through the quoted passage in "cloak," "click of the hooves," and "clutching." The Borgia murder recurs obsessively in the remainder of the canto. It is presented twice more with added detail, intruding upon the contemporary historical account of the murder of Alessandro de' Medici by *his* kinsman Lorenzino de' Medici (in 1537), and entwining itself with allusions to the murder of Agamemnon. The clock-tick echoes again in the last and longest glimpse Pound gives of the Borgia murder: "Hooves clink and slick on the cobbles./ Schiavoni . . . cloak . . ." [24] The emphasis on the clicking hooves of the murderer's horse as measuring mechanical time seems to stem from the image of time as a "barb," one of whose meanings is barbary horse. The image of time as a kind of horse recurs ironically in another incident described in the canto. For Pound, disorder in the body politic ultimately shows up in a perversion of the arts, so that the poetaster Mozarello receives poetic justice when "smothered beneath a mule." Fittingly, he is destroyed for his artistic sterility by a mule, the sterile offspring of jackass and mare and an ironic version of the *barb* of time.

The ascent to Neoplatonic light has changed into a descent into the darkness of time ("Tiber, dark with the cloak"), and the "fire" of passion is replaced by the "ice" in the lowest circle of Dante's hell, where "*Caina attende.*/ The lake of ice there below me"; Caina, one of the four divisions of the lowest circle of Dante's *Inferno*, contains betrayers of their kindred. Mechanical time, bad poetry (meter without meaning), history as a record of moral perversion, and Dante's *Inferno* are all closely associated with one another for the first time in this first of the important "time" cantos.

The insistence on the imagery of *descent* to characterize time or history is carried on in this last half of the canto in climactic fashion. First, the corpse of Borgia is plunged down into the Tiber. The historian Varchi of Florence then relates one of Lorenzo's initial plans to murder Alessandro by having him thrown from a wall, whereupon we are plunged into the "lake of ice" of Caina. Mozarello falls beneath a mule, but then Pound describes his death as "a poet's ending,/ down a stale well-hole." The canto ends on the note of death, "*Ma se morisse!*"

24. *Schiavoni*: the church at the place where a watchman saw Borgia's body dumped into the Tiber.

Pound views the Renaissance generally as a period of moral, political, and aesthetic disorder in comparison with the golden age of the troubadours, when poetry flourished and "The air was full of women." [25] Canto 5 is linked in a number of ways to the second great "time" canto, Canto 7, which is concerned with an examination of *modern* Europe in the light of the time concept. The most important link is the theme of the Florentine tyrant Alessandro's passivity in the face of a death foretold to him "thrice over" by his astrologist Del Carmine. Alessandro, like Acrisius, Astyages, and Cambyses, had his doom prophetically revealed to him, but unlike these legendary tyrants, he failed even to *try* to exert his will against destiny. As opposed to the perverted will of Lorenzo, Alessandro's "abuleia," or willlessness, is in Pound's view the particular mark of modern civilization. Renaissance man acted out of misdirected passion; modern man, his natural passions almost totally suppressed (Canto 7 dates back to 1921), does not act.

25. Canto 5, p. 18.

CHAPTER III

Rooms Against Chronicles

THE WHOLE of Cantos 4–7, published as a single unit in *Poems 1918–21*, seems to have been intended as a distinct sequence introducing in highly concentrated form the theme of time that would dominate the entire first phase of the poem. It is obvious that the cantos succeeding this group tend to single out particular themes or subjects and treat them in more and more extended fashion, whereas Cantos 4–7 dart dizzyingly over whole ranges of history and literature and cryptically fuse seemingly unrelated subject matters. The likeliest reason for such fusion would be that Pound wished to give the time-theme general applicability to all the other themes he would individually develop thereafter.

The unpublished letters of Ezra Pound to John Quinn, in the John Quinn Memorial Collection of the New York Public Library, cast light on Pound's intentions in this group of cantos. That Cantos 4–7 were composed as a "group" emerges, first, from their time of composition. Having written no new cantos since early 1917, when he finished the first version of the now largely discarded Cantos 1, 2, and 3, Pound suddenly gathered his energies into a concentrated effort and produced all of Cantos 4–7 during the latter half of 1919. He submitted them all to *Dial* in March, 1920, and in his cover letter he all but insists on the publication of at least Cantos 5–7 *as a unit*.

The motif he mentions as unifying them is the murder of Alessandro de' Medici by his brother Lorenzo. Pound points out that the subject begins in Canto 5 and concludes Canto 7.

His selection of the Medici murder as the unifying theme of Cantos 5–7 interestingly suggests his conscious preoccupation with the more general theme of mechanical time in these cantos. It was, after all, another Renaissance murder, that of Giovanni Borgia, which introduced in Canto 5 the vision-piercing "clock-tick"—and the subject-rhyme of the Medici murder inevitably carries forward the theme of time through Canto 7.

As to Canto 4, Pound felt that it could be printed separately (it had in fact been published privately on October 4, 1919). Its themes and subject matter, however, are carried over into Canto 5, whose opening theme of time cannot be understood apart from it. One's sense of the unitary nature of Cantos 4–7 is supported, then, by Pound's own testimony. It is also clear that Pound placed a high value upon these cantos. For example, in a letter to Quinn of October 1920 he says, "I at any rate think Canto VII the best thing I have done." If we remember that Pound is here placing Canto 7 above his finest earlier productions, including the *Cathay* volume and the *Propertius* and *Mauberley* sequences, we recognize our responsibility as readers to pay very close attention to it. (See Appendix A for quotations from Pound's letters to Quinn relevant to these early cantos.)

Canto 7 seems to complete a diptych with Canto 5. The latter's complex presentation of time, imbued with the tone of the Renaissance, is supplemented by another portrayal of time that borrows its main imagery from the modern wasteland. It is perhaps more accurate to say that some of the main imagery of Canto 7 resembles important images in Eliot's *Waste Land*, which Pound was editing about two years after he had completed Canto 7.[1] Eliot had of course read Canto 7 and may

1. See Myles Slatin, "A History of Pound's 'Cantos I–XVI,' 1915–1925," *American Literature* XXXV (May 1963), 188. Slatin quotes from an unpublished Yale letter written by Pound to his father on December 13, 1919, in which the poet states that he had *completed* Canto 7. We

have been directly influenced by it in composing *The Waste Land*. (One critic, noting that in these poems "The two poets share a vision of men as husks, shells, and pods," unfortunately assumes, in spite of the weight of chronological evidence to the contrary, that *The Waste Land* influenced Canto 7.[2]

As in Canto 5, the general theme of Canto 7 is the violence done to love and beauty by the perverted will of society, and the poet's attempt to retrieve the living vision of Aphrodite from beneath the dead weight of time. The first line, "Eleanor (she spoiled in a British climate)," suggests the general theme of the canto and at the same time links it with the Eleanor-Helen-Aphrodite motif of Canto 6. Pound has been carefully working his Love-theme and Time-theme into contrapuntal climaxes against one another. As for the Love-theme, we have seen the Aphrodite of Canto 1 merge into Helen-Eleanor and other figures in Canto 2. The legends of the troubadours, blended with the classical passion myths of Canto 4, are a collateral development of the Eleanor theme and re-emerge more explicitly and powerfully in the Pieire de Maensac episode of Canto 5. Finally the troubadour and Eleanor themes converge climactically in Canto 6 in celebration of the power of passion and poetry to liberate body and spirit from social bondage.

One of the most difficult passages of Canto 7 immediately follows the first line, Eleanor giving way now to Helen the destroyer, as Aeschylus's (and Homer's) old men see her:

> Ἕλανδρος and Ἑλέπτολις, and
> poor old Homer blind,
> blind as a bat,

---

know that Pound saw a first draft of *The Waste Land* (the fabulous first version, owned by the New York Public Library) in the fall of 1921, months *after* the August, 1921, publication of Canto 7, in substantially its present form, in *Dial*. Thus any resemblance between the two poems can be due only to the *Zeitgeist*, to previous literary talk between the two poets, and to the influence of Canto 7 on the Eliot poem rather than vice-versa.

2. Guy Mattison Davenport, Jr., "A Reading of I–XXX of the Cantos of Ezra Pound" (Ph.D. dissertation: Harvard, 1961), p.290.

Ear, ear for the sea-surge;
            rattle of old men's voices.
And then the phantom Rome,[3]
            marble narrow for seats
"Si pulvis nullus" said Ovid,
"Erit, nullum tamen excute."
Then [4] file and candles, e li mestiers ecoutes;
Scene for the battle only, but still scene,
Pennons and standards y cavals armatz
Not mere succession of strokes, sightless narration,
And [5] Dante's "ciocco," brand struck in the game.

The passage ends with telescoped quotations from Flaubert's
Un Coeur Simple. The critic George Dekker does an excellent
job in analyzing it as "a highly condensed, peculiarly Poundian
history of mimesis from Homer to Flaubert." [6] In addition to a
condensed commentary on the great poetic styles of various
eras, however, the passage gives us brief glimpses of the *spiritual
states* of the historical periods represented. I believe that a
study of the passage from this point of view will ultimately
prove the more fruitful for an understanding of the canto.

Aeschylus puns on Helen's name in the *Agamemnon,* calling
her Ελέναυς (ship-destroying), ἔλανδρος (man-destroying), and
ἑλέπτολις (city-destroying). In the *Iliad* Homer reports the same
head-shaking attitude of the old men of Troy towards this
dangerous Helen, the most beautiful woman in the world.
In spite of his blindness, Pound is saying, Homer's great aural
imagination, his musical sensitivity, enabled him to appreciate
profoundly the earth-shaking, invincible power of beauty. Helen
becomes incarnate in the literally earth-shaking "sea-surge," the
sound of which Homer captured magnificently in the onomato-
poeic *poluphloisboio,* a rendition which Pound himself tried to
reproduce in English for many years with only partial success.

3. The Faber and Faber edition reads "phantom of Rome."
4. "To" in the Faber and Faber edition.
5. "To" in the Faber and Faber edition.
6. George Dekker, *The Cantos of Ezra Pound: A Critical Study*
(New York, 1963), p. 16.

This surge of the sea against the beach is responsible for the very "rattle" of the old men's fear-ridden voices, as though they are mere pebbles tossed by the power of beauty, impotent to resist it. That this is the intention of the lines is made clear halfway through the canto, when Pound, recalling us to the beginning again by repeating the epithets given Helen in the *Agamemnon*, writes: "The sea runs in the beach-groove, shaking the floated pebbles,/ "Eleanor!" The myth of the destruction of Troy gives meaning to the catastrophic events of human history by taking for granted that the noble but dangerous power of sexual passion is at the root of social behavior. Aphrodite is a force for either destruction or creation (how she affects man depends on the state of his will), but in either case there is no question in the mind of Homeric Greece of her awesome power in human affairs. The *holism* of the archaic imagination is evident in its representation of the polar opposites. Aphrodite (Venus) and Ares (Mars)—creation and destruction—as lovers.[7]

After Homeric Greece, Ovidian Rome is a "phantom." "Noble forms, lacking life," and "dead concepts, never the solid, the blood rite," Pound says of Roman civilization in Canto 25. The quotation from Ovid's *Artis Amatoriae* concerns the sexual opportunities afforded by the narrow seats of the Roman theatre and reads in unabbreviated translation:

> And if perchance, as will happen, a speck of dust falls on your lady's lap, flick it off with your fingers; and if none fall, then flick off—none; let any pretext serve your turn.[8]

7. Edgar F. Racey, Jr., in an unpublished dissertation "Pound's *Cantos*: The Structure of a Modern Epic" (Claremont Graduate School, 1963), p. 27, writes: "Traditionally, the gods, particularly Venus and Mars, have stood as metaphoric representations of the two-fold rhythm that men have observed in all things, and the Greeks, apparently aware that it is impossible completely to separate creation and destruction, conceived of the two as lovers."

8. *The Analyst*, No. IV, p. 3.

The words *phantom, nullus, nullum* emphasize the emptiness of such cheap sexual opportunism, a "game" which provides fitting comment on the vicious, empty blood-letting of the gladiatorial "games," or combats, going on in the arena. The narrowness of the seats suggests the shrunken stature of both Venus and Mars, who in this cynical Roman society of *panem et circenses* have lost their original mythic significance. The "dissociated sensibility" of the Roman no longer recognizes that social order is based on the creative interaction of the will and nature, of Mars and Venus—of the *Yang* and *Yin*, if we may use the Chinese equivalent. Mars and Venus in separation lose their higher values and degenerate into base forms of physical collision providing cheap, ephemeral thrills for a spiritually moribund society. The result of such a split sensibility is the diminished "being" of "husks" that ought to have been men, as Pound makes clear in the rest of the canto.

Then the Provence of the troubadours and the France of the *chansons de geste* are weighed with slightly qualified approbation against Ovidian Rome. In "files and candles, e li mestiers ecoutes" ("and the [sacred] mysteries heard"), an allusion to the Catholic Middle Ages, the "mysteries" are appreciated once more. However, Pound implies that in spite of the "candles" the mysteries are not *seen*, are not directly experienced in their fullness as once at Eleusis. The dark, unattractive, otherworldly religion of medieval Europe deprived itself of the full Eleusinian vision through its scorn of temporal values (the religious fanaticism of a *geste* like the *Chanson de Roland* represents, for Pound, the perverse extreme of such a world view[9]). As a result, the life-affirming, ebullient *secular* world of the Middle Ages, especially as its spirit is revealed to us in troubadour poetry, was much better able than the Church to experience and incarnate a type of the original Eleusinian ecstasy and vision: "Scene for the battle only, but still scene." The lusty secular spirit of the age shows itself in the romantic gusto that

9. Pound returns to satirize the fanatical Roland in Canto 20.

the troubadours felt even in war.[10] The Provençal phrase "cavals armatz" alludes to Bertran de Born's poems that glorify war;[11] in de Born's poetry, Pound says, "The passages on the joy of war . . . enter the realm of the universal."[12] Inspired by his exalted emotion toward his lady-love, the troubadour poet could occasionally see some noble significance in war, could bring Venus into union with Mars once again, as did the Hellenes. In spite of the official Catholicism, "Provençal song is never wholly disjunct from pagan rites of May Day," Pound says; ". . . the spirit was, in Provence, Hellenic."[13]

The romantic and aesthetic emotions applied to the description of battle in troubadour poetry save such work from the meaningless relation of "mere succession of strokes, sightless narration." The line seems to be a multiple allusion: first, perhaps, to the unflagging butchery in blind Homer's combat descriptions in the *Iliad*; secondly, to the gladiatorial combats barely noticed by Ovid's preoccupied spectators; and thirdly, very possibly to the Christian fanaticism of the early French epic in which the love-theme is almost totally absent, as in the *Chanson de Roland*.[14]

More importantly, "mere succession of strokes" recalls the imagery of clock-time of Canto 5, where the strokes of mechanical time become the death-dealing sword-strokes that kill Giovanni Borgia ("Clock-tick pierces the vision"). Where the mythic, holistic vision does not inform the will, human activity

10. Compare George Dekker's perception with regard to these lines, *Cantos of Ezra Pound*, p. 18.

11. Particularly to the poem beginning "Be·m platz lo gais temps de Pascor" ("Well pleaseth me the sweet time of Easter"). In that poem the resurgent beauty of nature affects the poet with an *aesthetic* regard for the panoply of knights and horses arrayed in a field.

12. *The Spirit of Romance*, p. 46.

13. Ibid. p. 90.

14. See also Dekker, *The Cantos of Ezra Pound*, p. 18, who says that the line "is perhaps contemptuous reference to the *Chanson de Roland*."

becomes an empty and destructive "succession of strokes" aptly
regarded as mechanical time. Through the ill-fated house of
Atreus in the *Agamemnon*, Aeschylus projects his vision of history as a bleak and hopeless "succession of strokes" fated to
continue indefinitely through the generations (halted only by
divine intervention in the *Eumenides*). Allusions to the *Agamemnon* run all through the *Cantos*. They appear at first in
counterpoint with the murder of Giovanni Borgia, where they
provide a mythical embodiment of the theme of mechanical
time. Thereafter, they always appear in relation to historical
materials to reinforce, by the suggestion of a mythic prototype,
the theme of historical evil that is first given major treatment in
Canto 5. We remember that the first line of the passage we
have been considering here quotes epithets from the *Agamemnon* on the destructiveness of Helen, whose abduction
served to continue the series of disasters that befell the house of
Atreus. It may not seem far-fetched then to assume that in the
phrase, "mere succession of strokes," Pound has further condensed a direct allusion to one of his favorite passages in the
Agamemnon, lines 1344–5, quoted in telescoped form in Greek
in Canto 5 but reading in full translation:

Chorus
Silence: who cried out that he was stabbed to death within
the house?
Agamemnon
Ah me, again, they struck again. I am wounded twice.[15]

Pound alludes further on in the *Cantos* to later lines in the
same scene (1404–6), and perhaps in "mere succession of
strokes" we also hear an echo of lines 1429–30, spoken by the
Chorus in prophetic condemnation of Clytemnaestra:

15. The translation quoted is that by Richmond Lattimore in *Greek
Tragedies*, Vol. I, eds. David Greene and Richmond Lattimore (Chicago,
1960), pp. 48–49.

> Yet to come is stroke given for stroke
> vengeless, forlorn of friends.[16]

Dante's vision of the souls of great Christian warriors ascending to the higher realization of peace and justice, imagized in the sparks flying upwards from the " 'ciocco,' brand struck in the game," closes this passage at—for Pound—the high point of the poetry of Christian Europe. Dante's Neoplatonic vision of the One, the Light from which all things radiate and to which all things reascend, his vision of God as "supreme Love and Intelligence" [17] contrasts with the ascetic gloom of "li mestiers ecoutes." The "brand struck in the game" counterpoints the "mere succession of strokes." The stick Dante strikes with strikes a *light,* and his poetic vision attempts to redeem the games of love and war in a mythico-philosophic synthesis fully equal, in its own way, to the poetic synthesis achieved by the philosophically unsophisticated, purely mythic imagination of Homer. Dante represents the highest spiritual reach of his own age; the Neoplatonism which informed the finest spirits of his time (e.g. Cavalcanti), attained in him its grandest expression.

A space intervenes between the reference to Dante and the following line, Flaubert's "un peu moisi, plancher plus bas que le jardin." What especially seems to be missing is the whole period of the Renaissance, but Pound has already given us a highly idiosyncratic summation of that period in Canto 5, in his clipping from the historian Varchi and in his references to the poetasters Mozarello and Barabello. In Pound's view, European poetry was in decline from the Renaissance through the nineteenth century, when prose became the higher art. In an essay of 1914 he says:

> Flaubert and De Maupassant lifted prose to the rank of a finer art, and one has no patience with contemporary poets

16. Ibid. p. 51.
17. Ezra Pound, *Impact*, p. 133.

who escape from all the difficulties of the infinitely difficult art of good prose by pouring themselves into loose verses.[18]

Flaubert's prose, characterized by the accurate presentation of carefully selected detail, is as charged with significance as the language of poetry. The three-line pastiche from the fourth paragraph of *Un Coeur Simple* [19] suggests a civilization mildewed (*moisi*) and fallen into decay, its floor or foundation literally sinking into the earth for lack of sustaining vitality. The phrase "sous le baromètre" seems to have as subject "The old men's voices" of the following passage, as though the precise barometer of Flaubert's prose vision prophesied the spiritual wasteland of the twentieth century. Later lines in this canto connect what seems to be the same middle-class French living-room with Pound's concept of time as *descent*, as a *sinking* into death:

> Low ceiling and the Erard [20] and the silver,
> These are in "time." Four chairs, the bow-front dresser,
> The panier of the desk, cloth top sunk in.

In the passage following the excerpts from Flaubert, "the great domed head" of Henry James, active critic rather than passive victim of the times, arises in self-willed "weighted motion" to countervail the *downward* pressure of time,

> And the old voice *lifts* itself
> weaving an endless sentence. [Italics mine.]

James is a "phantom" in the sense that he had recently died (1916) and in the sense that he resembles the shade of Tiresias,

18. Ezra Pound, "Vorticism," in *Modern Criticism: Theory and Practice*, edited by Walter Sutton and Richard Foster (New York, 1963), p. 133.

19. The translation given in *The Analyst*, No. IV, p. 4, of the lines in French is as follows: "A little musty, the floor lower than the garden./ Against the panelling, a straw armchair,/ an old piano, and under the barometer . . ." Note also that *moisi* (musty) suggests line 1, Eleanor as "*spoiled* in a British climate." [Italics mine.]

20. *Erard*: a celebrated make of French piano.

"drinking the tone of things" as the Theban drank blood in order to gain strength for prophecy. The Jamesian style, too, like Flaubert's, is a *barometer* (Gr. *baros*, weight), for it moves "with weighted motion" (a translation of the following "*Grave incessu*"), measuring the weight, the atmospheric pressure, or, in Jamesian parlance, "the tone of things" that characterized late Victorian society. Pound places James in a room which flaunts the tawdry taste of the late nineteenth century in architecture and the arts, "beneath the columns of false marble,/ The modish and darkish walls,/ . . . and the paneled wood/ Suggested" rather than real. Everything is *unreal*, imitation: what is "modish" is a mere shadow of a shadow, a cheap imitation of what has been out of fashion for millennia. The shade of James has more substantial *weight* than this mere shade of a shade which represents the spiritual state of Victorian society. James's phantom is the type of the living spirit, the "active will" of the still living dead poised against the "Dry casques" of the modern dead-though-alive who are "moved by no inner being," as they are described at length in the second half of the canto.

The following lines, beginning "We also made ghostly visits," seem to be based, in the autobiographical sense, on Pound's change of residence from London to Paris in the winter of 1920–21, after an absence of seven years. One senses a general indebtedness in these lines to the atmosphere of James's ghost stories. The theme of the passage, registering his disappointment with the cultural climate of post-war Paris, is expressed in "Knocking at empty rooms, seeking for buried beauty." The "sun-tanned" beauty of Eleanor-Helen-Aphrodite is no longer to be found in the old "rooms" redolent of death: "The wilted flowers/ Brushed out a seven year since, of no effect." On one level, the "wilted flowers" probably refer to the atmosphere of Eliot's early poetry since Eliot rather than Pound is the true heir of James, as Dekker points out.[21] Allusion to Eliot is significant in relation to Paris, however, because of Eliot's importation of the poetic modes of French Symbolist

21. Dekker, *The Cantos of Ezra Pound*, pp. 20–21.

poetry into English. Pound is perhaps saying here that not only is Eliot's early style "of no effect" any more for the poet in search of Beauty, but that the decadent pre-war style of French symbolism [22] is equally useless and was "brushed out" seven years before by the cataclysm of World War I. It becomes clear in the next lines that Pound has been speaking of a nostalgia for a dead poetic style from whose "empty rooms" Beauty no longer answers to the modern poet's needs:

> Damn the partition! Paper, dark brown and stretched,
> Flimsy and damned partition.

An outmoded poetic style is the paper partition which must be torn aside if "buried beauty" is to be revived.

It is important to realize that Pound has not dropped the idea of time as suggested in "mere succession of strokes" earlier in the canto. Mechanical time at that point became associated with both bad poetry and the meaningless destruction of war. Here, too, Mars does violence to Venus, World War I has buried Helen, but Helen is to be revived by a fresh poetic effort that will again abolish time.

The method by which poetry is to be revitalized—by which the "damned partition" of a dead style is to be torn down—can be gathered from the following short stanza:

> Ione, dead the long year
> My lintel, and Liu Ch'e's [lintel].[23]
> Time blacked out with the rubber.

These lines dramatically reverse the mood of frustration built up to a shouting climax just the moment before. The passage, though difficult, is not obscure, since Pound is alluding to two

22. In his essay "Vorticism" of 1914, Pound says: "The symbolists . . . degraded the symbol to the status of a word. . . . One can be grossly 'symbolic,' for example, by using the term 'cross' to mean 'trial.' " *Modern Criticism*, eds. Sutton and Foster, p. 133.

23. Bracketed word omitted in the Faber and Faber edition.

of his own early poems, one entitled "Ione, Dead the Long Year," and the other "Liu Ch'e," a translation of a poem by the fourteenth-century Chinese poet of that name.[24] Both poems are on the subject of lost love, but in their successful use of image and tone they capture permanently the *feeling* of love, so that Love itself outlasts the death of the particular object of love, defying time. Both poems succeed in employing the *image*, which Pound defines as "that which presents an intellectual and emotional complex in an instant of time." [25] In 1914 Pound mentions Liu Ch'e in just this connection:

> Ibycus and Liu Ch'e presented the "Image." Dante is a great poet by reason of this faculty, and Milton is a wind-bag because of his lack of it.[26]

The "rubber," or the poet's eraser, a metonym for the labors of translation and revision, re-creates by an effort of will and love Liu Ch'e's own deathless expression of love and thereby blacks out over five centuries of time.

"Lintel" appears to be another use of metonymy for the doorway or window of the poet's unobstructed vision after his labors of renewal have cut down the flimsy "partition" of time. "Lintel" comes into English via Old French for "threshold," and as such is an allusion to the last line of "Liu Ch'e," in which the clinging memory of the poet's lost love is presented as "A wet leaf that clings to the threshold." [27] Pound is playing an etymological prank. Just as a word for "threshold," through process of linguistic evolution, becomes exalted into its higher

24. See *Personae*, pp. 108 and 112.

25. *Modern Criticism: Theory and Practice*, p. 134n.

26. Ibid. p. 132.

27. I am indebted to Hugh Kenner for this "threshold" identification. He rightly cautions me against unnecessarily complicating the "lintel" passage, but I think it necessary to explain (as I attempt to do in my succeeding remarks) why Pound preferred to use "lintel" when he could himself have avoided complications and used the simpler, equally disyllabic "threshold."

counterpart, a lintel, so does a particular lost love, both in Pound's case and in Liu Ch'e's, rise from the earth to become permanently recaptured through the time-defying " 'sculpture' of rhyme." As the supporting beam which carries the whole weight of the structure above the poet's "window," *lintel* suggests the quality of love which sustains the artist's vision and prevents the poetic superstructure from collapsing.

The absence of a sustaining, time-abolishing "lintel" in the civilization of the nineteenth and twentieth century is indicated in the imagery of sham support and sinking in the following lines (italics mine):

> The Elysée *carries a name on*
> And the bus behind me gives me a *date for peg*;
> *Low ceiling* and the Erard and the silver,
> These are in "time." Four chairs, the bow-front dresser,
> The panier of the desk, cloth top *sunk in*.

The Palais de l'Elysée, where the President of the French Republic resides, is a mockery of timeless Elysium, whereas the modern bus, making its rounds with clock-like precision, reminds the poet of nothing but mechanical time. There is irony in the transiency of any particular "date" serving as "peg" or support for the poet seeking a "lintel" that withstands time.[28]

A snatch of conversation then introduces the general statement of theme towards which all the previous images have been tending:

28. The line under discussion, "And the bus behind me gives me a date for peg," seems to me to be a subtle modernization of these lines in Marvell's "To His Coy Mistress":

> But at my back I always hear
> Time's winged chariot hurrying near.

The context is similar to Pound's—the theme of Love against Time—and the polarity of love and war central to Marvell's poem is prominent in Canto 7 as well. Eliot echoes the same lines in *The Waste Land*, when Tiresias says, "At my back from time to time I hear," not the sounds of chariots, but of today's "horns and motors" (ll. 196–97).

> "Beer-bottle on the statue's pediment!
> "That, Fritz, is the era, to-day against the past,
> "Contemporary." And the passion endures.
> Against their action, aromas. Rooms, against chronicles.
> Smaragdos, chrysolithos; De Gama wore striped pants in Africa
> And "Mountains of the sea gave birth to troops."

The beer-bottle defiling the statue signifies the irreverence of
the present toward the past. The values of the present center on
consumption as opposed to creation; our will is directed toward
momentary satisfaction of appetite rather than sustained self-
sacrifice for the production of enduring works. The empty bottle is the emptiness and puniness of the self-complacent contemporary Ego (a "shell" containing "A dryness calling for
death") in isolation from the enduring values of the past. The
beer-bottle is in time, the statue in the realm of the permanent.
The same time-theme informs *Hugh Selwyn Mauberley,* finished
not long before the completion of Canto 7:

> The "age demanded" chiefly a mould in plaster,
> Made with no loss of time,
> A prose kinema, not, not assuredly, alabaster
> Or the "sculpture" of rhyme.[29]

The speaker, who is obviously in favor of the statue in the "beer-
bottle" passage just quoted, is addressing one "Fritz," apparently a German (the name is World War I slang for a German
soldier), and therefore likely to invite identification with the
beery values of the present and the vicious militarism which set
out to destroy the humanistic values of the past.[30]

29. *Personae*, p. 188.
30. The only trouble with such an identification, however, is the
fact that there is overwhelming biographical evidence to the effect that our
"Fritz" is not a German, but a Dutch art historian named Fritz Vanderpyl
(mentioned unmistakably in Cantos 74 and 80), a friend of Pound's
during the poet's Paris days (see *The Analyst*, No. VI, pp. 4–6). However,
if the allusion is to Vanderpyl, why, then, did not Pound identify him in

But "the passion endures," the urge to create the statue outlasts the destruction of statues; the empty beer-bottle ultimately
shatters against the solid stone. "Against their action, aromas."
An aroma is something which delicately lingers, like a memory,
when a beautiful woman is no longer physically present. An
aroma defies time, symbolizing the passion that endures, whereas "action" (parallel to the following "chronicles" or events of
history) most often leaves behind nothing but destruction. The
word "action" here is equivalent to the *kinema* (Gr. "motion")
that the "age" prefers to "the 'sculpture' of rhyme" in the passage just quoted from *Mauberley.*

"Rooms, against chronicles." The controlling image of
Canto 7 is *rooms.* Up to now we have seen mildewed rooms,
empty rooms, and old men's rooms that are to dominate the
latter half of the canto. Pound makes much metonymically of
parts of rooms as well (partitions, lintels). Rooms have become
ambiguous symbols for states of civilization and for the states of
artistic sensibility presiding in judgment, through acts of creation that are equally acts of criticism, over those states of civilization. Rooms contain the "tone of things," aromas, or else
wilted flowers whose aromas have long gone. *Chronicles* are
bald records of events listed in chronological order, "mere succession of strokes, sightless narration," a list of occurrences connected meaningfully by nothing except the mere fact of having
"a date for peg." Rooms may betray the spirit of a civilization,
but chronicles can reveal only the unanalyzed "march of
events." [31] Because of their intimation of privacy, rooms reveal
the relationship between the subjective self and the objective or
public forms of a given society, whereas chronicles offer only the
public record. Chronicles stand for *history* in the sense of

the canto in some unambiguous way? To look at Pound the poet simply
as autobiographer, in this passage as in many others, may be to limit
unduly the levels of interpretation that the intentional vagueness of the
text makes possible.

31. *Hugh Selwyn Mauberley,* l. 17.

mechanical time; rooms suggest time-defying *poetry*. Pound is, after all, playing on the double meaning of the Italian *stanze*: "stanzas" of poetry are "rooms." He uses the like image persistently but crudely in the scrapped first version of Canto 1:

> (I stand before the booth, the speech; but the truth
> Is inside this discourse—this booth is full of the
> marrow of wisdom.)[32]

And again, several pages later:

> Or shall I do your trick, the showman's booth, Bob Browning,
>
> . . .
>
> And set the lot, my visions, to confounding
> The wits that have survived your damn'd *Sordello?* [33]

The use in Canto 7 of partitions preventing entrance to rooms, doors of "empty rooms" whose empire handles do not twist "for the knocker's fall," and lintels sustaining doorways through which vision is possible—all are foreshadowed in the use of the "gate" image of the first version (since rejected) of Canto 2. There Pound is seeking entrance into the spiritual wisdom and poetic sensibility of "the ancient people," [34] and the way he discovers is "through the old tales and poems. Artistic creation is a gateway into the past": [35]

> Another gate?
> And Kumasaka's ghost come back to tell
> The honor of the youth who'd slain him.

32. "Canto I," *Poetry* X (June 1917), p. 113. Note that this early version of Canto 1 was still an integral part of the poem when Canto 7 was first published (in *Dial* of August, 1921) and was not definitely rejected till about two years later.

33. Ibid. pp. 117–18.

34. "Canto II," *Poetry* X (July 1917), p. 180.

35. Max Halperen, "A Structural Reading of *The Cantos* of Ezra Pound" (Ph.D. dissertation: Florida State University, 1959), p. 35.

Another gate.

> The kernelled walls of Toro, *las almenas*;
> Afield, a king come in an unjust cause.[36]

The conflict between poetry and history, Spirit and Time, is the central one of the *Cantos*.[37] Mauberley, in retreat from the world of time, failed to exert a creative pressure against the tide of history which would have helped bring about cultural renewal and negate time. In the *Cantos,* culture "heroes" like Malatesta and Jefferson are types of the artist who does exert active pressure on the social environment and constructively imposes some measure of artistic order on the chaos of history. He is more or less successful in bringing history into conformity with poetry and bridging the gap between Spirit and Time, self and society. Mauberley is the type of the artist as "impressionist," whom Pound defines as "the toy of circumstance, as the plastic substance *receiving* impressions"; Malatesta is the type of the "vorticist," whom we are to think of "as directing a certain fluid force against circumstance, as *conceiving* instead of merely reflecting and observing." [38]

The first phase of the *Cantos,* Pound's *Inferno,* comes to a climax in Canto 30 and is characterized by the failure of the constructive will in the occident to maintain social order. The failure, an inability to keep self and society in harmony, is due to the loss of "order within." According to Pound, the Kung Canto (Canto 13) is the "announcement of backbone moral of the *Cantos.*" [39] Kung makes his main point in the following six lines:

36. "Canto II," *Poetry* X (July 1917), p. 185–86, quoted in Halperen, "A Structural Reading of *The Cantos*," p.35.

37. Note the beginning of Canto 8: " 'Slut! Bitch!' Truth and Calliope/ Slanging each other sous les lauriers."

38. "Vorticism," in *Modern Criticism,* p. 136.

39. Angela Chih-Ying Jung, "Ezra Pound and China" (Ph.D. dissertation: University of Washington, 1955), p. 69.

> If a man have not order within him
> He can not spread order about him;
> And if a man have not order within him
> His family will not act with due order;
> > And if the prince have not order within him
> He can not put order in his dominions.

The "key" to the "plot" of Phase One, Pound's *Untergang des Abendlandes,* is the decay in the West of the principle of Order Within. Time reigns where order fails.

The "beer-bottle" passage which began this discussion ends with two lines that continue to puzzle critics:

> Smaragdos, chrysolithos; De Gama wore striped pants in Africa
> And "Mountains of the sea gave birth to troops."

The Greek terms for "emeralds" and "topazes" probably stem from the *Elegies* of Propertius, but there is no reason to assume that the entire context of these words, in which Propertius jealously condemns the rich presents given his faithless mistress by a wealthy rival of his, necessarily colors Pound's mention of these gems. These stones are colorful enough in their own right, green and gold; gold is Aphrodite's color; and both stones together recall the central lines of Canto 5: "Topaz I manage, and three sorts of blue;/ but on the barb of time." I see in the mention of these stones a continuation of the contrast between the classic beauty of the past (the gem-like permanence of Propertian verse) and the "barb of time," particularly the decay of Renaissance poetry exemplified by Camoens's *Lusiads,* an epic which he would consider more as "chronicles" than as poetry. Pound mockingly paraphrases the line in the Portuguese epic which describes Vasco Da Gama's trunk hose, in order to expose Camoens's emphasis on the superficies of things. Pound has said that the value of the *Lusiads* "lies in its timeliness," that is, "it gives us the tone of the time's thought," voicing "a phase, a fashion of a people, and not their humanity." [40] The last line, a pseudo-quotation which mocks the bombastic style of Camoens, seems to me to have a further depth of meaning as a parody of the Latin of Horace:

parturiunt montes, nascetur ridiculus mus.

The "ridiculous mouse" is "troops," the waste of poetic energy in nationalistic celebration of war. Thus Pound continues to play on the theme of love against war as he mocks the exploits of Da Gama in his contempt of empty militarism. In the stones "smaragdos, chrysolithos" Pound sums up previous mention of the "statue," the classic "past," the enduring "passion" of love, and the "rooms" of *poetry* he places against the "chronicles" of *history*.

The canto continues now in a reprise of the Eleanor-Helen motif, and the Helen who has deserted a modern "Paris" now moves before the poet as "Nicea," appearing in his mind's eye in "all her naked beauty":

> And her moving height went before me,
> We alone having being.

The passion felt by the poet gives him "being" and confers the same substantiality upon his poetic vision. In contrast there are the

> Thin husks I had known as men,
> Dry casques of departed locusts
> speaking a shell of speech . . .
> Propped between chairs and table . . .
> Words like the locust-shells, moved by no inner being;
> A dryness calling for death.

40. *The Spirit of Romance*, p. 216.

Pound is playing upon the Neoplatonic idea that evil is not a force in itself but is an *absence of being*. The One which is Light radiates essence from itself and eventually the light weakens the farther it travels. Evil is no more than the degree to which the light of God's love shines more or less feebly in any created being. For Pound, too, evil is an absence of "being," qualitatively the absence of love, but in his view it is not natural for the spirit of man to be deficient in love, and if there is such a deficiency it is explicable in terms of a misdirection of the will.

Those men who are now husks and shells and casques have their own perverted wills to blame. Their upper middle-class setting, suggested by the *rooms* described in the ensuing *stanzas*, intimates that these dead men represent the British Establishment, the power élite. They are a power élite that have just enough "Life to make mock of motion." Their activity, their speech, is a meaningless "rattle: shells given out by shells." They suffer a paralysis of the will, an *abuleia* like that of Alessandro de' Medici, who is recalled from Canto 5 to sum up here, at the end of Canto 7, the general moral and spiritual paralysis of the European power élite in the twentieth century.

The imagery used to describe these wasteland figures of the British Establishment functions more specifically, it would seem, to suggest the guilt of "usury age-old and age-thick" (*Mauberley*), the guilt of Britain's upper classes vis-à-vis the horrors of the Great War. For the old men are described not simply as creatures "calling for death" to put an end to their "mock of motion," but as death-*dealing* zombies calling for the death of others. We notice that they have been "locusts," and traveling swarms of locusts destroy all vegetation in their paths. They symbolize specifically the locust-like scourge of war, because they are now 'Dry casques of departed locusts," and *casques* are helmets. They are *shells* "speaking a shell of speech," and their words echo the millions of rounds of ammunition they profitably manufactured and thereby contributed to

firing during World War I. Their war is responsible for the
temporary entombment of love and art in the modern wasteland:

> Square even shoulders and the satin skin,
> Gone cheeks of the dancing woman,
> Still the old dead dry talk, gassed out—
> It is ten years gone, makes stiff about her a glass,
> A petrefaction of air.

The "old dead dry talk" refers to the death-laden shells of
speech of "the tawdry class," and the phrase "gassed out" am-
biguously qualifies the "dry talk" as well as the "dancing
woman," so that the Establishment is also associated with the
use of poison gas that buried so much beauty during the war.

The guilt of the "tawdry class" is primarily the guilt of
omission. Passionless and compassionless, they failed to direct
any "force against circumstance" and followed the most lucra-
tive path of least resistance. Lorenzaccio, the murderer of Alessandro, is "more live than they" because his at least was the
guilt of commission. He acted out of passion, even though it
was perverted passion. In Canto 7 the modern *Inferno* is
brought into comparison with that of the Renaissance sketched
in Canto 5, and the twentieth century comes off by far the
worse. The inhabitants of Pound's wasteland would actually
have been denied a place in Dante's hell, for Dante includes
only *active* sinners in his circles of hell. Dante's hell is a place of
dignity and tragedy, and those "wretches, who never were
alive," [41] having done nothing worthy of praise or blame, are
kept just outside the depths of hell to avoid giving evildoers any
occasion to vaunt over them. Pound's allusion to these "Neu-
trals" of *Inferno*, III, is strangely parallel to Eliot's *Waste Land*
allusion to these same "wretches" when he describes the deni-

41. *Inferno*, I, l. 64. (Pound's "Lorenzaccio/ Being more live than
they," is a clear allusion to this passage.)

zens of his own Unreal City.[42] In Pound's view, the evil of
modern times results from abuleia, so that our image of hell can
only be of a spiritual state which, as he tells us in his first "Hell
Canto" (Canto 14) is "without dignity, without tragedy."

42. Line 63 of *The Waste Land* is a direct translation of *Inferno*,
III, ll. 56–7, which read as follows:
> . . . io non averei creduto
> che morte tanta n'avesse disfatta.

["I should never have believed death had undone so many."—Sinclair's
translation.]

CHAPTER IV

Loss of the Concrete Universal

IF THERE IS development of any sort between Cantos 8 and 30, it certainly does not proceed in a mechanically logical, straight line. If one examines these cantos in musical or organic terms, however, an aesthetically satisfying development does finally reveal itself. Its "shape" is not a straight line but a spiral, a spiral in which the themes established in embryo up through Canto 7 are continually reverted to and given more and more expanded treatment. We now become aware not only of parts of cantos and single cantos being played off against each other, but of groups of cantos functioning as single units in juxtaposition with other unitary groups of cantos. The question still remains, "What is the purpose of these structural complications, of these continual variations upon the same basic themes?" It seems to me that Pound's spiral method, by which the same themes recur in different contexts and are regarded from different points of view, suggests that a process of *clarification* is going on. Images cryptically flashed at the reader in the first several cantos are enlarged upon and juxtaposed in new combinations so that facet after facet of their significance is progressively revealed. What is at first dark grows clearer and brighter. This organic method, which resembles the exfoliation of a rosebud, is perfectly suited to a poem whose main purpose is to record the growth of the poet's consciousness—not as it appears to the poet upon afterthought, "recollected in tranquility," but as it actually occurs, *in statu nascendi*. The method is not essentially different from Eliot's non-logical method in *The Waste*

Land, in which the repetition, expansion, and varied collocation
of images finally results in clarity.

Pound's increasing awareness of the decay of Western culture, his consciousness of Western man's loss of sensibility and
consequent incapacity for constructive action, is seen developing both in breadth and in depth throughout the first thirty
cantos. The more he becomes aware of the *scope* of the degen-
erative process, the more he becomes aware of the root *cause* or
causes of such decay in our society.

Development in scope of the theme of decay takes place
along the two lines distinctly established in Cantos 5 and 7, an
alternation of Renaissance with modern materials. The enlarged
scope of Pound's awareness is first made evident in the Malatesta cantos (8–11), which Pound calls

> openly volitionist, establishing, I think clearly, the effect of
> the factive personality, Sigismundo, an entire man.[1]

Sigismundo Malatesta, fifteenth-century condottiere and patron
of the arts, was in Pound's view one of the last of Western civilization's "whole" men—*polumetis,* or many-minded, like
Odysseus, a man whose sensibility united art and politics, the
contemplative and the active life, in holistic synthesis. Malatesta achieved, in spite of endless political and military distrac-
tions, a lasting monument dedicated to his beloved mistress and
third wife, Isotta degli Atti. The Tempio Malatestiano at
Rimini is evidence of a creative will that was able to withstand
the forces of time, the endless intrigues, petty rivalries, wars,
and shifting loyalties of Italian city-states forever at each other's
throats:

> The Tempio Malatestiano is both an apex and in verbal
> sense a monumental failure. It is perhaps the apex of what
> one man has embodied in the last 1000 years of the occi-
> dent. . . .
> In a Europe not YET rotted by usury, but outside the

1. *Guide to Kuchur,* p. 194.

then system, and pretty much against the power that was . . . Sigismundo cut his notch. He registered a state of mind, of sensibility, of all-roundness and awareness. . . .

You can contrast it [the Tempio] with St. Hilaire. You can contrast it with ANY great summit done WITH the current of power.[2]

The point Pound makes is that there is a limit to how much any one man can do *against* the current of power. If a man like Malatesta had lived in a society that fostered his efforts, he would have achieved artistic wonders, like the great medieval cathedrals, that stagger the imagination. Malatesta is a tragic figure, and in his portrayal a whole new range of tragic emotion enters the *Cantos*. (Unusual insight is afforded into the genesis and structure of the Malatesta Cantos in a letter from Pound to Quinn of August 1922. Extracts of this previously unpublished letter appear in Appendix A.)

The tragic destiny of Malatesta resonates later in these cantos in the tragic portraits of Niccolò d'Este and of the decay of Venice. The modern scene is in comparison "without dignity, without tragedy" and Pound develops it largely in comic terms, treating it for the most part in a tone of contemptuous irony. As he expands his scope, however, he also deepens his analysis. In the Malatesta cantos Pound directs his attention for the first time to the involvement of the Catholic church in the decay of the West. Sigismundo's chief antagonist emerges as Aeneas Silvius Piccolomini, Pope Pius II, "that monstrous swollen, swelling s. o. b."[3] who accuses Malatesta of all possible sins against man and God. Ultimately, the contrast Pound intends between the tyrannical Pope and the many-minded condottiere is that between two distinct sorts of religious sensibility. In *The Commentaries of Pius II* the Pope interrupts "a prolonged denunciation of the Lord of Rimini's evil life and works" to accord "grudging praise" to the Tempio:

2. Ibid. pp. 159–60.
3. Canto 10, p. 44.

Nevertheless, he built at Rimini a splendid church dedicated to St. Francis, though he filled it so full of pagan works of art that it seemed less a Christian sanctuary than a temple of heathen devil-worshippers.[4]

The Pope's praise, telescoped into *"templum aedificavit"* (Canto 8, p. 32), re-echoes down the winding corridors of the *Cantos*. For Pound, the seemingly pagan temple is product of a sensibility that harks back to a primitive, Dionysian form of Christianity, whereas the Pope represents the later, corrupt Christianity of dogmatism, tyranny, and the negation of life:

> There are [says Pound] . . . only two kinds of religion. There is the Mosaic or Roman or British Empire type, where someone, having to keep a troublesome rabble in order, invents and scares them with a disagreeable bogie, which he calls god.
> Christianity and all other forms of ecstatic religion, on the other hand, are not in inception dogma or propaganda of something called the *one truth* or the *universal truth*; they *seem* little concerned with ethics; their general object appears to be to stimulate a sort of confidence in the life-force.[5]

The Tempio, according to Pound, was an attempt to revitalize Christianity:

> Idea that there could be clean and beneficent Christianity restarted in Tempio Malatestiano. Country priest not the least disturbed that I shd. be making my farewells *solo ai elefanti*. Namely that I had come for friendly word with the stone elephants and not for altar furniture.[6]

Pound's distinction between the two types of Christianity, one life-affirming, the other life-denying, is at the root of his criticism of the West and is the most important single theme con-

4. Quoted in *The Analyst*, No. V, p. 14.
5. *The Spirit of Romance*, p. 95.
6. *Guide to Kulchur*, p. 301.

tributing to the over-all development of the time-theme in the
first thirty cantos.

The brief appearance in Canto 8 of the Byzantine philosopher Gemisthus Plethon serves to advance the Neoplatonic
theme of 'Iamblichus' light" that was set in opposition to the
forces of life-denying tyranny in Canto 5. Plethon, skeptical of
doctrinal Christianity, wished to reanimate Western culture
through a sort of Neoplatonic revival that would also involve a
revival of Greek mythology. His sensibility was of the life-
affirming, *holistic* sort expressed in the Tempio Malatestiano, a
temperament opposed to the dogmatic Aristotelianism that had
come to dominate the Church and Western thought in general.
"Greek philosophy," Pound says,

> and european in its wake, degenerated into an attack on myth-
> ology and mythology is, perforce, totalitarian. I mean that it
> tries to find an expression for reality without over-simplifica-
> tion, and without scission, you can examine a living animal,
> but at a certain point dissection is compatible only with
> death.[7]

Pound uses the word "totalitarian" to describe mythology in
exactly the same sense as I have been using "holistic." Holism is
opposed to the "scission" of reality by the abstract intelligence,
which, as Jan Smuts says, "has made the real concrete world of
matter and life quite unintelligible and inexplicable." [8] The
holistic theme, developed by symbolic means alone in the previous cantos, emerges now in Canto 8 at the level of philosophical generalization in the *"concret Allgemeine,"* the "concrete
universal":

And the Greek emperor was in Florence
            (Ferrara having the pest)
And with him Gemisthus Plethon

7. *Impact*, p. 126.
8. Quoted by Edmund W. Sinnott, "Introduction," *Holism and
Evolution* (New York, 1961), p. xiii.

> Talking of the war about the temple at Delphos,
> And of POSEIDON, *concret Allgemeine*,
> And telling of how Plato went to Dionysius of Syracuse
> Because he had observed that tyrants
> Were most efficient in all that they set their hands to.

The "*concret Allgemeine*" is quoted from Fritz Schultze's "definitive exposition" of Plethon's philosophy in *Geschichte der Philosophie der Renaissance* (1874). I quote the relevant passage in translation:

> Plethon is a complete Platonic realist in the Medieval sense. The universal is for him the final reality. But this universal is not abstractly general, as the Nominalists consider it, but the *concrete universal*, which includes in itself all particulars: it is not a mere abstract of all particulars, but the full totality of all particulars.

The loss of the Concrete Universal, the capacity for mythological or "totalitarian" thinking, as Pound would put it, is the key to social disorder in general and to the decline of the West in particular, as Pound pictures that decline in the first thirty cantos. The holistic view of reality common to Neoplatonism, and especially to Confucianism, is essentially *tolerant*; dualistic thinking is *intolerant*. Holism is inclusive, its scale of values admitting of infinite shades of gray between black and white. Dualism is exclusive, denying the complexities of the real and reducing the ambiguities of human experience to abstract moral and metaphysical categories that require men to make simplistic choices between supposed irreconcilables such as Good and Evil, Spirit and Matter, Time and Eternity. Metaphysical disorder in the Church, the spiritual center of the West, is for Pound the prime historical locus from which the degeneration of our civilization has proceeded. Western history is marred by the excesses of Christian fanaticism, which stem ultimately from dualistic intolerance. Disorder in Catholicism gave rise to

Protestantism, but for Pound the Protestant sects did no more than intensify the root disorder from which they were sprung. Catholic fanaticism gave birth to even more unnatural, life-denying forms of Protestant fanaticism. At least the medieval church had condemned economic injustices such as the practice of usury, but the individualistic excesses of Protestantism served rather to foster such economic vices, and the very meaning of "vice" became unhealthily narrowed. "The stink of non-conformist sects," Pound says, "has been in their losing the sense of all obscenity save that related to sex." He goes on to "define fanaticism as loss of the sense of gradations. Protestant sects are largely without a scale of values." [9]

The loss of the sense of proportion, the basis of Confucian "order within" in these early cantos, characterizes the post-medieval development of Christian thought and behavior in the West. We recall that in Canto 13 Kung says, "If a man have not order within him/ He can not spread order about him." For Pound, Christianity practises the reverse principle. "Christianity as practised," he has written, "resumes itself into one commandment dear to all officials, American Y.M.C.A., buro-crats, etc., 'Thou shalt attend to thy neighbor's business before attending to thine own.' . . . I refuse to accept ANY mono-theistic taboos whatsoever." [10] In Canto 13, after the passage on "order within," Pound writes:

> And Kung gave the words "order"
> and "brotherly deference"
> And said nothing of the "life after death."

In the *Cantos* so far we have seen fratricide rather than "broth-erly deference"; it remains to examine Kung's silence on the matter of a "life after death." Pound feels that the Christian emphasis on the afterlife is the worst of the doctrinal evils re-

9. *Guide to Kulchur*, p. 196.
10. *The Letters of Ezra Pound*, p. 183.

sulting from its dualistic orientation to reality. He says that
there is no "sense of social order in the teachings of the irre-
sponsible protagonist of the New Testament. . . . The concentration or emphasis on eternity is not social. The sense of responsibility [is] . . . expressed in Kung's teaching." [11]

I shall attempt to show that the major theme Pound develops between Cantos 8 and 30 is that disorder in the West is due
ultimately to metaphysical derangement in Christianity. The
orientation of Christian thought and feeling *against nature* is
the nexus between the Renaissance and contemporary materials
that dominate these cantos. Pound develops three main Renaissance subjects: the heroic, creative efforts of Malatesta against
the forces of political and moral chaos that finally overwhelm
him; Niccolò d'Este's tragic murder of his young wife Parisina
(who was a cousin of Sigismundo Malatesta); and the decay of
Venice, pictured in significant conjunction with the decay of
the Estes. The two main contemporary subjects he develops are
the "Hell" of usury and related evils (occupying most of Cantos
12–19), and the equally modern hell of intellectual and emotional impotence (concentrated in Cantos 27–29). The destructive tendencies of the Renaissance are associated with
Catholicism, at least insofar as we have initially analyzed the
opposition of the Plethon-Malatesta temperament to the religious sensibility of the Pope; the negative elements in the contemporary scene, however, are carefully associated with Protestantism. The particular connection Pound intends in these
cantos between Protestantism and usury is easy enough to point
out, so that I shall pursue this line of investigation first. I shall
reserve for subsequent treatment the crucial connection Pound
establishes between Renaissance disorder and the intolerant,
anti-natural dualism of a universal Catholic church that has lost
contact with reality.

The first specific link between Protestantism and usury

11. *Guide to Kulchur*, p. 38.

occurs in Canto 12, where usury as a theme is first openly mentioned in the *Cantos:*

> Jim X . . .
>> in a bankers' meeting,
>> bored with their hard luck stories,
>>> . . .
> Told 'em the Tale of the Honest Sailor.
> Bored with their proprieties,
>> as they sat, the ranked presbyterians,
> Directors, dealers through holding companies,
> Deacons in churches, owning slum properties,
> *Alias* usurers in excelsis,
>> the quintessential essence of usurers.

The "ranked presbyterians" recall the figures "Propped between
chairs and table" of Canto 7, whose significance now more
clearly emerges. Not only are Protestantism and usury linked,
but they are seen as *essentially* connected. Pound elsewhere
makes this same point: "Putting usury on a pedestal, in order to
set avarice on high [cf. "usurers in excelsis"], the protestant
centuries twisted all morality out of shape." [12] The "Tale of
the Honest Sailor" turns on the idea of sodomy. The sailor,
thinking he has given birth to a son, scrimps and saves till he
becomes owner of a line of steamers and then finally confesses
to his "son" on his deathbed:

> "I am not your fader but your moder," quod he,
> "Your fader was a rich merchant in Stambouli."

The sailor, formerly a "rowster" and "boozer," has become as
Protestant as any of the "ranked presbyterians" by denying
himself sensual pleasures in order to accumulate a fortune. The
implied resemblance between this former sodomist and the

12. Ibid. p. 256.

usurers at the bank meeting is the more subtle point of Jim X's wonderful anecdote, for, as Pound notes in one of his essays:

> Usury and sodomy, the Church condemned as a pair, to one hell, the same for one reason, namely that they are both against natural increase.[13]

The theme reaches final explicitness in the Usura Canto (Canto 45,), which condemns usury as "CONTRA NATURAM."

The first of the "Hell" cantos (Canto 14) describes the usurers and all their henchmen and cronies as "the perverts, who have set money-lust/ Before the pleasures of the senses," pictures them as "the vice-crusaders, . . . /waving the Christian symbols," and winds up with the image of "Episcopus, waving a condom full of black beetles." The nightmarish images of these Hell cantos are the prototypes for all the vignettes of contemporary life to be found in succeeding cantos. Announcing clearly the theme of *negative* metamorphosis, Pound says (Canto 14): "THE PERSONNEL CHANGES,/ melting like dirty wax,/ decayed candles," and we are reminded of Eliot's Bleistein staring from "protozoic slime" and of his "smoky candle end of time." [14]

But usurious Protestantism is, for Pound, the deformed child of Mother Church. The spiritual decay of the Catholic sensibility as the cause of all subsequent disorder in Western history is projected in these early cantos primarily through the Este materials, which are first announced in the last line of Canto 3: "Silk tatters, 'Nec Spe Nec Metu.'" The motto ("with neither hope nor fear"), found in rooms of the Este palace in Mantua, expresses the stoic ideal of self-restraint and balance that emerges later in the Kungian ideal of "order

13. *Impact*, p. 144.
14. T. S. Eliot, *Collected Poems 1909–1962* (New York, 1963), pp. 32–33.

within." But "silk tatters" are all that remains of former Este greatness. In this climactic line Pound foreshadows Renaissance decay and the whole theme of time first explicitly developed in Canto 5. In Canto 7 there is again brief allusion to the Estes,[15] but the specific cause of their decline, and with them the decline of the Renaissance, is first adumbrated in Canto 8. Toward the end of this canto, in which the Concrete Universal has been announced as the principle of order, allusion is made to the murder of the young and beautiful Parisina d'Este by her husband Niccolò. Whether he acted on proof or mere suspicion of her adultery with his favorite son Ugo is not known, but suddenly, in 1425, he had them both imprisoned for the offense and decapitated:

> and the sword, Paolo il Bello's,
>   caught in the arras
> And, in Este's house, Parisina
> Paid
> For this tribe paid always, and the house
> Called also Atreides'.

The first two lines quoted allude to the famous story of Paolo and Francesca (*Inferno*, V, 73–142), lovers who suffered a tragic end similar to that of Ugo and Parisina. The allusion to the unfortunate house of Atreus suggests the ill-starred houses of the Malatestas, the Estes, and, by extension, of all the noble families of the Renaissance; and it recalls also the Agamemnon motif entwined with other Renaissance tales of family bloodletting in Canto 5.

Since the Parisina murder becomes symbolic of Renaissance disorder in general, the loss of the Concrete Universal must

15. The phrase "E biondo," from the next to last line of Canto 7, probably alludes to the *Inferno* (XII, 109–112), where the blonde Obizzo II da Este, a murderous tyrant, is said to have been killed by his stepson. Report had it that he was strangled (in 1293) by his stepson in a quarrel over the latter's inheritance.

somehow be applicable to the mind of Niccolò d'Este, just as we have seen it to be applicable to the disordered mind of Malatesta's chief antagonist, Pope Pius II. What both minds have in common is violent antipathy to the expression of the natural passions. The idea that Niccolò's disordered mind exemplifies the general derangement of the Renaissance *Christian* sensibility emerges more clearly in Canto 20, when the Renaissance theme begins a powerful resurgence after being muted for some time in favor of the contemporary scene.

In Canto 20, after a passage celebrating the natural passions, Pound reverts to the murder of Ugo and Parisina. The interest now is specifically in the disordered *mind* of Niccolò d'Este, who is presented, as Pound has explained in a letter to his father, "in sort of delirium after execution of Parisina and Ugo." [16] He thinks first of the legendary founding of Atesten, a commune in Northern Italy, by a supposed ancestor who was one of the survivors of Troy. The following motif, " 'Peace! keep the peace, Borso,' " refers to the failure of his son Borso to keep peace between Sigismundo Malatesta and Federigo d'Urbino. The next passage is Este's confused but satirical recollection of the last moments of Roland, who, as Pound comments, "dies grumbling because he has damaged the ornaments on the horn [the "olofans"] and broken it." [17] The final images that pass across Este's consciousness telescope the effect Helen's beauty had on the Trojan elders with a similar scene from Lope de Vega's *Las Almenas de Toro*, with the exception that the king who unknowingly views his beautiful sister up on the walls of Toro is imagined by Este to have an erection. Este then damns himself, with allusion to the "arras" that in Canto 8 was made to serve as scene for the murder of Paolo and Francesca.

In spite of the seeming disjointedness of these images, there is method in Este's madness. He thinks first of the heroic *founding* of his line, of the creative past which comments so se-

16. *Letters*, p. 210.
17. Ibid. p. 211.

verely on his own destructive present. Next, he adverts to his son Borso's failure to keep peace as a symbol of his personal failure to keep order within his own family, and as a symptom of the anarchy into which the Renaissance was progressively collapsing. We are again forced to recollect Kung's dictum that "if a man have not order within him/ His family will not act with due order." The next passage in Este's "delirium" is an act of profound self-analysis. In satirizing Roland's Christian fanaticism and, by implication, the egotistical pride which prevented his trumpeting for help, Este is condemning the fanatical mentality in himself which resulted in his murder of the two human beings he loved most. Roland's anger at being defeated by the Moors should have been turned against himself rather than against the traitor Ganelon, since the unnecessary destruction of the flower of French manhood was within his own power to avert. He was ruled, however, by his abstract Christian hatred of the infidel to the extent that he lost all sense of proportion and destroyed almost everything and everyone he loved best, himself included. So, too, Este has lashed out in self-righteous, Christian violence at the two "infidels" whose deaths mean the death of all that he holds dear. (Canto 24 is much more explicit in connecting Este's act of murder with a perverted religious sensibility.) The following image, in which the king ("telo rigido") is unwittingly excited by the beauty of his own sister, represents in Este a sudden flash of empathy for the incestuous passion of his dead son. Because of Parisina's youth, Ugo must have regarded her much more as a kind of sister than as a stepmother, and Niccolò, as the "King," puts himself in Ugo's place. He recognizes the irresistible power of feminine beauty and natural passion which, in the legend of Helen and Paris, set off the chain of events mythically responsible for the founding of the Este family in the first place. Saying "Este, go' damn you," he is pronouncing judgment upon himself as a fanatical Roland whose religious sensibility has cut him off from all sense of reality.

Este's delirium ("'Keep the peace, Borso!'") introduces Canto 21, underscoring the theme of tragic disorder that runs through the following passages on the Medici family, whose unwise financial practices finally destroyed their greatness. The theme of Roland as the misdirected will out of touch with reality is subtly employed as the basis for the whole of Canto 22,[18] but the Este theme as such re-emerges more clearly in Canto 23. Here we have a major variation on the Niccolò-Parisina-Ugo affair. The canto begins with a quotation from Porphyry, a third-century Greek Neoplatonist, most of whose works, "including the most important, are lost, among them a treatise against the Christians in fifteen books, which was publicly burned under Theodosius II."[19] The phrase from the anti-Christian Porphyry, "Et omniformis . . . omnis/ Intellectus est" ("And every intellect is capable of assuming every shape"), combines with those of "Gemisto" Plethon in the following lines (e.g., "'Never with this religion/ Will you make men of (the greeks.'") to introduce the theme of this canto as a criticism of the abstract tendencies of Christianity in the light of a tolerant, plastic, polytheistic holism. The kind of "science" based on the abstractions of medieval scholasticism is contrasted unfavorably with the *concrete* science of experiment, which involves repeated exposure of mind and body to realities, no matter how dangerous:

> Invention-d'entités-plus-ou-moins-abstraits-
> en-nombre-égal-aux-choses-à-expliquer . . .

18. Although it is not possible here to develop a full analysis of Canto 22, an examination of all the episodes, however, does clearly reveal the theme of the canto to be the impotence of the "orthodox," legalistic word, the abstract official point of view, in face of a motley, contradictory, unofficial human reality which it can neither define nor control. The suggestion that this canto is a variation upon the theme of Roland receives further support when we take note that the conflict between Christian and "Moorish" sensibilities is central to it. The scene is conveniently laid in modern Gibraltar.

19. Oskar Seyffert, *Dictionary of Classical Antiquities*, revised and edited by Henry Nettleship and J. E. Sandys (Cleveland, 1956), p. 505.

La Science ne peut pas y consister. "J'ai
Obtenu une brulure" M. Curie, or some other scientist
"Qui m'a coûté six mois de guérison." [20]

After further images stressing mythological parallels to
the scientific quest for light or knowledge through experience,
Pound develops with lyrical intensity the theme of sexual love,
which is in his and Remy de Gourmont's view an "intellectual
instigation":

> And the rose grown while I slept,
> And the strings shaken with music,
> Capriped, the loose twigs under foot;
>
> . . .
>
> As we had lain there in the autumn
> Under the arras, or wall painted below like arras,
> And above with a garden of rose-trees,
> Sound coming up from the cross-street.

Presence of the "arras" tells us that these unspecified lovers are
Parisina and Ugo,[21] and the rose-cross opposition of the last
two lines may be a Rosicrucian symbol, filtered through early
Yeats, of the impalement of the rose of passion, love, art, the
Spirit itself, on the cross of Time—Pound's "cross-street" perhaps suggesting the *Christian* moral fanaticism of Este's extre-
mist behavior.

After this lyrical passage, the Este love-triangle is resumed
by implication in a significantly expanded version of Pieire de
Maensac's elopement with Tierci's wife (see Canto 5). The
Dauphin of Auvergne defended the troubadour lover and his
mistress against the armed attacks of Tierci, who

20. See Pound's *ABC of Reading* (New York, 1960), pp. 17–18, for
what amounts to commentary on this specific passage.
21. We recall the last lines depicting Niccolò d'Este's delirium in
Canto 20: " 'Este, go' damn you,' between the walls, arras,/ Painted to
look like arras."

> . . . never got Pierre nor the woman.
> And he went down past Chaise Dieu,
> And went after it all to Mount Segur,
>   after the end of all things,
> And they hadn't left even the stair,
> And Simone was dead by that time,
> And they called us the Manicheans
> Wotever the hellsarse that is.

> And that was when Troy was down, all right,
>   superbo Ilion . . .

"And that was when Troy was down" is exact repetition of the first line in Este's "delirium" (Canto 20) after he has caused his wife and son to be beheaded. Este is associated with Tierci, another husband who loses his wife to a young lover, and Tierci in turn is associated, in his frustrated retreat from Auvergne, with the fanaticism of the Albigensian Crusade. Pope Innocent III proclaimed the Crusade in 1208 for the purpose of annihilating fellow Christians accused of being "Manicheans." [22] Pound, switching to the point of view of those annihilated, indicates the insanity of a Christian consciousness so deranged by intolerant dogmatism that it could justify mass-murder in the name of God over mere abstractions. Tierci is pictured as joining the Crusade in its last stages, after the destruction of the

22. The Cathars of southern France, one of whose principal seats was Albi (hence the name "Albigenses"), were branded by the Church as guilty of the Manichean heresy. Whether or not this accusation was grounded in fact, the Cathars "took much greater account [in their religious practices] of the moral than of the dogmatic aspect of religion. . . . [They] were commonly known in Provence as 'the good men.'" Their teaching spread rapidly, and the papacy "saw in it a threat to the entire edifice of its power." "When Pope Innocent III proclaimed the Crusade against the Albigenses . . . , he provided an opportunity for which the covetous feudal barons of the North [including Simon de Montfort] had long lain in wait." "More than 300 towns and 200 castles were stormed or burned and all their inhabitants massacred." [Robert S. Briffault, *The Troubadours*, ed. L. F. Koons (Bloomington, 1965), p. 138ff.]

castle at Mont Segur and after the death (1218) of Simon de Montfort, leader of the Crusade. In this canto, then, Pound clearly links Renaissance disorder with root disorder in the intolerant Christian consciousness.

Canto 24 is altogether devoted to Niccolò d'Este. The main interest lies again in Niccolò's reaction to the beheading of his wife and son, but before this scene of delirious grief there is a long passage concerning a journey by Niccolò in his youth to Jerusalem. The point seems to be the contrast drawn between the sensuous delights he enjoyed during those parts of the voyage he spent in Greece and the disappointing filth of Jerusalem, including the commercialization of the holy places:

> And at Corfu, greek singers; by Rhodos
> Of the windmills, and to Paphos,
> Donkey boys, dust, deserts, Jerusalem, backsheesh
> And an endless fuss over passports;
> One groat for the Jordan, whether you go there or not,
>
> . . .
>   and
> "Here Christ put his thumb on a rock
> "Saying: hic est medium mundi."
>   (That, I assure you, happened.
>   Ego, scriptor cantilenae.)
> For worse? for better? but happened.
>
> . . .
>   and they had a bath
> When they got out of Jerusalem.

In drawing this picture of decay at the geographical heart of Christianity, Pound is obviously suggesting that the spiritual heart of Christendom had also fallen into decay by Este's time. The theme of Este's marriage and its tragic outcome is also suggested, rather ominously, in the allusion to the words of the marriage ceremony (Pound's "For worse? for better?"), which imply as well that the marriage of Western man to Christianity has turned out for the worse.

The following passage describes the insane grief of the Marquis of Ferrara over the death of his beloved Ugo, and a little further on Pound describes a subsequent decree of Este's by which "all women known as adulterous" were beheaded so "that his should not suffer alone." Renaissance violence and injustice bred more of the same, until finally the age of the great Renaissance families passed. In Pound's view, Este violence against nature resulted in the progressive emasculation of the later generations of this once noble family:

> After him and his day
> Were the cake-eaters, the consumers of icing,
> That read all day per diletto
> And left the night work to the servants.

The decay of Venice portrayed in Cantos 25 and 26 parallels the pattern established for Ferrara as a process of degeneration proceeding from within. In this extended portrait of Venice in decline, Pound at last takes up, in his spiral journey, the opening image of Canto 3, giving us the background for a full appreciation now of that early glimpse we had of a beloved Venice whose "gondolas cost too much."

The Renaissance triptych is complemented by three further panels from contemporary life whose purpose is to reveal modern man as self-castrated, insensitive to beauty, and alienated from his own body. The "abuleia" of the husks and locust-shells of Canto 7 is given expanded treatment now in Cantos 27–29. If the types chosen for satire are in large part small-town, middle-class *Americans*, the reason is chiefly Pound's desire to emphasize the deterioration of the Western mind during "the protestant centuries." The utter inflexibility of the average American mind, closed to the challenge of new experience, is adroitly summed up in the "ligneous solidness" of the old lady from Kansas in Canto 28. Transplanted to Europe, she sits in the "railway feeding-room in Chiasso" run by her daughter's Swiss husband and responds to nothing, frozen to her bench as if "waiting for the train for Topeka" forever.

Canto 29 develops in clear philosophical terms the Neoplatonic theme Pound has been building all through the poem in holistic challenge to the fragmented Western spirit. The allegorical figure of Lusty Juventus, the eternal life-force as manifested in the spirit of youth, looks from "the planks" (used for coffins) up "to heaven" as he stands and speaks "before the residence of the funeral director/ Whose daughters' conduct caused comment." It is clear, especially in the context of the rest of this canto, that the respectable and ridiculous "old man" who "did not know how he felt" personifies the Protestant consciousness. The fanatical aversion of the Puritan temperament to the pleasures of the senses has historically made it a "funeral director" indeed, for its main business has been *burial of the human body* (at which it has not been entirely successful: witness the old man's daughters). " 'Moral' was narrowed down to application to carnal relations," Pound says elsewhere in criticizing the Protestant centuries.[23]

Juventus' "criticism" of the old man emerges clearly in the following metaphysical utterance:

> "Matter is the lightest of all things,
> "Chaff, rolled into balls, tossed, whirled in the aether,
> "Undoubtedly crushed by the weight,
> "Light also proceeds from the eye.

In this passage of anti-materialistic paradoxes the "aether" is pictured as the active, spiritual essence of things responsible for the constant metamorphosis of matter, whose ever-changing forms are passing embodiments of the supreme spirit or life-force. Juventus plays on the "lightness" of matter in the Neoplatonic sense (reinforced by the last line) that matter is in essence Light, an aspect of the holistic structure of the universe in which all phenomena are ranged on a graduated scale according

23. *Guide to Kulchur*, p. 256.

to the degree to which they embody the spirit of God (who is Light). Secondly, the physical heaviness of matter is contrasted with its metaphysical *lightness*, its lack of the inherent power to act on its own as a principle in opposition to "aether" (life-force, spirit, or Light). In this sense it is mere "chaff"— "crushed by the weight" of the living grain (the aether which, paradoxically, is physically so light). These lines, taken in their dramatic context, serve as a complex criticism of the Protestant consciousness. The "funeral director" takes "matter," the human body, too *gravely* (if I may be permitted a pun consistent with the tenor of the whole passage). His obsessive concern with burying the body signifies the Protestant "belief," if behavior attests to belief, that the body manifests a will *contrary* to that of the spirit and perhaps even more *powerful* than that of the spirit, considering how few mortals are predestined to salvation. This sort of religion, in Pound's view, reflects the loss of all sense of proportion. The perverted sensibility of Protestantism (and of its parent, late-medieval Catholicism) was unable to recognize that spirit operated *in* nature, *through* the body, so that the Protestant suppression of the body resulted in the suppression of the spirit as well: we remember, in this connection, Pound's belief that the emotions, passion, love, are an "intellectual instigation."

The function of the quoted passage, then, has been to give a metaphysical "explanation" near the terminal point of the first thirty cantos of the contemporary *Inferno* portrayed in them so far. The "ligneous solidness," vagueness, effeteness, and other personality derangements of the figures in Pound's Protestant sketches are traced to an underlying cause, an inherently intolerant dualism that strikes out fanatically against nature without perceiving that an attack against nature is necessarily a mutilation of spirit, and ultimately a revulsion against God. The Renaissance *Inferno* collaterally presented in these cantos is by implication subject to the same root analysis. I do not mean to suggest that Pound, in introducing Juventus' speech, is breaking into prose commentary on what he has thus far accom-

plished in strictly poetic terms. If he had wished to do so he
would have presented these lines in a less cryptic, more explicitly logical mode of discourse. But I have already indicated
that these lines heighten the dramatic tension between Juventus and the funeral director. Dramatic complication and sly,
witty ambiguity run all through Juventus' words. First of all,
we recall that *Lusty* Juventus is speaking to a "funeral director/
Whose daughters' conduct caused comment." The "comment"
is not only neighbors' gossip but Juventus' speech itself, which
is on one level a confession to the old man of having enjoyed
his daughters' favors. The old man reacts vaguely to the comment on his daughters' conduct, but Juventus presses the point:
" 'What I know, I have known,/ 'How can the knowing cease
knowing?' " The sexual sense of the verb "to know" is sufficiently obvious in the context. Juventus continues:

> "Matter is the lightest of all things,
> "Chaff, rolled into balls, tossed, whirled in the aether,
> "Undoubtedly crushed by the weight.

The lightness of the girls' behavior and the ease of conquest is
suggested in the first line. The second line is syntactically ambiguous enough to permit of a sexual meaning for "balls,"
which is overtly used in that sense in the very next canto
("Balls for yr. honour!"). "Into" can be read as "into contact
with," and the resulting physical ecstasy is suggested by
"tossed," "whirled," and "crushed." *Aether* derives from the
Greek verb *aithein,* to kindle or burn, and the combination of
chaff with fire suggests the power of passion over the flesh.

Sexual desire and Protestant repression of desire is the
canto's main subject. The old men, the locust-shells of Canto 7,
reappear now as "cicadas":

> Languor has cried unto languor
>   about the marshmallow-roast
>
>   .   .   .
> The cicadas continue uninterrupted.

With a vain emptiness the virgins return to their homes
With a vain exasperation
The ephèbe has gone back to his dwelling,

. . .

The gentleman of fifty has reflected
            That it is perhaps just as well.

From this passage until nearly the end of the canto, the tone and imagery is Prufrockian. As in Eliot's poem, the sea provides the major metaphors for sexual desire:

The young seek comprehension;
The middleaged to fulfill their desire.
Sea weed dried now, and now floated,
            mind drifts, weed, slow youth, drifts,
Stretched on the rock, bleached and now floated;
Wein, Weib, TAN AOIDAN
Chiefest of these the second, the female
Is an element, the female
Is a chaos
An octopus
A biological process
            and we seek to fulfill . . .
TAN AOIDAN, our desire, drift . . .

. . .

Our mulberry leaf, woman, . . .

In these lines Pound is consistently equating woman to nature, a mindless dynamism to which man must in some sense surrender himself in order to fulfill himself. She is amorphous *Matter*, a primitive manifestation of the life-force roughly equivalent to the blind chaos of the Unconscious; and the spirit or constructive will of man is forever engaged in the struggle to give her permanent, meaningful form. She is the passive "mulberry leaf" which the creative will transforms into the silk of art (TAN AOIDAN, song). (Actually, it is impossible to reduce what Pound implies about "the female" to a coherent philosophical definition—an "octopus" is not a "chaos," for example,

—but the imagery does concur in denying to the female, *qua* female, the possession of conscious intelligence.) Deprecating the body in favor of an abstraction called "spirit," the Protestant consciousness endeavors to starve itself to death. The bewildered poet comments on this psychological phenomenon in the conclusion to the passage under discussion:

> And I, "But this beats me,
> "Beats me, I mean that I do not understand it;
> "This love of death that is in them."

Up to this point, Pound's main concern in the *Cantos* has been to picture the loss of the Concrete Universal. He has been at pains to develop the idea that both body and spirit must exist in harmony if the individual is to live a rich, creative life and if a civilization is to preserve its vitality. He portrays the Western mind as having lost its flexibility, its sense of proportion, its capacity to understand body and spirit as a continuum. The prime cause of the degeneration of Western culture, Pound suggests, is the loss of order within a Church that became increasingly abstract and dogmatic in its approach to a manifold, Protean reality. As it lost contact with reality it began to split up into Protestant sects which did no more than magnify the spiritual maladies of the Mother Church. As the One, the Universal Church, fell to pieces, the existence in Europe of an all-round, "entire man" became more and more impossible; the environment became too hostile to permit any more Sigismundo Malatestas. Pound's general condemnation of the Renaissance as a time of decadence bears witness to the powerful effect of pre-Raphaelite doctrine on his views of art and history. The following statement by Pound from the *ABC of Reading* should reveal the essential criterion by which he judges Renaissance art:

> . . . the painters of the Quattrocento, intent on their MAIN subject, Virgin sitting on bed with child, etc., *unity in picture*. Renaissance decadence: painters intent on painting a bit of

drapery, this or that bit of a picture, or chiaroscuro or what not.[24] [Italics mine.]

Disorder in the Church's apprehension of reality, Pound would argue, is reflected in the fragmented sensibility apparent in Renaissance art.

Canto 30, the subject of the next chapter, is a grand reprise of the themes developed through the previous twenty-nine cantos. Its function is to tie together the elements that have been receiving separate elaboration, and finally to connect the whole vision of the European *Inferno* with the metaphysical theme of time that had been introduced in Cantos 5 and 7. The unifying historical theme of the first thirty cantos, the idea that the social, moral, and aesthetic disorder of Western civilization is traceable to decay within the Church, receives final emphasis in the emphatic final line of Canto 30:

Il Papa mori.[25]

With these three words, "The Pope died," Pound sums up the tragedy of the West and what he envisions as the cause of that tragedy, the loss of responsible spiritual leadership.

24. *ABC of Reading*, p. 132.
25. An accent mark above the *i* in "mori," denoting the past tense, is mistakenly omitted.

CHAPTER V

Time is the Evil

BEFORE launching into the second phase of the poem, Pound felt the need for a concentrated statement of what he had tried to achieve thematically thus far. Such a "statement" is provided by Canto 30, which on one level is a résumé of major themes, while on another it functions as a transition to Phase Two. On a third level, however, the canto accomplishes a significant advance in the poem's total significance. Two major themes are recapitulated, the theme of time, and the theme of disorder in the Christian sensibility; but their sudden juxtaposition now throws both into a new light. The "point" that the first thirty cantos have been striving to make, the logical aim of their unfolding, finally crystallizes in Canto 30, the climax of Pound's *Inferno*.

Like Cantos 5 and 7, Canto 30 is a major "time" canto. The first part, concluding with the lines on "Messire Alfonso," is one of the most perplexingly beautiful passages in all of the *Cantos* and is therefore well worth the effort of explication. A single line emerges as the most difficult to understand and yet the most demanding of our attention, as though it were the key to all the rest: "Time is the evil. Evil." The repetition of "evil" seems simply to follow the lyrical pattern of repetition that appears throughout this whole section of the canto ("Compleynt, compleynt," "Artemis, Artemis," "A day, and a day"), but there is probably some further significance to the repetition in this line. Pound seems to be directing us to proceed from the contemplation of specific evils ("the evil.") to the concept of abstract evil itself ("Evil."); we are to advance from the particular to the general.

Particular evils are obviously embodied in the surrounding passages, but it is up to the reader to discover what they have in common that should spell out the general concept of evil itself. An examination of Artemis' beautiful "Compleynt Agaynst Pity," and the passages concerning Paphos, the murdered Ignez de Castro, and Madame *Hyle*, should "define" *evil* for us. We should then equate the definition we have formed to the abstraction, Time. It is perhaps strange that a poet so opposed to the type of mind that works primarily in abstractions should in his own poetry engage in highly abstract statement, but we ought to keep in mind Pound's precise attitude toward abstract statements: "An abstract or general statement is GOOD if it be ultimately found to correspond with the facts." [1] We must now examine the poetic "facts" to see if they shed light on the generalization.

Pity seems to be the specific evil in the Artemis passage; murder, that in the Ignez stanzas; and abuse of money power, the evil connected with the mysterious "Madame *Hyle*." No immediately apparent common denominator emerges, and we are forced to a closer inspection of each passage.

Artemis' "Compleynt" has received a good deal of critical attention. Donald Davie describes it as a "haunting mediaeval pastiche" which reverses "Chaucer's 'Complaint unto Pity' into an argument for a proper ruthlessness." [2] Clark Emery notes Pound's comment on Dante's *Inferno* XX:

> When Dante weeps in pity for sorcerers and diviners, Virgil shows classic stoicism:

1. *ABC of Reading*, p. 25.
2. Donald Davie, *Ezra Pound: Poet as Sculptor* (New York, 1964), p. 131.

Art thou, too, like the other fools? Here liveth pity when it is well dead. Who is more impious than he who sorrows at divine judgment? [3]

Emery equates this Pity, by which all things in Artemis' forests are "growne awry," to "sentiment, a lack of savagery in intellectuals, a false tolerance" that interferes "with the exercise of justice." [4] Finally, M. L. Rosenthal indicates that the idea Pound is attempting to communicate in Artemis' song against Pity is that Pity is a form of sentimentality, and "*sentimentality* is . . . a fraudulence of communication, the stylistic counterpart of usury." [5] These critics examine the passage from various angles, casting different but complementary lights upon it. The lines are so rich, however, that they seem indefinitely capable of interpretation. Only full quotation will do justice to the beauty of the song as well as suggest its complexity:

> Compleynt, compleynt I hearde upon a day,
> Artemis singing, Artemis, Artemis
> Agaynst Pity lifted her wail:
> Pity causeth the forests to fail,
> Pity slayeth my nymphs,
> Pity spareth so many an evil thing.
> Pity befouleth April,
> Pity is the root and the spring.
> Now if no fayre creature followeth me
> It is on account of Pity,
> It is on account that Pity forbideth them slaye.
> All things are made foul in this season,
> This is the reason, none may seek purity
> Having for foulnesse pity

3. *The Spirit of Romance*, pp. 134–35. Quoted in Clark Emery, *Ideas into Action*, p. 121.

4. Emery, *Ideas into Action*, p. 121.

5. M. L. Rosenthal, *A Primer of Ezra Pound* (New York, 1960), p. 27.

And things growne awry;
No more do my shaftes fly
To slay. Nothing is now clean slayne
But rotteth away.

Artemis is presented here primarily in her roles as goddess of the hunt and goddess of nature. She prunes excess and thereby maintains the "purity," health, and beauty of nature. In that sense she is symbolic of the self-regulatory principle in nature, the ecological balance by which nature maintains itself in a sort of timeless perfection. She is also representative of the principle of order in man, by which the will brings the emotions into harmony with the intellect. Pity is a type of emotional excess, a "false tolerance," by which order in external nature as well as in human nature is subverted. Pound is thinking of the concept of Pity as it appears in medieval love poetry, where the lover often resorts to the lady's sense of pity for his sufferings as reason for her to bestow her favors on him—an unmanly appeal, as it seems to us, and an unnatural motivation for physical love. Pity, therefore, violates the order of nature, whose self-regulatory pattern of birth, copulation, and death is founded upon the immanent will of the universe itself, a necessity in things that appears ruthless, perhaps, but is in fact the profoundest wisdom.

"Pity" appears in a paradoxical light. Its *effect* is regarded as equivalent to that of the most vicious political jealousies, such as those which resulted in the murder of Ignez de Castro, a lady of the court whom the young Pedro, heir to the Portuguese throne, had secretly married.[6] Pity *also* murders: "Pity slayeth my nymphs," cries Artemis. A clear distinction is made between the "clean" slaying practised by Artemis and the "foul" slaying wrought by Pity. Killing is necessary to the ecological balance of nature; the excessive proliferation of any one element is prevented and harmony is maintained. Pity, however, by sparing "so many an evil thing"—dangerous excess which should be

6. *The Spirit of Romance*, p. 218.

b6rfj

destroyed—paradoxically causes "the forests to fail" by upsetting nature's balance. The intention of Pity is good, but misguided, and its effects are murderous.

"Pity befouleth April," laments Artemis. "All things are made foul in this season." She means the hunting season, for soon she cries, "No more do my shaftes fly/ To slay." Although all wild creatures were sacred and dear to her, the Greeks considered her favorite beast to be the hind, which was hunted during the month of March-April (called by most Greeks *Artemision*, but named *Elaphe-bolion*, or "deer-shooting," by the Athenians).[7] We have already understood Pity to be a violation of nature, but Pound examines this violation more precisely now: what Pity violates is man's proper regard for the *seasons* and for the sacred activities man should perform in due season in order to maintain the balance of nature and the ecological balance between man and nature. Two major principles of Confucian ethics are that man should act in due proportion and *in due season*. Pound's translation of the *Chung Yung* ("Unwobbling Pivot") reveals the supreme importance of a reverent attitude toward the seasons in the Confucian ethical system:

> Chung Ni (Confucius) said: The master man finds the center and does not waver; the mean man runs counter to the circulation about the invariable. . . .
> The master man's axis does not wobble. The man of true breed finds this center in season, the small man's center is rigid, he pays no attention to the times and seasons, precisely because he is a small man and lacking all reverence.[8]

The great new theme which emerges in the "Compleynt" is the characterization of the natural order in terms of the seasonal cycle, the process of *organic time*. The *Cantos* hereafter shall concentrate on the development of the concept of organic time.

7. Seyffert, *Dictionary of Classical Antiquities*, p. 71.
8. Ezra Pound, trans., *Confucius: The Great Digest and Unwobbling Pivot* (New York, 1951), pp. 103–5.

It now becomes important to show that Pound intends, in this passage, a major confrontation between nature as organic time and "evil" as mechanical time.

It is sufficiently clear by now that the "evil" Pound depicts in this passage is man's *violation of nature,* but have we any evidence to warrant our equating this concept of Evil to the abstraction "Time"? If our analyses of Cantos 5 and 7 have any validity, the reply must be an affirmative one. These central, early cantos are preparations for the present climactic statement that "Time is the evil." Cantos 5 and 7 establish the meaning of "time" as any destructive process originating in the disordered will of man that violates the natural order. Mechanical time holds sway where man has lost his mythological, holistic perception of reality. It holds sway where man's many-leveled response to his biological and social environments is distorted as a result of a false conception of reality. "Pity," for Pound, suggests both sentimentality—a disordered emotional response to reality—and the damaging effects of sentimentality on nature and society.

Pity's violation of the mythological or holistic perception of reality is implied when Artemis says, "Pity slayeth my nymphs." The various nymphs of wood, stream, and mountain are the poetic and religious projections of a "primitive" sensibility which sees nature suffused with divine forces whose operations are beautiful and often benevolent toward man. The dualistic mentality destroys the nymphs because it refuses to accord divinity to nature; filtering God out of nature, it sets nature and spirit in sharp opposition. The natural expression of human emotion becomes distorted so that Pity, for example, lights upon an unworthy object, and love—as Pound remarks in Canto 29—becomes the love of death. Pity, as a matter of fact, seems to be the obverse of the emotional frigidity displayed by some of the American types in Cantos 28–29 who are the helpless victims of an impoverishing dualism. As I tried to point out when in Canto 7 I discussed the love-and-war, Venus-Mars polarity, the arbitrary cleavage of nature and spirit, mind and body, results in the shrunken significance of both. The ultimate effect of the dualistic vision of reality is the definition of man as "a ghost in a corpse."

This discussion of the dualistic mentality leads to what I consider the most important single idea embodied in Artemis' "Compleynt." In the conflict between Artemis and Pity, Pound is presenting the tragic contrast between the Greek mythological apprehension of the world and the succeeding Christian, theological world-view. In one of his essays Pound has described the holistic Greek mentality as "the Mediterranean sanity,"

> the radiant world where one thought cuts through another with clean edge, a world of moving energies . . . untouched by two maladies, the Hebrew disease, the Hindoo disease, fanaticism and excess.[9]

By the "Hebrew disease" Pound means "ANY monotheistic taboos whatsoever. . . . I consider the *Metamorphoses* a sacred book, and the Hebrew scriptures the record of a barbarian tribe, full of evil." [10] In Pound's view there have been two major elements bringing disorder into Christianity. The abstractions of Aristotelian logic-chopping displaced the influence of Neoplatonism in its theology, and the "Hebrew disease" of fanaticism, as he calls it, rose to the ascendancy in its ethic as *practised*, if not in actual theory:

> I am not inveighing against the best Christian ethic or against the quality of Western mind shown in Bishop Grosseteste's treatise on light [a Neoplatonic work]. I am against the disorderly tendencies, the anarchy and barbarism which appear in poor christian teaching, fanaticism and superstition.[11]

9. *Literary Essays of Ezra Pound*, ed. T. S. Eliot (Norfolk, 1954), p. 154.

10. *Letters*, p. 183.

11. Pound, *Impact*, p. 138.

Thus far this study has made it apparent that the main focus of attack in the *Cantos* has been the Christian sensibility and its historical ramifications. Pound's letters make it clear that as early as 1918, when the first cantos were being shaped, he was obsessed with

> the belief that most of the tyrannies of modern life, or at least a lot of stupidities, are based on Xtn taboos, and can't really be got rid of radically until Xtianity is taken lightly and sceptically, until, that is, it drifts back into the realm of fairy-lore and picturesque superstition (mostly unpicturesque, at present).[12]

One of the points that will emerge in the following chapters is that Pound never relents in his criticism of Christianity, a criticism which is by and large constructive.

In Artemis' "Compleynt" the *Cantos* achieve an important thematic advance. Not only does the "Compleynt" bring into focus the radical criticism of Christianity Pound has been engaging in all along, but it serves to establish the Christian sensibility as "the evil" which the reader is to identify with "time." Time in Cantos 5 and 7 applied generally to *any* violation of nature proceeding from the misguided will of man; now, in Canto 30, time in the Western world is identified exclusively with the evil effects of the Christian consciousness.

The Christian *concept* of time is itself, for Pound, a perversion of reality. Christians oppose Time to Eternity, the temporal to the spiritual, and an intolerant dualism necessarily disparages the temporal world, that is, all earthly things, as inherently evil. Although Greek philosophy also distinguished between Time and Eternity, Time, for Plato, was "the moving image of Eternity," inferior to the unmoving world of ideas but in no sense opposed to it. Christianity makes no value distinction between nature and history, between the geocosm and the microcosm; man and earth were both corrupted by the "Fall,"

12. *Letters*, p. 141.

and are therefore both included, without distinction, under the rubric of time. For the Greeks, however, nature deserved special consideration as an imitation of the divine:

> The Greek holds that motion and becoming are inferior degrees of reality, in which identity is no longer apprehended—at best —save in the form of permanence and perpetuity, hence of recurrence. The circular movement that ensures the mainte- nance of the same things by repeating them . . . is the most immediate, the most perfect (and hence the most nearly divine) expression of that which, at the pinnacle of the hierarchy, is absolute immobility. According to the celebrated Platonic defi- nition, time, which is determined and measured by the revolu- tion of the celestial spheres, is the moving image of unmoving eternity, which it imitates by revolving in a circle.[13]

Pound's Artemis represents the mysterious power that in- sures the orderly procession and God-like, eternal return of the seasons. She embodies, at the same time, archaic man's concep- tion of the beauty of nature's cyclic time-pattern and his rev- erent awareness of nature's immortality. For the Christian, the beauty of nature became suspect and its immortality was denied by the doctrine of its corruption. For the first time in the *Cantos*, therefore, the forces of order and disorder come into conflict in terms of two opposed views of time, mechanical time versus organic time, and complementarily in terms of two op- posed world-cultural views, the dualistic Christian as against the holistic Greek. The central conflict of forces in the poem thereby achieves a higher degree of philosophical definition. Simultaneously, we can now begin to see that the structure of the first thirty cantos exhibits true development, that the full effect of Canto 30 rests upon the accumulation throughout the previous cantos of effects more specialized and limited in scope.

13. Henri-Charles Puech, "La Gnose et le temps," *Eranos-Jahrbuch* XX (Zurich, 1951), pp. 60–61. Quoted in Mircea Eliade, *Cosmos and History*, p. 89n.

Examination of the passages immediately following the "Compleynt" reveals further development of some of the major ideas discussed above. Actually, the next stanza is a continuation of the "Compleynt," but from a new point of view. Paphos was famous for the worship of Aphrodite, whose archetypal voice pours scorn upon her misguided representative in Christian times, a Christian "Venus" who violates what is proper to the seasons of human life by suppressing her youthful desires and sacrificing her femininity in the fruitless task of keeping an old man's "embers warm." In the first part of the "Compleynt," we saw Pity as disruptive of the principle of *order* (Artemis); now we see Pity operating against the natural expression of sexual *energy* (Aphrodite). Christianity, Pound is saying, has managed to pervert the two fundamental forces— Kungian order and Eleusinian energy—whose harmonious conjunction is necessary if a civilization is to flourish. The violation of natural order, the violation of natural energy—either or both characterize mechanical time.

The bafflement of the "young Pedro," unnaturally and unseasonably bereft of his love, is similar to that of the "young Mars," who has lost his Venus to Pity:

> Time is the evil. Evil.
> > A day, and a day
> Walked the young Pedro baffled,
> > a day and a day
> After Ignez was murdered.

> Came the Lords in Lisboa
> > a day, and a day
> In homage. Seated there
> > dead eyes,
> Dead hair under the crown,
> The King still young there beside her.

In *The Spirit of Romance* Pound summarizes the historical events concerning Ignez and Pedro which Camoens treats of in the *Lusiads*:

Constança, wife of Pedro, heir to the throne of Portugal, died
in 1345. He then married in secret one of her maids of honor,
Ignez da Castro, a Castilian of the highest rank. Her position
was the cause of jealousy, and of conspiracy; she was stabbed
in the act of begging clemency from the then reigning Alfonso
IV. When Pedro succeeded to the throne, he had her body
exhumed, and the court did homage, the grandees of Portugal
passing before the double throne of the dead queen and her
king, and kissing that hand which had been hers.[14]

Pound did not consider Camoens's treatment of the theme vital
as art. It had "the beauty of words and cadences, and of expression, not the beauty of that subtler understanding which is
genius." In spite of his splendor, Camoens failed. "Every age
. . . yields its crop of pleasant singers, who know the rules, and
who write beautiful language and regular rhythms; poetry completely free from the cruder faults: but the art of writing poetry
which is vitally interesting is a matter for masters." [15] If we ex-
tend the concept of mechanical time to the realm of verse, we
can see that Pound regards Camoens's poem as itself an example of mechanical time, an empty succession of "regular
rhythms" uninformed by understanding. So, too, in an analogous way, the image of Ignez selected by Pound may be meant
to embody the concept of mechanical time, in that she is a life-
less body, a form emptied of meaning. In any case, the act of
murder, the most extreme of all violations of nature, seems to
be the embodiment of the concept of mechanical time most
immediately intended in this passage, for it is put into the same
relation with "time" in this instance as was the murder of
Giovanni Borgia in Canto 5. Further, Pedro's morbid clinging
to the dead past, a variation on the general idea of "Pity" conceived of as sentimentality, intensifies the meaning of time as a
violation of nature, a "love of death" (Canto 29). Pedro reminds one of Dido in the previous time-canto, Canto 7:

14. *The Spirit of Romance*, p. 218.
15. Ibid. p. 219.

> Dido choked up with sobs, for her Sicheus
> Lies heavy in my arms, dead weight
> Drowning, with tears, new Eros.

Dido's morbid attachment to a dead husband, Pedro's to a dead wife, both prevent the spiritual renewal that alone abolishes time.

The theme of "dead weight" overpowering the living, violating the order of nature, is as important to the next passage in Canto 30 as it has been to all the preceding:

> Came Madame ῬΥΛΗ
> Clothed with the light of the altar
> And with the price of the candles.
> "Honour? Balls for yr. honour!
> Take two million and swallow it."
>   Is come Messire Alfonso
> And is departed by boat for Ferrara
> And has passed here without saying "O."

On the historical level, the Madame "Matter" alluded to is Lucrezia Borgia, and Messire Alfonso is Alfonso d'Este, prince of Ferrara, Lucrezia's third husband. In the first three lines she is pictured in church, arrayed for her wedding, for which she herself has paid. The next two lines reveal that she has purchased her husband as well. Alfonso

> feels that his honor is thereby compromised. He is advised to pocket the dowry and swallow his pride. . . . The marriage was arranged by Ercole d'Este, Alfonso's father, and Pope Alexander VI, Lucrezia's father, and took place, by proxy, in Rome, with the considerable pomp the Borgias could stage. Alfonso married by command [the alliance was politically advantageous].

The last three lines refer to the fact that Alfonso, "having kept aloof from the entire proceedings . . . covertly visited the extravagant procession that brought Lucrezia to Ferrara, looked at his bride, and departed again." [16]

Lucrezia's conduct became respectable once she had settled in Ferrara,[17] but during her appearance in this canto Pound chooses to represent her in her former light as a crass, hypocritical, domineering arch-villainess. The significance, however, of the name Pound gives her, Madame "Matter," is not immediately clear. The Greek *Hyle*, Pound notes, developed in meaning from "uncut forest, and the stuff of which a thing is made, [to] matter as a principle of being." [18] Guy Davenport, whose historical scholarship I have been indebted to, reads Madame *Hyle* as

> Mother Nature, "my Lady Forest," *Hyle* normally means "forest," but can also mean "nature," "timber," or even "ordure," and Pound uses this latter meaning in [Canto] LXXVII ("the army vocabulary contains almost 48 words/ one verb and participle one substantive *hyle*"). In philosophy [it] meant the material world.[19]

The *Annotated Index* lists these meanings: "Wood, woodland, wood cut down, stuff, material, matter."

Madame *Hyle* can be understood in both concrete and abstract terms. As "My Lady Forest" she is Artemis' forests "growne awry" and "made foul in this season" of the Renaissance, the living wood turned to "ordure," perhaps. As rotting timber, she is like the exhumed Ignez, a corpse raised to a position of command.[20] But Artemis' forests have fallen into decay because of the prevailing Christian attitude of irreverence to-

16. Guy Mattison Davenport, Jr. "A Reading of I–XXX of the Cantos of Ezra Pound" (Ph.D. dissertation: Harvard University, 1961), p. 454.

17. Emery, *Ideas into Action*, p. 122.

18. Impact, p. 121 n.

19. Davenport, "A Reading of I–XXX of the Cantos," p. 453.

20. Compare the "husks" and "shells" of Time in Canto 7.

ward nature. Lucrezia, who might have flowered into a Venus under a different religious and moral tutelage, is "growne awry" into a brassy vampire. A disintegrative dualism has, by a process of false abstraction, transformed Mother Nature into Madame "Matter," and the blatant Lucrezia stands defiant in the church, an image of Matter opposed to Spirit, even lording it over the Spirit, the tail wagging the dog. In Canto 29 Lusty Juventus, now the thwarted "young Mars," said, "Matter is the lightest of all things,/ Chaff, rolled into balls, tossed, whirled in the aether," but the Christian distrust of Matter invested it with so much importance as the ubiquitous principle of Evil that the principle of Spirit grew energically pale beside it. Ironically, whereas Juventus described matter as "the lightest of all things," treating it *lightly* in comparison to the Neoplatonic *Light* of the One, Madame "Matter" is "Clothed with the light of the altar," arrogating to herself the energic candle-power that the Church once possessed when it was a spiritually vital organism. Values are topsy-turvy in Pound's Renaissance world. The light that shines in the Church is a materialistic one; money outshines honor. In the philosophy of Scotus Erigena, one of Pound's favorite medieval Neoplatonists, matter was not even recognized as a separate principle of being. "Matter itself, far from being the means by which we can know the essence in things, is quasi-being, the cause of nothing." [21] In Lucrezia's world it is the Prime Mover.

In the final "O" that Alfonso is too passive even to utter, we become aware of the fate of the Estes and of all the noble families of the Renaissance: reduction to a cipher. After Niccolò d'Este, Pound says in Canto 24, came the impotent "cake-eaters." The fanatical violence of the Renaissance resulted in figurative self-castration; the loss of order implies the dissipation of creative energy. Lucrezia's colloquial "Balls for yr. honour!"

21. Gordon Leff, *Medieval Thought from St. Augustine to Ockham* (Harmondsworth, Middlesex, 1958), p. 70. Quoted in Dekker, *The Cantos of Ezra Pound*, p. 84, as a partial gloss to Canto 90.

suggests, not so subtly, that her captive husband lacks just those manly virtues, popularly associated with the testicles, which give substance to the word *honor* and make it mean more than mere concern for social respectability. Lucrezia's subjugation of Alfonso is backed up by the full authority of the Church, who happens to be her father, the Pope Alessandro Borgia briefly mentioned at the end of the canto as dying. The idea once more emerges, in this new perspective, that the disorder of the Renaissance began with disorder in the Church; befouling the innocence of nature, the Church transformed her in men's minds into Madame Matter, an evil principle that is no more than a projection of the mental disorder which fathered it. Nature so deranged takes its vengeance on man; *hubris* is visited with *nemesis*; the suppressed *Yin*, the female, erupts violently against the oppressive *Yang*, the disordered "male" will. The relationship between Kung and Eleusis, order and energy, is undermined.

The juxtaposition of Madame "Matter" with the spiritual "light" of the Church represents in condensed form the Christian doctrine of dualism—Matter versus Spirit, Time versus Eternity—that for Pound ultimately destroyed the Church itself. In the image Pound presents, Madame Matter is meant, finally, as a new and more accurate name to replace "Mother Church." Madame Matter, by her vulgar modernity of expression, suggests that *she* is now the religion of modern times: "Balls for yr. honour!/ Take two million and swallow it." Modern finance replaces earlier fanaticism. The theme of time not only embraces the Renaissance but also the modern inferno, and in the abrupt shift of tone that ushers in the voice of Madame Matter, Pound achieves a sudden, jarring fusion of Catholic and Protestant themes, of the unworldly intonation of *Gloria in excelsis* with the sober stridency of his "usurers in excelsis" of Canto 12.

"Il Papa mori." Commenting on the end of Canto 30, Emery says that "the Pope's death and the allusion to printing hint at things to come in later cantos: the rise of Protestantism, the shift from an Italy-centered to a Britain-centered world," and, of course, to emphasis on the theme of usury.[22] Pound draws upon a letter from Girolamo Soncino, the great printer, to his patron Cesare Borgia, describing the creative craftsmanship of the printers and cutters of new type-fonts assembled in his workshop in the town of Fano, where Soncino established himself in 1501.[23] The letter was sent to Cesare, the Pope's son, in July, 1503,

> And in August that year died Pope Alessandro Borgia,
> Il Papa mori.

In a sense, the printing press did indeed kill and replace what the Pope had so long represented for Europe. The Church, with its magical formulae, had exercised the only sort of control over nature that man had ever conceived possible—until the Renaissance, when the European mind became intoxicated with the possibilities suggested by *mechanical* means of controlling the external environment. The abstract, Christian world-view gave way, however, to another artificial system of apprehending and controlling reality. Marshall McLuhan has summed up the effect of the printing press, "the first mechanization of a complex handicraft, and . . . the archetype of all subsequent mechanization," almost as if he were commenting on its meaning for Canto 30:

> The uniformity and repeatability of print permeated the Renaissance with the idea of time and space as continuous measurable quantities. The immediate effect of this idea was to desacralize the world of nature and the world of power alike. The new technique of control of physical processes by segmentation and fragmentation separated God and Nature as much as Man and Nature, or man and man.[24]

22. Emery, *Ideas into Action*, p. 123.

23. Davenport, p. 455.

24. Marshall McLuhan, *Understanding Media: The Extensions of Man* (Signet Books: New York, 1966), p. 160.

Soncino's printers are the final variation in the canto on the theme of mechanical time. Pound, playing on the name of the town (Fano di Cesare) where Soncino had set up shop, calls it first "Caesar's fane," then speaks of Soncino having brought his printers "in Fano Caesaris." The fact that his craftsmen are "working in Caesar's fane," i.e. literally the *church* of Caesar, has multiple implications. First of all, the prince Caesare Borgia is his patron. Secondly, we are reminded of Madame Matter's presence in the church of her father, Pope Alexander Borgia, a church that has become the church of *Caesar* rather than remained the church of God. The printers, like Madame Matter, represent the forces of mechanical time that, nourished by the Church, become its nemesis. Among his printers, Soncino boasts of "a die-cutter for greek fonts and hebrew." Giving tremendous impetus to the rise of Protestantism, the type-font succeeded the holy-water font, and the modern West was baptized in printer's ink. Pound's attitude toward Soncino is hardly negative, however. Soncino was a great craftsman, and neither he nor his workers were responsible for the historical forces of fragmentation (developing out of Protestantism, according to Pound) unleashed by their craft. Never without a sense of humor, Pound ends Canto 30 with "Explicit canto/ XXX," punning on the printer's "30." [25]

25. The pun is noticed by Max Halperen in "A Structural Reading of *The Cantos* of Ezra Pound" (Ph.D. dissertation: Florida State University, 1959), p. 161.

PART TWO

Purgatorio

TIME AS ORDER

CHAPTER VI

Attention to the Times and Seasons

THE FIRST PHASE of the *Cantos* comes definitely to an end, an *announced* finish, in Canto 46, where Pound says

> This case, and with it
> the first part, draws to a conclusion,
> of the first phase of this opus, Mr Marx, Karl, did not
> foresee this conclusion . . .

The second phase, however, has been gaining the ascendancy since Canto 31, gathering momentum even as the "first part" thumps to a resounding summation in the Usura Canto (Canto 45). A few lines after those quoted above, Pound makes it clear that he has been developing the second phase, or "case," simultaneously with completing the first:

> This case is not the last case or the whole case, we ask a
> REVISION, we ask for enlightenment in a case
> moving concurrent, but this case is the first case:
> Bank creates it ex nihil.

The "concurrent" second case being developed, as I have outlined in my introduction, is that a truly *enlightened* nation bases its prosperity upon the adjustment of its economic practices to the rhythms of nature or organic time. I consider Cantos 31–46, therefore, primarily as a period of transition leading us from the full force of Phase One, attained in Canto 30, to the great plateau of the second phase, which begins at Canto 47.

Pound's *Purgatorio* is a vast stretch of poetry extending from Canto 31 through 71. Very uneven in quality, it contains some of the most arid pages he has ever written as well as some of his best, most sustained triumphs of lyricism up to *The Pisan Cantos*. I use the word *Purgatorio* for this phase of the poem because the dominant note is now one of hope, whereas the previous cantos, Pound's *Inferno*, have emphasized the theme of darkness and despair. The Confucian principles of order, largely inoperative in the panorama of decay we have just witnessed, are now to be presented as ideas which at certain historical moments have been successfully put into action.

Pound will attempt to show that through proper "direction of the will" in its leaders, any social organism can abolish the evils of mechanical time and put all its energies to creative rather than destructive uses. He will not only be illustrating the principles of Confucian order as already enunciated in Canto 13, but he will examine history in the light of a much more profound reading of Confucianism than he manifested in the earlier cantos. He will be concerned to show that "order within" is based on the precise observation of the nature of things, and that an understanding of the nature of things depends further on an awareness of nature's *way*, the Tao, which Pound translates in his *Confucius* as "the process." The "process" manifests itself in the cosmic cycles and seasonal rhythms of nature. If men live in harmony with nature's rhythms, if a leader is a "master man," as Confucius puts it, and "pays . . . attention to the times and seasons" in what he decrees for his people, then society will achieve a maximum of creative order. The enemies of art and society have been represented as forces of mechanical time; the perception of organic time is now presented as the key to their vanquishment.

My intention in the present chapter is to trace the time-theme as Pound develops it between Cantos 31 and 46. In an earlier comment I described this stretch of sixteen cantos as a transitional group in which the Confucian theme of organic time rises in contrapuntal reply to the theme of usury, the economic evil which Pound considers the root of the modern *Inferno*. Before the Confucian aspect of these cantos can be fully appreciated, however, the reader should have a general grasp of the historical subject matter, often obscure, which Pound employs so intensively in this section. I believe that most of the background can be gathered inductively from the poetry, but to present this material now should ultimately render my exposition of the time-theme more coherent.

The main subject of these cantos is economic history, particularly the history of banking practices at certain periods in the history of the United States, England, and Italy. Pound has stated clearly the reason for his obsessive interest in economics:

> Most social evils are at root economic. I, personally, know of no social evil that cannot be cured, or very largely cured, economically.[1]

Between Cantos 31 and 37 Pound treats the period of American history, from the Revolution to the Civil War, during which a heroic struggle was waged by several American presidents against the monopolistic designs of the forces of usury. The war against the financiers, and particularly against the first and second Banks of the United States, was fought successfully between the presidencies of Jefferson and Van Buren, but with the Civil War came the triumph of usury. In 1944, in a pamphlet written in Italian, Pound listed what he thought to be the highlights of American economic history. I quote that portion relevant to the cantos under discussion:

> 1620–1750: Beginning and development of colonial prosperity . . . This prosperity stimulated gluttony, and the London monopolists tried to impose their monetary monopoly;
>
> 1750–1776–1788: Preparation for the Revolution, formation of the American system;

1. *Impact* (Chicago, 1960), p. 86.

1789: Washington president. Struggle between Hamilton, conservative agent of finance and Jefferson's democratization. . . .

1801–1825: Jefferson and his disciples in the White House. The Louisiana Purchase. Second war against England.

1829–1841: Jackson and Van Buren in the White House. Fight between the banks and the people. The people won;

1841–1861: . . . Debts contracted by the South to New York bankers and elsewhere. . . . From 1861 war of secession, triumph of finance . . .[2]

Jefferson's solution to the problem of usury is stated emphatically in a single italicized line in Canto 40: "*If a nation will master its money.*" Max Wykes-Joyce summarizes Pound's Jeffersonian position: "The chief function of the bank in Pound's economics is to distribute credit," and "there is nothing save economic ignorance to prevent the State from issuing credit, without paying interest to the bankers."[3]

For his American history materials, Pound draws heavily on only a few sources. Cantos 31–33 are quarried mainly from the correspondence between Adams and Jefferson. Canto 34, the John Quincy Adams canto, comes from the selected edition of *The Diary of John Quincy Adams*, 1794–1845 (New York, 1928). Canto 37, the Martin Van Buren canto, is a pastiche of fragments from *The Autobiography of Martin Van Buren* (Washington, D. C., 1920).[4]

Speaking of the Jefferson-Adams correspondence, Pound says that

2. "An Introduction to the Economic Nature of the United States," trans. Carmine Amore, in *Impact*, pp. 35–36.

3. Max Wykes-Joyce, "Some Considerations Arising from Ezra Pound's Conception of the Bank," *An Examination of Ezra Pound*, ed. Peter Russell (Norfolk, 1950), pp. 224–25.

4. William Vasse, "American History and the Cantos," *The Pound Newsletter*, No. 5, ed. John Edwards (Department of English, University of California at Berkeley, January, 1955), p. 14.

nothing surpasses the evidence that CIVILIZATION WAS in America, than the series of letters exchanged between Jefferson and John Adams, during the decade of reconciliation after their disagreements.[5]

"The sanity and civilization of Adams-Jefferson," Pound goes on to say, "stems from the encyclopedists":

You find in their letters a varied culture, and an omniverous [sic] (or apparently so) curiosity. And yet the "thinning," the impoverishment of mental life shows in the decades after their death, and not, I think, without cause.[6]

The implied cause is no doubt a process of cultural decay which Pound would connect with the rise of tolerance for usury. The cosmopolitan awareness of Adams and Jefferson in *economic* thinking was especially dangerous to the usurers and the related forces of obscurantism:

They both had a wide circle of reference, of knowledge, of ideas, with the acid test for hoakum, and no economic inhibitions. The growth of economic inhibition, I mean specifically in the domain of THOUGHT, is a XIXth century phenomenon to a a degree that I believe inhered in no other century.[7]

Martin Van Buren appears prominently only in Canto 37, where he is protagonist in the people's struggle against Biddle's Bank (the second Bank of the United States). The main reason Pound resuscitates Van Buren is to galvanize interest in his memoirs:

Van Buren's memoirs, the records of the American bank war, the death struggle between the bank and the people, were written around 1860, and never got printed till 1920.[8]

5. *Impact*, p. 167.
6. Ibid. p. 177.
7. Ibid. p. 182.
8. Ibid. p. 144.

The sixty-year delay in publication was not, according to Pound, accidental. "The real war," he explains,

> was the war between the bank and the people, waged and won for the people by Jackson and Van Buren. This is the fact that explains the silence of 'history' and the small respect paid to Van Buren throughout the whole period of American decadence, which dates from Lincoln's assassination.[9]

Another reason for Pound's exclusive reliance on these documentary materials for the composition of the American history cantos is his desire to stimulate interest in them as literature, as the best literature, in his opinion, produced in America at the time. He sees "Not only our American history but our literature in the correspondence of J. Adams, Jefferson, J. Q. Adams, Van Buren." [10] Ever the iconoclast, his intention is consciously to junk our accepted literary heritage and provide us with the true one, the one in which he sees the most vitality, the most relevance to social reality, and therefore the greatest validity as poetic statement. These documents comprise the true American literary renaissance for Pound, as they do not, for example, for F. O. Matthiessen.

Of less interest, perhaps, to the American reader is the barrage of documentary excerpts on Italian banking which fills out most of Cantos 42–44. These cantos trace the history of equitable, non-usurious banking practices in Italy from the foundation of the Monte dei Paschi (Bank of the Grasslands) by Cosimo I of Tuscany in the early seventeenth century through the late eighteenth-century reforms of the Grand Duke of Tuscany, Pietro Leopoldo, and the continued good works of his successors in the early nineteenth century—especially Ferdinando III, who undid the years of economic havoc wrought by the Napoleonic occupation of his duchy. In Canto 41 Mussolini

9. Ezra Pound, *America, Roosevelt and the Causes of the Present War* [Money Pamphlet No. 6] (London, 1951), p. 12.
10. *Guide to Kulchur*, p. 264.

arises as the new hope for Italy, and by extension for all of Europe and America, whose corruption by the forces of usury we have been witnessing through Cantos 35, 37, 38, and 40. Mussolini is the man who Pound feels will quash the greedy money-ogres and lead Italy on to cultural rebirth. The Mussolini of Canto 41 and of Pound's *Jefferson and/or Mussolini,* a prose work written during the same year (1933), is meant by the poet as a challenge to America to judge its present by the standards of its past. In the book just mentioned, Pound poses the following rhetorical question (originally all in italics, which I omit):

> Do the driving ideas of Jefferson, Quincy Adams, Van Buren . . . FUNCTION actually in the America of this decade to the extent that they function in Italy under the DUCE?
> The writer's opinion is that they DON'T.[11]

For Pound, Mussolini is a type of the Odysseus *polumetis,* the many-minded, all-round, "entire man," like Sigismundo Malatesta, who did not allow the demands of expedience to compromise his fundamental need to create a work that would endure. "Mussolini," says Pound, "is the first head of state in our time to perceive and to proclaim *quality* as a dimension in national production. He is the first man in power to publish any such recognition *since* . . . Sigismond Malatesta." [12] In his ability and desire to harmonize the practical with the enduring, he is likened to Jefferson, who in turn is more than once in the *Cantos* associated with Malatestan all-roundness (see, for example, Canto 21, p. 97). Both Jefferson and Mussolini are regarded primarily as *artists* whose medium happens to be politics. Praising Jefferson for effecting the Louisiana Purchase, Pound considers that in so doing, Jefferson exhibited the justifiable

11. *Jefferson and/or Mussolini: L'idea statale: Fascism as I Have Seen It* (New York, 1935), p. 104.
12. *Impact,* p. 87.

opportunism of the artist, who has a definite aim, and creates out of the materials present. The greater the artist the more permanent his creation.[13]

Mussolini, too, must be considered as a creative artist:

I don't believe any estimate of Mussolini will be valid unless it *starts* from his passion for construction. Treat him as *artifex* and all the details fall into place. Take him as anything save the artist and you will get muddled with contradictions.[14]

Ultimately, all of Pound's "heroes" are variations upon the central idea of the Confucian prince, whose sense of order is based upon a clear perception of concrete reality.

The time-theme I wish to explore stems from Pound's conception of the Confucian hero as the master man who pays "attention to the times and seasons." The early American leaders whom Pound admires are presented as examples of the Confucian master man. Appropriately enough, the very beginning of Canto 31 introduces us emphatically to the new major theme:

> Tempus loquendi,
> Tempus tacendi.

These words, inscribed on the tomb of Isotta degli Atti in the Tempio Malatestiano, link the American cantos with the preceding cantos concerning the European Renaissance and bring Malatesta and Jefferson into one focus. The source of the lines is Ecclesiastes, iii, 7: "a time to keep silence, and a time to speak." Because of the importance of this quotation in announcing what I regard as the fundamental theme of the second phase of the *Cantos*, I reproduce most of the passage from which it is taken and which it inevitably calls to mind (Eccl. iii, 1–8):

13. *Jefferson and/or Mussolini*, pp. 15–16.
14. Ibid. p. 34.

To every thing there is a season, and a time to every purpose under the heaven: a time to be born, and a time to die;
a time to plant, and a time to pluck up that which is planted;
a time to kill, and a time to heal; a time to break down, and
a time to build up; a time to weep, and a time to laugh; a
time to mourn, and a time to dance; . . . a time to get, and
a time to lose; a time to keep, and a time to cast away; a time
to rend, and a time to sew; a time to keep silence, and a time
to speak; a time to love, and a time to hate; a time of war,
and a time of peace.

In spite of Pound's occasional fulminations against the
Hebrew contribution to Christian culture, he has not hesitated
to draw upon Hebraic wisdom when it corresponds to insights
he has derived from other cultural contexts. It is apparent from
the above quotation that Pound's "Tempus loquendi,/ Tempus
tacendi" (reversing the original order of phrasing in the Bible)
is not meant to be restricted literally to the acts of speaking and
keeping silence. The idea that "To every thing there is a season,
and a time to every purpose," is implicit, and we can not help
noting the resemblance of this Biblical observation to Kung's
advice about acting in accord with "the times and seasons."
Pound seems clearly to be broaching the conception of organic
time, the idea that all things in nature have their proper moments of fruition, and especially in the context of the present
canto, the corresponding idea that all human actions have their
appropriate times, that "the readiness is all." The idea arises in
immediate contrast to the theme of mechanical time developed
in Canto 30, in which Pity, artificially prolonging the life of
"embers" by denying young love its seedtime, imposes with
devastating effect an unnatural time-pattern upon organic reality.

The only other instance I find in Pound's writings of the use
of "Tempus tacendi," the Latin phrase, occurs in a letter in
which he cautions himself to keep silent, to avoid for the present printing half-baked speculations on a subject he has not

mastered, the influence of Jewish ethical ideas on modern life. Although he will keep *publicly* silent on the subject, "I doubt," he says, "if any single ethical idea now honoured comes from Jewry." [15] In this letter Pound equates the time for keeping silence to the time needed to gather knowledge, a period that must precede the "Tempus loquendi" if the final speaking out is going to be at all effective. In Pound's *Confucius*, Kung makes the same point, giving practical and ethical significance to the time for silence (italics mine):

> In all affairs those which are calmly prepared make a solid base, and those which are not prepared run to ruin before they are ripe; *speeches calmly prepared are not empty*, affairs thought out in tranquility are not sabotaged later . . . ; action well considered beforehand does not bring anguish and a well thought mode of action is not interrupted from internal causes.[16]

Other bits of external evidence also point to a Confucian interpretation of "Tempus tacendi" as the time a man needs to attain "order within," after which must come the complementary "Tempus loquendi," the time for effective, creative action. With respect to the alleged "abuses" of the Confucian system, Pound has denied that they are "inherent in the principle of Confucius," saying that they

> are incompatible with the root. This I don't propose to argue save with someone who has passed the *Pythagorean time of silence* [italics mine]. The putting order inside oneself first, cannot be omitted from Confucian-Mencian practice if that is to be valid.[17]

Pythagoras is one of Pound's "Confucian" heroes (he appears again as a Confucian in Canto 98, p. 45). The "Pythagorean

15. *Letters*, p. 341.
16. *Confucius*, p. 165.
17. *Impact*, p. 140.

time of silence" is explained by Flavius Philostratus in *The Life of Apollonius of Tyana,* one of Pound's important sources for the *Rock-Drill* cantos, in which Apollonius emerges as a major "Confucian" culture-hero. "The followers of Pythagoras," says Philostratus,

> accepted as law any decisions communicated by him, and honoured him as an emissary from Zeus, but imposed, out of respect for their divine character, a ritual silence on themselves. For many were the divine and ineffable secrets which they had heard, but which it was difficult for any to keep who had not previously learnt that silence also is a mode of speech.[18]

Asked by his Pythagorean teacher, Euxenus, "why so noble a thinker as he and one who was master of a diction so fine . . . did not write a book," Apollonius replied, "I have not yet kept silence," and he thereupon imposed absolute silence on himself for five whole years.[19]

"Tempus loquendi,/ Tempus tacendi" represents, then, the two fundamental, interdependent principles, *thought* and *action*, the period of gestation preceding birth, the successful birth implying the completed gestation. I believe that the "loquendi" and "tacendi" are another embodiment of the *Yin-Yang* philosophy which, underlying Confucian thought, I see as underlying the *Cantos.* In Chinese thought,

> the *Yang* and *Yin* came to be regarded as two cosmic principles or forces, respectively representing masculinity, activity . . . for the *Yang,* and femininity, passivity . . . for the *Yin.*[20]

No better single piece of *internal* evidence is available for the Confucian bearing of "Tempus loquendi,/ Tempus ta-

18. Flavius Philostratus, *The Life of Apollonius of Tyana,* with an English translation by F. C. Conybeare, [The Loeb Classical Library], Vol. I (London, 1948), Bk. I, i.

19. Ibid. Bk. I, xiv.

20. Fung Yu-Lan, *A Short History of Chinese Philosophy* (New York, 1948), p. 138.

cendi" than the echo of these phrases in the entirely Confucian context of the Chinese Cantos (52–61). Among Confucianist maxims attributed to various Tang emperors, Pound lists several by Fou-Y, and I note especially: "War, letters, to each a time" (Canto 54, p. 31). The Chinese Cantos themselves serve as an extended commentary on this brief but highly charged apothegm, but I revert to Pound's prose for enlightening comment on the importance of the time-element in the Confucian conception of war:

> "In the *Spring and Autumn* there are no righteous wars, some are better than others." Spring and Autumn is the title of Confucius' history text book.[21]

("Confucius' history text book" is actually the work of Tung Chung-shu entitled *Ch'un Ch'iu Fan-lu,* or *The Copius Dew in Spring and Autumn.*[22]) Pound goes on to say, "There are times for politeness and times for prompt action. Discretion in perceiving the when is basic in Confucianism." [23]

In relation to Canto 31 and those cantos immediately following, "Tempus loquendi,/ Tempus tacendi" announces the fine balance between thought and action that Pound considers responsible for the greatness of leaders like Thomas Jefferson and John Adams, constructive geniuses who made viable the concept of an independent America. A statement Pound made during the early 'thirties, the period of composition of Cantos 31–41, reveals that the principle of "balance between thought and action" was at the core of his prescription for any good statesman:

21. *Impact*, p. 127.

22. Ch'u Chai and Winberg Chai, eds. and translators, *The Humanist Way in Ancient China: Essential Works of Confucianism* (New York, 1965), p. 354.

23. *Impact*, p. 128.

Obviously no best, no even good, governing class can be spineless . . . The term "good" in either case must include a capacity for action; some sense of relation between action and mere thought or talk.[24]

The same idea appears in Pound's *Jefferson and/or Mussolini*, where once again the governing class is judged on its capacity to harmonize thought and action:

When the nucleus of the national mind hasn't the *moral force to translate knowledge into action* [italics mine] I don't believe it matters a damn what legal forms or what administrative forms there are in a government. The nation will get the staggers.

And any means are the right means which will remagnetize the will and the knowledge.[25]

The end sought for is the "Tempus loquendi," the time of creative *action*. But creative action comes about only through the efforts of those who appreciate the value of the "Tempus tacendi" and practise creative silence. "C'est toujours le beau monde qui gouverne," says Pound: "Or the best society, meaning the society that, among other things, reads the best books, possesses a certain ration of good manners and, especially, of sincerity and frankness, modulated by silence." [26]

Canto 31 reveals in flashes the diversity of intellectual interests and the capacity for effective action that marked the personalities of Thomas Jefferson (who gets the lion's share of attention in this canto) and John Adams. Jefferson is pictured as avid for information, aware of "the state of things," and effective in translating *knowledge into action*, successful in ex-

24. Ezra Pound, *ABC of Economics* (London, 1933), p. 69.
25. *Jefferson and/or Mussolini*, pp. 94–95.
26. *Impact*, p. 50.

ploiting the creative potential of any given moment. The canto
begins:

> Tempus loquendi,
> Tempus tacendi.
> Said Mr Jefferson: It wd. have given us
>   time.
> "modern dress for your statue. . . . .

(The last line introduces a lengthy, truncated excerpt from a
letter "to General Washington, 1787" in which Jefferson asks
for information that would enlighten him as to the possibilities
of an Erie Canal project: "I consider this canal,/ if practicable,
as a very important work.")

In the third line, one is struck almost immediately by the
lack of any clear antecedent for the pronoun "it," but if one
ceases to look for what is not there one does finally apprehend
what *is* there, emphasis on the word "time," which is given a
line all to itself—emphasis, that is, on Jefferson's general awareness of the need for the "tempus tacendi," the need for the
proper time in which to prepare for effective action. The following line, a reference to a statue to be built in honor of Washington, shows us Jefferson's sense of timeliness, his awareness of
the creative possibilities of his own historical moment. His wide-
ranging sensibility gives broad cultural significance to the *political* revolution then in progress by perceiving the analogous need
for *artistic* revolution. People are not political animals and then,
coincidentally, artistic animals; they are inseparably both at
once, and true revolution affects every aspect of the seamless,
living tissue of a culture. Breaking the shackles of political tyranny calls for an equivalent overthrow of the tyranny of a dead
classicism in sculptural style. In the midst of political revolution, Jefferson's mind ranges from perception of the need for reform in the arts to similar perceptions with regard to improving
the nation's commerce by means of an Erie canal. Jefferson

exemplifies one of Pound's favorite Confucian principles: *Make It New:*

> In letters of gold on T'ang's bathtub:
>   As the sun makes it new
>   Day by day make it new
>   Yet again make it new.[27]

Not only does Jefferson exploit the potentialities of the moment at home, but he sees that the time is ripe for a constructive move abroad to stabilize the financial condition of the new-born American nation. Aware that France is on the eve of revolution, he forms a plan (successfully carried out, as we see in the John Adams Cantos, 62–71) to get a loan from Holland:

So critical the state of that country [France]
moneyed men I imagine are glad to place their money abroad.
Mr Adams could borrow there for us.
This country is really supposed to be on the eve of XTZBK49HT
        (parts of this letter in cipher)
        Jefferson, from Paris, to Madison, Aug. 2, 1787.
            (Canto 31, p. 4)

As these examples indicate, Pound's intention to amplify the opening "tempus"-theme, the Confucian ideal of "discretion in perceiving the when," achieves unmistakable realization in the particulars of the canto. Jefferson's capacity to translate knowledge into action is repeatedly represented by excerpts stressing his awareness of "the times and seasons." I add to the examples already given the following passage (italics mine):

". . this was the state of things in 1785 . . ."
                                                (Mr Jefferson.)

27. *Confucius*, p. 36.

. . met by agreement, about the close of the session—
Patrick Henry, Frank Lee and your father,
Henry Lee and myself . . . to consult . . *measures*
circumstances of times seemed to call for . . .
produce some channel of correspondence . . . this was in '73.
                                                Jefferson to D. Carr

I would like to conclude this discussion of Canto 31 with an appreciation of certain lines in it that stand out above all the rest for their general appeal. Pound repeats at length an amusing anecdote reported by Adams to Jefferson:

"Man, a rational creature!" said Franklin.
"Come, let us suppose a rational man.
"Strip him of all his appetites, especially his hunger and thirst.
"He is in his chamber, engaged in making experiments,
"Or in pursuing some problem.
"At this moment a servant knocks. 'Sir,
" 'dinner is on the table.'
" 'Ham and chickens?' 'Ham!'
" 'And must I break the chain of my thoughts to
" 'go down and gnaw a morsel of damned hog's arse?
" 'Put aside your ham; I will dine tomorrow;'
Take away appetite, and the present generation would not
Live a month, and no future generation would exist;
and thus the exalted dignity of human nature etc. . . .
                    Mr Adams to Mr Jefferson, 15 Nov. 1813.

The political hustle-bustle of the canto suddenly gives way to a relaxed moment of hilarity in which the historical protagonists emerge, at last, in flesh-and-blood fullness. But I do not think the anecdote is intended solely to provide comic relief. We get, in addition, a conception of man as *animal rationale*, a creature whose dignity rests not on the rejection of appetite, but on the reconciliation of the demands of appetite with those of reason. "I suspect," Pound has said, "that the error in educational systems has been the cutting off of learning from appetite." [28]

28. *Guide to Kulchur*, p. 98.

The creature of pure thought says, "Put aside your ham; I will dine tomorrow," but Adams implies that man as a rational *animal* must recognize that there is a time to think, and a time also to dine. The anecdote gives clear, effective expression, I think, to Pound's own holistic conception of man as a body-mind continuum. In his essay on Cavalcanti, for example, he speaks approvingly of the "Tuscan aesthetic": "The conception of the body as perfect instrument of the increasing intelligence pervades. The lack of this concept invalidates the whole of monastic thought." [29]

Canto 32, consisting almost entirely of snippets from the letters of John Adams, makes heavy use of animal imagery in a pattern of amusing contrasts between man as rational animal and man as mere animal. The theme of the canto, as stated in the first two lines, is a variation upon "Tempus loquendi,/Tempus tacendi":

"The revolution," said Mr Adams,
"Took place in the minds of the people." [30]

The idea that creative change in society is only a reflection of what takes place in the minds of the people is carried out in the animal images. The conscientious breeding of finer and finer strains of domestic animals is associated with Adams and with America generally. Americans "are in the constant practice of

29. "Cavalcanti," in *Literary Essays of Ezra Pound*, ed. T. S. Eliot (Norfolk, 1954), p. 152.

30. The uncut version of this passage as it appears in the original letter (Adams to Jefferson, August 24, 1815) reads as follows: "What do we mean by the revolution? The war? That was no part of the revolution; it was only an effect and consequence of it. The revolution was in the minds of the people, and this was effected from 1760 to 1775, in the course of fifteen years, before a drop of blood was shed at Lexington." (*The Life and Works of John Adams*, Vol. X [Boston, 1856], p. 172). [Quoted in James P. Shannon, "Canto XXXIII" (p. 1), one of a series of Yale glosses on the *Cantos*, prepared and mimeographed at Yale University under the direction of Norman Holmes Pearson.]

changing the/ characters and propensities of the animals we raise for/ our purposes." The idea of positive metamorphosis embodied in this animal image is echoed in Adams' concern "for civilizing the indians." His idea is that real elevation of their state of civilization is not to be accomplished by the old method of "religious ministrations," but by a concrete process of education which motivates them from within and thereby effects real inner change:

> The following has been successful. First, to raise cattle
> whereby to acquire a sense of the value of property . . .
> arithmetic to compute that value, thirdly writing, to . . .
> keep accounts . . .
> fourth to read Aesop's Fables, which are their first delight.

In contrast, the contemporary rulers of Europe are pictured as having fallen from human status into that of "mere animals":

whether in a stye, stable or state-room, [they]
let everything bend before them and banish whatever might
lead them to think . . . and thus are become as mere animals. . . .
Cannibals of Europe are eating one another again. . . .

Mindless, they are transformed into animals as if by the wand of Circe, whose major entrance into the poem in Canto 39 is thus anticipated and rendered at least partially intelligible.

Repeatedly, the intelligence of American leadership during the early stages of our nationhood is counterpointed with the ignorance of contemporary European statesmen. Bonaparte, for example, is singled out for his ignorance of economics, but the implication is that such ignorance is symptomatic of a habit of mind which resulted in his defeat. The theme of Bonaparte's ignorance is introduced in Canto 31 and developed at some length in Canto 34 through excerpts from the letters of John Quincy Adams, minister to Russia from 1809 through 1811:

> En fait de commerce ce (Bonaparte) est un étourdi,"
>   said Romanzoff.

Napoleon's disastrous defeat in Russia was due to an over-extension of himself in space ("he must always be *going*.") as well as improper calculation of the time factor ("French army 500 thousand, the Russian 300 thousand,/ But counting on space and time.").

The intellectual portrait of Quincy Adams is not confined to his political astuteness but is intended to reveal him as an all-round intelligence, "many-minded," passionately concerned with literature, economics, even plant life, and conversant with these subjects in detail. His observations on plant life are of particular interest because they embody Pound's new emphasis on the theme of organic time:

Black walnut, almond planted in spring
take two months precisely to vegetate to the surface.
This has been (May 26th) a harassing day
but I perceived a tamarind heaving up the earth
in tumbler number 2, and in tumbler number one, planted. . . .

                        . . .
Reading Evelyn's "Sylva" and making
Trivial observations upon the vegetation of trees until dark.

If we look ahead to the presentation of Confucian ethics in Canto 99, we read:

> The Venerated Emperor
>   watched things grow with affection,
> His thought was not dry on a shelf.[31]

Using images from nature, Pound presents Adams as a "master man" who pays "attention to the times and seasons." His thought is grounded in the nature of things, not abstract and "dry on a shelf."

31. *Thrones: 96–109 de los cantares* (New York, 1959), p. 47.

Canto 35, reintroducing the modern *Inferno*, presents the
theme of disorder specifically in terms of Confucius's "mean
man" who is incapable of acting in due season, as we discover in
the opening image:

> Mr Corles was in command of machine guns
> but when the time came to fire
> he merely lit a cigarette and walked away from his
> battery and seated himself in a field,
> So some subaltern gave the order to fire
> and Mr Corles did not suffer the extreme penalty
> because his family
> was a very good bourgeois family in Vienna
> and he was therefor sent to a mind sanatorium.

The invented name "Corles" may be read as "core-less," indica-
tive of a man without a center. The "times and seasons" passage from the *Unwobbling Pivot* to which I find frequent need
to refer helps further identify this man without a core or center
as Confucius's "mean man":

> Chung Ni (Confucius) said: The master man finds the
> center and does not waver; the mean man runs counter to the
> circulation about the invariable. . . .
> The master man's axis does not wobble.

One suspects that Pound's folksy use of the term "wobble" in
his translation of the *Chung Yung* as *Unwobbling Pivot* (1945)
may stem from the present canto, which goes on to indict the
upper middle classes of Central Europe for their sentimentality,
a "sensitivity without direction" that Pound absurdly associates
with Jewishness and makes responsible for a cultural blight he
sums up as "the general indefinite wobble."

The canzone "Donna mi prega," in Pound's view a touchstone of aesthetic and intellectual order, rises in the following
canto in sharp contrast to the picture of general disorder we

have just witnessed. Cavalcanti's poem, which Pound has described as "a scholastic definition in form, . . . clear and definite," [32] stands in judgment upon "the general indefinite wobble" of Central European civilization after the First World War. The poem is a definition of human love, the *"accidente"* ("accident" in the philosophical sense) which Pound translates in the third line as "affect" to avoid "introducing an English word of *double entente*." [33] George Dekker, who has studied the poem at length, gives the following clear summary of the theory of love it develops:

> Cavalcanti's theory of Love . . . holds that the essential form of Love is held in the memory, and that human passion is an "accident" . . . which occurs when the ideal form seems to be embodied in a particular woman.[34]

Pound considers it "quite possible that the whole of it [the canzone] is a sort of metaphor on the generation of light." [35] The first passage in the canzone which suggests the love-light equation is the following:

> Where memory liveth,
>   it [Love] takes its state
> Formed like a diafan from light on shade
> Which shadow cometh of Mars.

Pound considers the poem's light imagery due to Neoplatonic influence, especially the supposed influence of Grosseteste's *De Luce et de Incohatione Formarum*.[36] Other Neoplatonic influences, such as that of Plotinus, are suggested in Pound's comment on the passage:

32. "Cavalcanti," *Literary Essays*, p. 161.

33. Ibid. p. 159.

34. *The Cantos of Ezra Pound: A Critical Study* (New York, 1963), p. 89.

35. "Cavalcanti," *Literary Essays*, p. 161.

36. Ibid. p. 158.

> Da Marte ["of Mars"]: . . . there is a Neoplatonic grada-
> tion of the assumption of faculties as the mind descends into
> matter through the seven spheres, *via* the gate of Cancer: in
> Saturn, reason; in Jupiter, practical and moral; in Mars, the
> "spirited"; in Venus, the sensuous. Cf. Dante's *voi ch'inten-*
> *dendo il terzo ciel movete.* Macrobius, *In Somnium Scipionis;*
> and Plotinus, *Ennead.*[37]

Neoplatonism, as I have pointed out in an earlier chapter, identified in Pound's mind with a holistic acceptance of the various
levels of existence, with a balanced appreciation of both matter
and spirit, with the "conception of the body as perfect instrument of the increasing intelligence." Pound's essay on Cavalcanti makes it clear that he sets the "radiant world," "the
Mediterranean sanity" of the Tuscan poet against the "fanati-
cisms and excess that produce Savonarola, asceticisms that
produce fakirs, St Clement of Alexandria, with his prohibition
of bathing by women." He goes on to say that "after asceticism,
that is anti-flesh, we get the asceticism that is anti-intelligence,
that praises stupidity as 'simplicity,' the cult of *naïveté.*" [38]
Cavalcanti's poem evidences a holistic sensibility in which divine Love and human physical love are not incompatible opposites but are related in much the same way that the sun is related to the light of the sun that reaches earth. Cavalcanti is
demonstrating harmony, rather than opposition, between the
spirit and the body. A single line in the passage following
Pound's translation of the canzone sums up the holistic bearing
of the poem: "Sacrum, sacrum, inluminatio coitu" (a sacred
thing, a sacred thing, the cognition of coition).[39]

37. Ibid. p. 184.
38. Ibid. p. 154.
39. The line recalls two phrases from the Cavalcanti essay: "the
conception of the body as perfect instrument of the increasing intelligence," which I have already quoted, and a phrase from Avicenna, one of
the philosophers whom Pound supposes to have influenced the thought
of the canzone: "Amplius in coitu phantasia."

Aside from his final version of Cavalcanti's *Canzone d'Amore* in Canto 36, Pound made a previous attempt at translation which is available in *The Literary Essays of Ezra Pound* (pp. 155–57) and in *The Translations of Ezra Pound* (pp. 132–41). The main difference is that the first version keeps fairly close to the Italian original, whereas that in Canto 36 is a much freer rendering. Although I do not intend to examine all the changes, it appears that some were made to bring the canzone in line with the time-theme that Pound is developing in this section of the *Cantos*. The canzone (and Canto 36) opens as follows:

> A lady asks me
> > I speak in season
> She seeks reason for an affect, wild often
> That is so proud he hath Love for a name.

The second line, "I speak in season," seems clearly to carry forward the theme of the "tempus loquendi" from Canto 31. Cavalcanti is ranged alongside Jefferson as author of a great and permanent creation (the canzone was considered a *"capolavoro, a consummation of métier"* [40]) because he, too, knew that "readiness is all," that the time had come for him to speak because he had passed the time of preparatory silence, of intellectual maturation. I can attribute no other significance to "I speak in season," especially when one considers that there is no precedent for it in Pound's previous version of the canzone:

> Because a lady asks me, I would tell
> Of an affect that comes often and is fell
> And is so overweening: Love by name. [41]

Neither does the Italian text hint at any such possibility of translation:

40. "Cavalcanti," *Literary Essays*, p. 170.
41. *The Translations of Ezra Pound*, p. 133.

> Donna mi priegha
>
>   perch'i volglio dire
> D'un accidente
>   che sovente
>   è fero
> Ed è si altero
>   ch'è chiamato amore.[42]

I shall take note of one other subtle change that took place between the first and final translation of the canzone. Pound writes,

> Unskilled can not form his [Love's] image,
> He himself moveth not, drawing all to his stillness.
>   (Canto 36, p. 28)

In comparison, the previous version reads,

> None can imagine love
>   that knows not love;
> Love doth not move, but draweth all to him.[43]

Introduction of the word "stillness" draws attention to the nature of Love as a metaphysical entity, an Absolute very much like, or equivalent to, the Unmoved Mover. In this case, Pound is making explicit and emphatic a concept which is implicit in the description of Love that the line actually provides. (Pound's first version of the line in question is a closely literal rendition of the Italian: "E non si mova/ perch' a llui si tirj.") There would be no need to draw attention to this passage, except for the fact that "stillness" has already become one of the more heavily charged words in the *Cantos*. It is the metaphoric and conceptual center of the only sustained vision Pound has yet offered us of a paradise—the light-filled world of gods, god-

42. Ibid. p. 132.
43. Ibid. p. 139.

desses, and great men that occupies the whole of Canto 17. The major setting of that canto is Venice, whose palaces rising out of the canals he sees as a "white forest of marble." His vision of Venice is entirely numinous:

> Flat water before me,
> > and the trees growing in water,
> Marble trunks out of stillness,
> On past the palazzi,
> > > in the stillness,
> The light now, not of the sun.

Stillness is not merely the setting of these stone palaces, but the mysterious element out of which they are organically gener-ated, like trees. The stillness is associated with preternatural light, just as is Love, in Canto 36, which draws all to its stillness and must be "taken in the white light that is allness." The first use of "stillness" in the poem occurs in Canto 2, where we can readily see its genetic relationship to Canto 17. The marble forest of Venice is anticipated by the underwater coral tree that once was the sea-nymph Ileuthyeria:

> The swimmer's arms turned to branches,
> > . . .
> The smooth brows, seen, and half seen,
> > now ivory stillness.

The development of the theme of stillness is a perfect example of Pound's structural method, which I have described as a "spiral" progression. Themes, images, do not merely recur, but gather deeper and deeper meaning, and this meaning tends to become increasingly explicit as the poem unfolds. The theme of stillness achieves climactic philosophical importance at the end of Canto 49, where it stands in illuminating relationship to the theme of time:

> The fourth; the dimension of stillness.
> And the power over wild beasts.

I reserve discussion of Canto 49, however, to Chapter 8. For the present I shall continue to trace out the theme of organic time as it gains prominence in this transitional section of the *Cantos*.

In Canto 37, Van Buren, who succeeded in persuading Congress to establish an independent United States treasury, takes his place in Pound's American Hall of Fame as the last hero in the war against the U. S. Banks. He is shortly to be replaced, in the contemporary setting of Canto 38, by C. H. Douglas, whose theory of Social Credit Pound rather testily advances as a blinding light in the modern darkness of munitions manufacturers, exploiters, and vile politicians. There is allusion in this canto to Mussolini, the hero of Canto 41, in a rather cryptic time passage. The following lines occur after about two pages of relentless exposure of war profiteers and various evil politicians:

> "The wood (walnut) will always be wanted for gunstocks"
> And they put up a watch factory outside Muscou
> And the watches kept time. . . . Italian marshes
> been waiting since Tiberius' time . . .

"Walnut" alludes to Quincy Adams's loving attention to the times and seasons of plant growth in Canto 34:

> Black walnut, almond planted in spring
> take two months precisely to vegetate to the surface.

But later in Canto 34 (p. 21) we get the following abrupt image: "Gun barrels, black walnut . . ." Evidently Pound is implying that nature, which is a touchstone of sanity for the "master man," is perverted by the "mean man" to the uses of death. The "watch factory" which follows at the heels of "gunstocks" suggests the modernization of Russia through the violence of revolution. Through Lenin's destructive-creative genius, the country was blown out of the Middle Ages and Russian watches at last "kept time" with the pace of twentieth-century history. Pound saw much less moral ambiguity in the genius of Mussolini, who continued the process of creative modernization by draining the Pontine marshes. In the last issue of *The Exile* (1928) Pound writes:

STATECRAFT
    Practical men like Lenin and Mussolini differ from inefficients . . . in that they have a sense of time.[44]

He means, for example, that Lenin's revolution depended on an existing train and telegraphy system which he was able to use to constructive advantage in toppling the old régime. Much of the remainder of Canto 38 deals by way of contrast with those whose mental watches do not keep time ("His Holiness," complacently ignorant of electricity; the Austrian mentality, inflexibly antique): and it is such men, institutions, and nations that are portrayed throughout the canto as the willing witless victims of international usury and its cousin enterprises, the international munitions cartels.

Canto 39, the second poetic high point in this group of cantos, forms an interesting pair with Canto 36. "Donna mi-prega," as I understand it, is used by Pound as an affirmation of sexual love, an image of spiritual wholeness that stands opposed to the ascetic, dissective tendencies manifest in Aristotle, Aquinas (both of whom Pound condemns at the end of the canto), and all those who would deny the life-force. The descent of Love (or Light) into the flesh, which thereby partakes of divinity, is now in Canto 39 complemented by a powerful obverse image of ascent: from the flesh—and through the flesh —into Light. We get just this image in the fertility rite that concludes the canto:

44. Ezra Pound, *The Exile*, No. 4 (Autumn 1928), p. 3.

> Beaten from flesh into light
> Hath swallowed the fire-ball
> A traverso le foglie
> His rod hath made god in my belly.

The imagery of organic time is prominent in this canto. Order and disorder in man are depicted symbolically in terms of his relationship to the seasons. For "plot" Pound enlists Book X of the *Odyssey* in which Odysseus, aided by Hermes, foils the magic of Circe and transforms her into his willing concubine and mentor. The moral significance Pound gives to this episode appears to be that Odysseus-Everyman, in entering into a harmonious relationship with Circe, strikes a balance between the two opposing tendencies in his nature: the ascetic response of the mind, which cautions him to reject the powerful lure of sexuality; and the imperious desires of the body, which urge total self-abandonment to sensual pleasure. Forrest Read, Jr. sees Odysseus as striking a middle way between the "man-destroying passion" embodied in the self-indulgent Elpenor and the "man-destroying intellect" represented by Eurilochus.[45] Disorder in the sense of total devotion to the appetites is underscored by imagery of confusion in the sequence of the seasons:

> Girls talked there of fucking, beasts talked there of eating,
> All heavy with sleep, fucked girls and fat leopards,
> Lions loggy with Circe's tisane,
> Girls leery with Circe's tisane
>
> . . .
>
> Spring overborne into summer
>   late spring in the leafy autumn.

Circe seems to represent sexuality in particular and nature in general. The harmony achieved by Odysseus, who indulges the

45. Forrest Read, Jr., "A Man of No Fortune," in *Motive and Method in the Cantos of Ezra Pound*, ed. Lewis Leary (New York, 1954), p. 103.

demands of his body without forgetting that in due season he must resume the rigors of his manly mission, symbolizes Pound's ideal of psychological and social order, the holistic reconciliation of opposites. The creative consequences of such achieved order are embodied in the closing scene, where the ecstatic act of love between Odysseus and Penelope, at long last reunited, is dignified as a sacred rite that guarantees the rebirth of spring and of God or the gods (Adonis, Tammuz, Zagreus—Frazer's gods of the vegetation cycle):

> "Fac deum!" "Est factus."
>> Ver novum!
>>> ver novum!
>> Thus made the spring.

It is with "spring/ sharp in the grass" that Odysseus undertakes the rites appropriate to spring. Here is no confusion of seasons, but total reverence for "the times and seasons." The will of Odysseus, governed by Confucian wisdom, has achieved harmony with nature—with his personal, physical nature, and, ultimately, with the nature of things generally. The seasonal metaphor that Pound uses to express this harmony here assumes religious significance. Soon what in the transitional cantos are subordinate metaphors, mere occasional images of organic time, will come into prominence and take the center of the stage, no longer as mere metaphors but as principal subject. Organic time will become the impersonal "hero" against which the deeds and thoughts of men will be measured in many cantos to come.

Circe emerges in this canto on the literal plane as the ambiguous symbol of sexual allure. She herself, however, does not represent sexual excess. As the all but irresistible object of man's physical cravings, she becomes a force for either good or evil depending on what man himself wants to make of sex. As symbol of nature in general—and probably of all of reality, social and cosmic, with which man must learn to cope—she will appear

malevolent both to those who inordinately fear her and to those
who blindly surrender their will to her power. To those who
learn to strike a balance between their intellectual and appeti-
tive selves she will appear benevolent, affording unalloyed pleasure and, ultimately, wisdom. Odysseus, achieving harmony
with Circe, gains knowledge from her (he must visit Tiresias in
the underworld) that points his way toward "home" in the
sense of arming him with what he needs to revitalize the decayed cultural heritage. In the portrait Pound gives of Circe, the
emphasis is on her power to affect man constructively. In dis-
cussing the end of Canto 1, I indicated that the first phase of
the *Cantos* was prophetically represented by the sirens and the
second by Circe. The sirens, an image projected upon chthonic
nature by the disordered minds of those who constitute Pound's
Inferno, represent nature as a source of danger to be either
avoided at all costs or totally suppressed. Circe, as a constructive
guide to man, is the higher vision of nature which will dominate the second phase of the *Cantos*. The main female embodiment of the sirens in the first phase of the poem was Helen of
Troy, feared as a destroyer by the various "old men" of Pound's
Hell. Circe, a more nearly holistic image of nature, incorporates
the lower vision but transcends it in offering herself to man in a
potentially positive light. I must stress, however, that she symbolizes nature as a morally *neutral* entity whose energy is converted to good or evil uses by the will of man.

At the end of this transitional sequence, the figure of Helen
is finally freed of the onus of defamatory epithets she has had to
bear up to now, and these epithets are now transferred to usury:

> helandros   kai heleptolis   kai helarxe.[46]
> Hic Geryon est. Hic hyperusura.

This dissociation has become necessary because of the thematic
development registered in Canto 39. Feminine allure is there
"exonerated" of intrinsic responsibility for the disorder in

46. "Destroyer of men, and destroyer of cities, and destroyer of gov-
ernments."

human affairs so frequently charged to woman. The evil which has been attributed to woman, or to the biological nature of things which woman embodies (and which a poet like Eliot regards as evil), is traced instead to the anti-natural institution of usury.

In Canto 40 the barb of time intrudes again upon the poetic vision. The cheap, transient productions of the usury-ridden modern world, "Out of which things" the poet is "seeking an exit," appropriately include the primary symbol of mechanical time:

> haberdashery, clocks, ormoulu, brocatelli,
> tapestries, unreadable volumes bound in tree-calf,
> half-morocco, morocco, tooled edges, green ribbons,
> flaps, farthingales, fichus, cuties, shorties, pinkies
> et cetera.

The poet fittingly continues his voyage by identifying his own journey with the "periplum" or "voyaging around" of Hanno, whose world is mythic, heroic, Odyssean, a world of brutally direct confrontation of man with nature. In this world "folk wear the hides of wild beasts," rather than flaps and farthingales. "The clocks," included in Pound's list of useless, stuffy, Victorian fripperies and equally transient ladies' fashions, symbolize the wasted lives and the meaningless stream of experience in the modern world. In Hanno's world, the measure of time is days of purposive sailing; time is a process of continual discovery and creation (colonization):

> Men of Lixtae came with us to interpret
> for 12 days sailing southward, southward by desert
> one day sailed against sun, there is an harbour
> with an island 15 miles in circumference,
> We built there, calling it Cyrne
> believing it opposite Carthage as our sailing time
> was the same as from Carthage to the Pillars.

Hanno's periplum has transitional significance for the poet-voyager in more ways than one. It is a voyage of colonization and conquest—specifically, of African territory. Not accidentally, it directly introduces the Mussolini Canto, Canto 41. It appears that the long-pursued Italian policy of African colonization, given new impetus under *Il Duce,* is here glorified by a classic prototype wherein Hanno too sets up house among the Libyans and attacks the Ethiopians. Of course, the objection here might be raised that since this canto was published in 1934, Pound could not have known of Mussolini's conquest of Ethiopia in 1935. The answer is that anyone reading newspapers during the period could easily have foreseen Mussolini's Ethiopian venture, even though he may not have been able to predict its date. "For years he had threatened a push to the east," says John Gunther. "The campaign should have surprised nobody. . . . He needed room—colonies—for Italy to expand in. But his habit of bluster had, lamentably enough, persuaded folk in Western Europe that he was bluffing." [47]

After Pound's praise of Mussolini in Canto 41, three cantos (42–4) explore examples of Italian banking practice founded on just principles. Max Wykes-Joyce says that the Monte dei Paschi (Bank of the Grassland) was "founded for the good of the whole people by Cosimo I of Tuscany," who accepted "as security the grazing lands belonging to the city [Siena]." [48]

47. *Inside Europe,* rev. ed. (New York, 1938), p. 215.

Mary Evelyn Townsend tells us

"with the beginning of the thirties, Mussolini evidently determined upon drastic action in Ethiopia. In 1932, Grandi, then minister of foreign affairs, gave warning in a ringing speech to the senate: 'We cannot tolerate that Italy as a colonial factor be overlooked'; and Il Duce, himself, indicated Abyssinia as a field for conquest in 1934 when he pointed out that there was no room for expansion to the north or west; hence, 'Italy must turn to the south and east.' By the summer of 1934 also Italy was markedly increasing her armaments in her colonies; Ethiopia was reorganizing her military forces and conflict was imminent." (*European Colonial Expansion Since 1871* [New York, 1941], p. 148.)

48. See Russell, *An Examination of Ezra Pound,* p. 219.

"The lesson" of the Monte, says Pound, "is the very basis of solid banking. Credit rests *in ultimate* on the abundance of nature, on the growing grass that can nourish the living sheep." [49] In Canto 43 (p. 12) he writes:

> there first was the fruit of nature
> there was the whole will of the people.

The phrase that appears on the next page, "Grass nowhere out of place," a motif repeated elsewhere in the *Cantos,* means that nature is the ground of economic sanity.

The significance of all this economic analysis is that the poetry subtly shifts its focus from admiration of the Great Man who creates or restores social order to concern for the plight of the common man, the anonymous masses who are always the saddest victims of social disorder, which for Pound is "at root economic." Thus, amidst all the document-snipping in Canto 42 which reveals how the Monte dei Paschi was founded in justice, there is a single, brief strain of "poetry" which should command all our attention:

> wave falls and the hand falls
> Thou shalt not always walk in the sun
> or see weed sprout over cornice
> Thy work in set space of years, not over an hundred.

These lines explain the urgency of the surrounding documentation. Man is seen in his natural setting, subject to the rhythms of cosmic time that measure out his pathetically limited lifespan. Man at best lives in harmony with the elemental rhythms that delimit him, depending for his economic well-being on the adjustment of his activities to the productive rhythms of nature. Usury ignores man's dependence on nature, forcing him into an artificially accelerated rhythm of production that exhausts his

49. *Impact*, p. 147.

resources before they can be replenished. Pound has therefore defined usury as

> a charge for the use of purchasing power, levied without regard to production; often without regard even to the possibilities of production.[50]

Usury forces a mechanical rhythm upon organic processes, killing the goose that lays golden eggs by squeezing it in a vise to help it along. The same idea is expressed in Mencius' parable, related by Pound, of "the man who pulled up his corn because it didn't grow fast enough, and then told his family he had assisted the grain." [51] Pound is saying, in "wave falls and the hand falls," that man is limited pathetically enough by the rhythms of organic time: why, therefore, should his life be cut even shorter by economic injustices which throw him out of phase with those absolute cosmic rhythms?

It was Pound's economic studies which finally enabled him to associate the plight of the artist, with whom he is most concerned in the first thirty cantos, with that of the common man, both of whom are prevented from realizing their productive potential by a social system that operates contrary to nature, "CONTRA NATURAM" (Canto 45). In Canto 27 Pound treated scornfully "the labours of tovarisch," the masses who are capable of rising up to destroy their visible oppressors but have never built anything, "Laid never stone upon stone." And Pity, in Canto 30, became identified entirely with sentimentality. Now, however, the tragic chord that first sounded in the *Cantos* for the beleaguered artist-hero, Malatesta, is transposed into a key of tragic pity, completely unsentimentalized, for the fate of the average man subject to economic tyranny but unable to rise and shake off the real tyrant, whom he does not recognize.

50. *Selected Poems of Ezra Pound* (New York, 1957), p. 182.
51. *Impact*, p. 126.

With "wave falls and the hand falls" the theme of organic time has subtly assumed far more than metaphorical importance. From Canto 30 onward, imagery of the times and seasons exists in part to characterize the well-ordered mind as one that pays precise attention to realities. In other words, such imagery has had primarily psychological import. Jefferson's capacity to act in due season focuses attention not on the broader implications of the concept of organic time itself, but causes us to reflect rather on the finely ordered intelligence that could judge accurately just *when* to act. Beginning with Canto 42, however, but more clearly with Canto 46, the seasonal rhythms of external nature as a major determinant in human affairs become the main object of study. Nature as the key to order becomes our main concern. The focus shifts to the unsophisticated man in general, in his relationship to the natural environment on which he depends for physical as well as religious sustenance. This new, ecological emphasis achieves brilliant expression for the first time in Canto 46. Wishing to explore the permanent bases of social order, Pound picks up the "camel driver" theme that has lain dormant since Canto 4 (p. 16), where the camel drivers look down disapprovingly at the mechanical symmetry of the "plotted streets" of Ecbatan, a city of sterile order. The scene in Canto 46 is contemporary England, a conversation at tea in a "suburban garden":

Said Abdul Baha: "I said 'let us speak of religion.'
"Camel driver said: I must milk my camel.
"So when he had milked his camel I said 'let us speak of religion.
And the camel driver said: It is time to drink milk.
'Will you have some?' For politeness I tried to join him.
Have you ever tasted milk from a camel?
I was unable to drink camel's milk. I have *never* been able.
So he drank all of the milk, and I said: let us speak of religion.
'I have drunk my milk. I must dance.' said the driver.
We did not speak of religion." Thus Abdul Baha
Third vice-gerent of the First Abdul or whatever Baha,
the Sage, the Uniter, the founder of a religion.

The Bahaist's attempt to convert the Arab camel driver is futile. He can make no progress because the Arab is acting out in front of him the profounder natural religion that he lives every day. For his very existence, the camel driver must adjust the sequence and tempo of his daily activities to accord precisely with the unalterable, cyclic rhythms of organic time. For his own good and the good of his camel the driver must milk the animal at a certain time each day. The "time to drink milk" cannot be bypassed because the driver is no doubt thirsty at precisely this time, and the milk will go sour if he does not soon drink it. He "must dance" after drinking milk, probably because he is in excellent spirits now that his thirst is satisfied, and his dance is an instinctive celebration of the never-failing order of his existence. It is a religious expression, in the profoundest sense, of thanks to the God who reveals his goodness through the perfect and unremitting synchronization of his camel's biological needs with his own. The Bahaist is potentially a disrupter of this harmony between the driver and nature. He desires to impose an abstract religion upon the driver, one which has nothing to do with the palpable conditions of his existence. Bahaism, which seeks to unify all religions under one banner, is for Pound intolerant of the individuality of cultures, each of which develops its own gods out of the local soil, gods that are more real than the abstract, monotheistic concept of God which Pound regards as the Hebrew blight that infected Christianity with fanaticism.

In the space of a few lines, Pound modulates the theme of Bahaism to that of usury, quoting the chief founder of the Bank of England as saying that the Bank (I omit Pound's underlining)

> Hath benefit of interest on all
> the moneys which it, the bank,
> creates out of nothing.

For Pound, Bahaism is a type of spiritual usury, taking a man's soul in exchange for a few dry abstractions founded upon nothing. The danger in all abstract systems, as Pound sees it, is the separation of thought from the living context of reality, and the consequent crippling of living processes by the subjection of their natural rhythms to unendurable artificial strains.

Pound's main theme from now on, up to the Pisan sequence, will be his insistence that a rational social order, by which all men may realize to the full their creative potential, is possible if those who govern base their conduct and principles upon reverent regard for nature's "times and seasons." He will be at pains to stress that the standard for order in the ego and order in society is the visible order of nature. His "hero" will be, in a sense, nature itself, which teaches wise men their wisdom, but it may be equally profitable to regard Pound's hero from now on as the healthy society, one that lives in harmony with the cosmic clock. The deeper understanding he had been gaining of Confucianism and economics during the thirties enabled him to project a vision of the earthly paradise in terms more concretely rooted in social reality than were available to him in the early cantos, where the terms of his paradisal visions are purely personal, mythic, and aesthetic.

CHAPTER VII

Man, Earth, and Stars

THE NEW PHASE of the poem is definitely in the ascendant beginning with Canto 47, the first major statement of the cosmic and ecological significance of organic time. Canto 49, directly complementary to 47, transposes the time-theme into the Chinese setting that is to characterize the following sequence of cantos, in which Chinese history is related from a strictly Confucian point of view. Not since Canto 13 has the Confucian underpinning of the poem achieved explicit statement, and even there it was a static, anticipatory sort of statement, a seed that would sprout only at the proper time and under the right conditions. The moment for giving it full development was determined by dramatic considerations. Pound first had to lay bare in explicit, forceful detail, the workings of Usura in history and its ominous significance for mankind as the presumed fountainhead of evil; he had to tear the veil off the face of the enemy to reveal it in its full loathsomeness. Only then would an historically concrete, lengthy elaboration of the Confucian antidote to Usura's poison be dramatically effective.

Cantos 47 and 49, twin peaks of poetic achievement, are fully equal to their pivotal task of launching the poem in its new thematic direction. The "twins" analogy is intended to be more than just a figure of speech. Close study reveals their complementary natures, and even a superficial glance at the exactly similar endings of these cantos ("the power over wild beasts") invites the suspicion that they are the two halves of a diptych.

Canto 47 is an extremely sophisticated unit of poetry. A limited number of themes make their appearance, then intermingle in a series of variations and striking musical developments that cry out for comparison with the involutions of the fugue. Odysseus's descent into hell is the basic theme of the canto, so that the Nekuia, the theme which opened the first phase of the *Cantos,* is now called upon once more to announce the formal beginning of the second. The next theme, a sort of fugal response growing out of the first, is the performance of certain magical rituals which imitate the death of Tammuz-Adonis, the god of vegetation, who disappears into the underworld each autumn and leaves the earth barren behind him: the small red lamps that "float seaward" symbolize the blood of the dying god. A third theme is the complementary ritual of raising "gardens of Adonis," which also were intended to secure the rebirth of the god by imitative magic. These gardens furnish "the best proof," according to Frazer, "that Adonis was a deity of vegetation, and especially of the corn." They

> were baskets or pots filled with earth, in which wheat, barley, lettuces, fennel, and various kinds of flowers were sown . . . Fostered by the sun's heat, the plants shot up rapidly, but having no root they withered as rapidly away, and . . . were carried out with the images of the dead Adonis, and flung with them into the sea or into springs. . . .
>
> . . . All these Adonis ceremonies . . . were originally intended as charms to promote the growth or revival of vegetation.[1]

Pound expresses this agricultural theme in two lines:

> Wheat shoots rise new by the altar,
>   flower from the swift seed.

If Adonis is a god "especially of the corn," then the Adonis theme, indeed the whole agricultural theme of the canto grows

---

1. Sir James George Frazer, *The Golden Bough: A Study in Magic and Religion,* one-volume edition (New York, 1960), p. 396.

out of the main Nekuia theme with which the canto begins, for Circe directs Odysseus "to hell/ And to the bower of Ceres' daughter Proserpine." In the corresponding passage in the *Odyssey* (quoted at length in Greek in Canto 39) Ceres, the goddess of corn and of agriculture, foundress of law, order, and civilization, is not mentioned, so that Pound clearly introduces her to set the stage for the agricultural theme that follows.

After the initial exposition of these three "themes," as I have called them (the Nekuia, and the magical rites imitating the death and rebirth of the vegetation god), the canto falls into a second and then a third clearly demarcated exposition of the same three themes in the same order as first introduced, but each time a theme reappears it has been transfigured by what has gone before. The nearly mathematical device Pound uses of structural repetition serves as a framework for consistent thematic evolution, so that nothing is ever really mechanically repeated. The following schema represents my conception of the three-part structure in which each main "exposition," to use fugal terminology, is divisible into three minor sections (themes A, B, and C). I have indicated the lines and have given the identifying motif that carries over most persistently for each of the three themes in spite of the changes these themes undergo:

I. First exposition:
   A. (1–14) Begins: "Who even dead . . ."
      Motif: "First must thou go the road/ to hell."
   B. (15–31) Begins: "The small lamps . . ."
      Motif: "By this gate art thou measured."
   C. (32–33) Begins with its motif: "Wheat shoots rise new by the altar."

II. Second exposition:
   A. (34–47) Begins: "Two span . . ."
      Motif: "To the cave art thou called, Odysseus."
   B. (48–62) Begins: "Begin thy plowing."
      Motif: "By this gate art thou measured."

C. (63–78) Begins: "And the small stars . . ."
Motif: "doth thy death year/ Bring swifter shoot?"

III. Third exposition:
    A. (79–89) Begins with its motif: "The light has en-
tered the cave. Io! Io!"
    B. (90–95) Begins: "Falleth."
Motif appears actually as last line (89) of A, a
means of fusing the two parts: "By this door have
I entered the hill."
    C. (96–109) Begins: "Think thus of thy plowing."
Motif: "When the new shoots are brought to the
altar."

Most motifs do not remain associated with a specific theme.
I refer to elements like the monster Scylla from the *Odyssey*;
the phrase "TU DIONA/KAI MOIRAI' ADONIN," i.e.
"You, Dione,[2] and the Fates [weep for] Adonis," from Bion's
Lament for Adonis; and the plowing instructions from Hesiod's
epic, *Works and Days*. Such motifs shift position in the basic
structure in accordance with the over-all movement of the canto
toward the progressive fusion and development of ideas implicit
in the opening exposition of themes.

The canto opens with a reworking of the boudoir scene of
Canto 39 in which Circe, bedded "in the dark" with Odysseus,
gives the hero directions for reaching his "road's end" by requir-
ing him to "sail after knowledge" to Tiresias in hell. Pound has,
of course, used the Homeric myth of Odysseus' sailing after
knowledge as the basic metaphor of the *Cantos* as a whole, but
a mental voyage into deepening insights specifically determines

2. Aphrodite's mother, but here Aphrodite herself. The first part of
the phrase, "TU DIONA" (You Dione), seems to be a slight invention
of Pound's. Mention of Aphrodite does not occur in the same passage in
Bion, the closest previous mention of her (as Cytherea) occurring eight
lines earlier (l. 88) than the "KAI MOIRAI" element of line 96. See *The
Greek Bucolic Poets* with an English translation by J. M. Edmonds, The
Loeb Classical Library (New York, 1928), p. 393.

the development of the present canto and seems to account entirely for its form. Odysseus-Pound (the "thou" and eventually the "I" of the canto) experiences a series of illuminations.

Before I discuss this progression of insights in detail, however, it might be helpful, in order to provide an overview of the thematic development of the canto, to examine the structural significance of the shift that takes place in the narrative point of view. Until part three, the narrating voice is that of Circe, who literally addresses Odysseus as "thou" at the beginning. The voice then becomes associated with that of Tiresias ("two span to a woman," etc.), whom Odysseus is assumed to have visited —as indeed he has in Canto 1—after leaving Circe. Tiresias, even more than Circe, is an oracular speaker who guides and teaches the voyager. Ultimately, Odysseus-Pound is left to himself when he becomes capable of the final vision, for which he has been well prepared. (The single typographical "break" in the poem occurs just at this significant point, between parts II and III.) Just as in Canto 31 of Dante's *Paradiso* Beatrice finally leaves the side of the poet, who has absorbed all the wisdom she has had to offer, so, too, the voice of Circe-Tiresias disappears and is replaced in part III by that of the poet, who has digested all the wisdom of his composite guide and is now capable of acting in his own right as guide to mankind (if not actually, at least in the narrative terms of the canto's "plot").

The second-person mode of address again appears in part III —even after the poet's voice takes over—and re-emphasizes the wisdom ("Think thus of thy plowing") already dispensed in part II. This would be sheer repetition or mere reprise, as would much of the ending of part III, but for the fact that it is the fully initiated poet-voyager, now become the hierophantic guide, who is using the second-person pronoun to lead the neophytes, mankind in general, along the same path of knowledge which he himself has successfully trodden.

The "course of instruction" which the voyager, at the outset a neophyte, undergoes takes him from the dark bed of Circe through the "overhanging dark" to Tiresias, and on to view the spectacle of the religious-magical rites intended to revive the dead god Adonis. If the reader follows this voyage, he realizes that Pound is suggesting a connection between the Homeric myth of the Nekuia and religious rituals enacting the death and rebirth of a vegetation god. Mention of Proserpine in line 5 already implies that the descent of Odysseus is analogous to the descent of Proserpine, a vegetation deity like Adonis, to Hades. In this reading, the wisdom which Odysseus hopes to gain, so that he may safely reach home, does not consist simply of navigational directions from Tiresias but is embodied in the power which enables Proserpine to return to earth and fructify it for two-thirds of the year. Odysseus is really searching for the secret of the rebirth of vegetation—and ultimately, for the secret of cultural rebirth. Ceres and Proserpine are the goddesses whose rites were celebrated in the Eleusinian mysteries, so that the chthonic wisdom which Odysseus finally attains in his Eleusinian ecstasy (part III) is introduced at the very outset as the profounder object of his quest.

The function of part I of the canto, as it affects the reader, is to make him aware of the source of great literary myths such as Homer's in the religious rituals of the ancient world. The cycles of organic time, which determine the death and rebirth of vegetation, are at the source of the most vital cultural phenomena: religion and art. The Confucian precept of reverence for "the times and seasons" is thus already the implicit "lesson" of the canto, but this Confucian theme has yet to be explored in the depth of its cultural ramifications before the canto ends.

The most difficult line of part I, "By this gate art thou measured," becomes understandable in the light of this time-theme. The passage reads:

> The small lamps drift in the bay
> And the sea's claw gathers them.
> Neptunus drinks after neap-tide.

> Tamuz! Tamuz!!
> The red flame going seaward.
>   By this gate art thou measured.

At this point, Odysseus sailing off to hell becomes transformed into Adonis, or the lamps that represent him, drifting seaward from the bay in the outgoing tide. George Dekker thinks that "in the present context 'this gate' refers, apparently, to a river mouth." [3] My own view is that because of the emphatic importance of the line, "By this gate art thou measured," in the present instance, and because of its even greater thematic role in part II, the literal interpretation of "gate" as estuary is insufficient. The "gate" must be that which *measures*, in an active sense, the dying of Adonis or the progress seaward of the lamps, and that can only be the outgoing tide.[4] *Tide*, of course, equals *time*; the tides are a measure of cosmic time, the lunar day; and implicit in the idea of ebb tide measuring death is the idea of consequent return or revival in flood tide. The progress of Odysseus, Adonis, vegetation, the tides, and the moon, is cyclical; their disappearance or death implies their return. The voice of Circe-Tiresias is telling Odysseus that although he is at the mercy of the tides, the tides are ultimately merciful. Nature's dangers, Scylla's snarling dogs in the lines that follow, are only one side, and not the most significant side, of the total picture of reality.

3. *The Cantos of Ezra Pound*, p. 39.

4. The Biblical tone of Pound's phrase suggests "strait is the gate" [Matthew 7:14]. The gate that Adonis takes toward the underworld is really the strait, or painful passage, "which leadeth unto life," even though it seems to lead only "to destruction." Pound's ironic allusion to Matthew has no Christian significance, but rather paganizes the New Testament in the same allowable sense that the Church Christianized the Old Testament. With respect to Odysseus, the "gate" is of course that between Scylla and Charybdis. Later on in the canto it will appear that the "gate" has profounder meaning as the sexual organs of woman, the gate through which man creates new life and himself enters into life. The gate which measures man is also, as we shall see, the grave.

The natural cycle of death and survival, approached in mythical terms in part I of the canto, is to be viewed in part II in its intimate relationship to the life of man as he actually lives it, and Odysseus becomes Everyman. The imagery is now sexual and agricultural, and the Adonis myth disappears because, in a sense, it is being ecologically "explained." The myth will reappear only in part III, with an increased resonance resulting from its implications having been concretely explored in part II.

The end of part I, "flower from the swift seed," provides the basis for the development of part II. "Seed" generates both the sexual theme of II A and the agricultural theme of II B. But the beginning of part II is also a return to the Circe-Odysseus episode at the beginning of the canto, whose sexual theme is now elaborated. Circe is generalized into womankind, and "woman" embodies the biological call of nature, the "biological process" of Canto 29, which all living things must obey. The human sex-drive is one aspect of an all-inclusive biological determinism which the brute force of the bull in the following lines seem to epitomize:

> Moth is called over mountain
> The bull runs blind on the sword, *naturans*
> To the cave art thou called, Odysseus,
> By Molü hast thou respite for a little,
> By Molü art thou freed from the one bed
>   that thou may'st return to another.

But one ought to distinguish the thought of Pound from the "naturalism" of writers such as Jack London. London's *The Call of the Wild,* for example, has as its naturalistic theme the reversion to nature, but Pound is interested in the progress of man from nature into civilization, from blindness into light. "The bull runs blind on the sword, *naturans* [in accord with nature]" suggests that all the art of man, the bullfighter, consists not in escape from nature or in naturalistic identification with nature, but in control of her blind motions, which man alone of all creatures is capable of predicting. The successful outcome of "the moment of truth" is entirely a matter of *timing:* the powerful lunge of bull against man is thus used by man to master the bull.

"Molü" is a complex symbol for that which frees man from passive subjection to nature and enables him to come into new and progressively more spiritualized relations with her. Sexuality is not to be rejected if man is to persist in harmony with nature (Odysseus must go from "one bed . . . to another"), but man is capable of evolving ever higher values from this basic relationship: Odysseus goes from the bed of Circe, which has raised him to an intermediate stage of wisdom, ultimately to the bed of Penelope, which represents the creative end of all wisdom, as we have seen in Canto 39.

Molü is the effective will, the refined intelligence, the sense of proportion man needs for creative action. The difference between man and nature is suggested more specifically in the last two lines of the stanza, which immediately follow those just quoted:

> The stars are not in her counting,
>> To her they are but wandering holes.

These lines complete the opening theme of the stanza, "Two span, two span to a woman,/ Beyond that she believes not," in which "two span" means whatever she can grasp in her two hands (or between her legs) as the limit of her interest in reality. Anything outside of her physical reach is "not in her counting," but the stars are in *man's* counting ("man" as opposed to woman, but more importantly, the race of man as opposed to nature). Pound implies that it was man's capacity to apply an objective standard of measurement, counting by the regular motions of the stars, to the biological and seasonal rhythms conditioning his physical existence, that rescued him from unconscious immersion in nature. For man, the stars do not "wan-der," but have a regularity that enabled him to fix the precise times for his all-important agricultural activities. Even though seasonal change has always been a valuable practical indicator of time, its gradualness does not provide a precise enough basis for such crucial calculations. "The seasons are composed of occupations and of climatic and other natural phenomena, and still preserve this concrete relationship and are therefore not definitely limited in duration." [5] Nilsson explains that "By the phases of the stars both occupations and seasons are regulated, and thus a standard is furnished by which to judge, and a limit is set to the indefiniteness of the phases of Nature." [6] Odysseus's success as a sailor is, of course, completely dependent on his ability to tell time and place from the stars.

The rise of civilization was greatly assisted by astronomical techniques of time-measurement, for the stars had all the regularity of movement man could require, and such knowledge, independent of local or temporary climatic conditions, was transmissible from generation to generation. The ability to measure time by the cosmic clock is a specific meaning for the Moly which rescued Odysseus from the pigsty. This is the whole point of the following passage (II B), which begins with Hesiod's instructions for attention to the stars in determining the precise times and seasons for plowing:

> Begin thy plowing
> When the Pleiades go down to their rest.
> Begin thy plowing
> 40 days are they under seabord,
> Thus do in fields by seabord
> And in valleys winding down toward the sea.
> When the cranes fly high
> think of plowing.

5. Martin P. Nilsson, *Primitive Time-Reckoning* (Lund, 1920, reissued 1960), p. 356.

6. Ibid. p. 348.

> By this gate art thou measured
> Thy day is between a door and a door.

Just as the image of descent to hell unifies the transition from the Nekuia to the Adonis ritual in part I, now the image of sexual intercourse with Circe ("To the cave art thou called, Odysseus") merges naturally with that of "plowing." The relationship here between coitus and plowing is not, for Pound, based simply on the age-old sexual sense of "plowing," but on the fact that plowing is alone equivalent in importance to coitus in ensuring the survival of man. It is with both procreation and agriculture that the myth of Adonis is concerned. Those who performed the magical rites connected with the death and rebirth of vegetation deities like Adonis

> often combined the dramatic representation of reviving plants with a real or a dramatic union of the sexes for the purpose of furthering at the same time and by the same act the multiplication of fruits, of animals, and of men. To them the principle of life and fertility, whether animal or vegetable, was one and indivisible. . . . These two things, therefore, food and children, were what men chiefly sought to procure by the performance of magical rites for the regulation of the seasons.[7]

Indeed, Pound's use near the end of part I of the phrase from Bion in which Aphrodite and the Fates weep for Adonis is intended to suggest the important sexual element in the ceremonies which is soon transposed into the sexual theme of II A. My intention in this discussion has been to show that the "woman" and "plowing" passages of part II grow out of themes already implicit and organically connected in part I.

Hesiod performs the vital job of transmitting knowledge that lies at the very core of the cultural heritage. The group of stars known as the Pleiades is the most important of the constellations for agricultural time-reckoning. Although it consists

7. Frazer, *The Golden Bough*, p. 378.

of "comparatively small and unimportant stars," the appearance of the group "coincides . . . with important phases of the vegetation." This is equally true of other stars, but the Pleiades are also more easily recognized than other, imaginatively created constellations, forming themselves "into a group without any aid from the imagination," [8] and therefore easily accessible as a means of time-measurement to the average peasant or farmer. Observation of other regularly recurring natural phenomena, like the flight of migratory birds, helps men determine certain seasonal points, the times for certain occupations, as in Hesiod "The cry of the migrating cranes shews the time of ploughing and sowing." [9]

The climactic lines of the passage quoted are

> By this gate art thou measured
> Thy day is between a door and a door.

Man's day is measured literally, Pound notes, by the two great cosmic "doors" that open to him in the morning and shut him in at night. Canto 49 makes this explicit:

> Sun up; work
> sundown; to rest.

But also implied are the doors that limit the period of man's life: the mother as entrance into the world and mother earth as exit. Finally, there is also the proper attitude of reverence that man should have for "the times and seasons" that measure his existence: man's day is between *adore* and *adore*. The religious theme of part I enters into the substance of part II as well. The "oxen" passage which follows manages a virtuoso time shift from Hesiod's Greece to contemporary Italy:

8. Nilsson, *Primitive Time-Reckoning*, pp. 129–30.
9. Ibid. p. 46.

> Two oxen are yoked for plowing
> Or six in the hill field
> White bulk under olives, a score for drawing down stone,
> Here the mules are gabled with slate on the hill road.
> Thus was it in time.

"The proper use of oxen" according to their capacities, says George Dekker, implies the moral necessity for the proper "treatment of human beings according to one's knowledge of their life span—which is . . . painfully short." [10] The cue for introducing a scene containing oxen is probably taken from Hesiod. Only a few lines after the "cranes" passage already discussed, Hesiod urges that one's oxen should be fed for the plowing task at hand.[11] Pound's personal observation of a plowing scene is juxtaposed with Hesiod's plowing directions to indicate the continuity of the past into the present, a live tradition that has endured in spite of the record of catastrophes normally associated with "history." "Thus was it in time" means, quite simply, that "it," or the relations between men, animals, and the earth in plowing, have been and have remained thus properly proportioned and harmonious. The implication is that this basic ecological harmony has managed to persist or reassert itself in spite of the forces of usury which undermine civilizations. A profound cultural optimism, a belief in an indestructible cultural minimum, the resiliency of man and nature against the destructive changes of history, is heard in the emphatic terseness of "Thus was it in time."

In the light of the ambiguity of the time-concept, as it has been developed in the *Cantos* up to now, further analysis would indicate that "in time" could mean, on the one hand, "simultaneous with but apart from and in spite of time-as-history (mechanical time)," and, on the other, "in accord with the pat-

10. *The Cantos of Ezra Pound*, p. 41.

11. See Hesiod, "Works and Days," *The Homeric Hymns and Homerica*, with an English translation by Hugh G. Evelyn-White, The Loeb Classical Library (New York, 1926), ll. 448–54.

tern of endless renewal that characterizes organic time." Pound
is saying, in this oxen passage, that even though the life of the
individual is pitifully limited "between a door and a door," the
race itself is immortal because the fundamental knowledge
needed for survival is indestructible. The lesson for Odysseus-
Everyman in all this is humility, but this is more properly the
theme taken up in the next section of the canto. Although the
theme of rebirth is implied in the oxen passage, it is given explicit development only in the following section (II C), which
like the end of part I deals with the theme of renewal but with
respect to man rather than to gods or vegetation. Part I has
concerned gods; part II concerns men (and, as we shall see, part
III will deal with men-as-gods).

Now, at the end of part II, Pound considers without re-
course to religious doctrines the sense in which man may be
assured of his immortality:

> And the small stars now fall from the olive branch,
> Forked shadow falls dark on the terrace
> More black than the floating martin
>   that has no care for your presence,
> His wing-print is black on the roof tiles
> And the print is gone with his cry.
> So light is thy weight on Tellus
> Thy notch no deeper indented
> Thy weight less than the shadow
> Yet hast thou gnawed through the mountain,
>   Scylla's white teeth less sharp.
> Hast thou found a nest softer than cunnus
> Or hast thou found better rest
> Hast'ou a deeper planting, doth thy death year
> Bring swifter shoot?
> Hast thou entered more deeply the mountain?

The passage is connected by a beautiful transition to the Hesiod-
plowing sequence: "And the small stars now fall from the olive

branch." The "small stars" recall the Pleiades, which one visual-
izes falling toward the horizon beneath the branch; but "small
stars" is also a perfect description of the small, white flowers of
the olive which are patterned in axillary groups and look like
stars. The relation of these short-lived spring flowers to the
branch is like that between the brief existence of individual
men and mankind.[12] They die, but they forever reappear; and
the olive branch, a symbol of peace, prepares for the reconciliation Pound wishes to establish between the individual and his
cosmic destiny in the next several lines. The "forked shadow"
that "falls" in the second line does an extraordinary job of fusing the olive tree itself, which is often forked in appearance and
grown in terraced orchards, with its "small stars" or falling
flowers, into a metaphysical image that particularly suggests the
forked image of a man and seems to imply that there is an
underlying unity or harmony between man's dual or "forked"
nature as both isolate individual and as minute fragment of a
far greater whole, mankind. Man, like Yeats's chestnut tree, is
neither leaf, blossom, nor bole, but a totality that transcends
any one of his separately regarded aspects.

If Pound could be asked for any metaphysical justification
for the pervasive holism of the *Cantos,* the present passage
comes as close to satisfying such a demand as great poetry can,
without degenerating into philosophy. The forked shadow of
tree and man gathers into it the shadow of the "floating martin" as well, concentrating the human, vegetable, and animal
realms into a unity. And the lesson to be learned from the martin is that of the transiency of the individual, man's need for
humility and for reduction of his emphasis on the Ego, which
in the Western world, at any rate, has become all-consuming.

The insignificance of any one man's "notch" on earth is
contrasted, however, with the fact that man has "gnawed
through the mountain," an act that Donald Davie partly iden-

12. One is reminded also of Pound's famous "petals on a wet, black
bough."

tifies with quarrying as a sort of first stage in sculpting.[13] The further implications of the image are the development of agriculture and the building of cities—indeed, the creation of civilization—as a notch in the earth much deeper and more nearly permanent than any made by a single individual. But man's softest "nest," his deepest and securest "planting," Pound says, is in the *cunnus*, the body of woman, whose concern is with the perpetuity of the race far more than it is with the survival of the individual. The womb of woman is the womb of civilization: "Hast'ou a deeper planting, doth thy death year/ Bring swifter shoot?" Is there any greater promise of life after death, of *cultural* continuity, Pound asks, than planting one's seed in the mountain of Venus? The function of part II has been to provide a corrective to the romantic emphasis on the Ego and to view those aspects of man's nature that correspond to the animal and vegetable realms (his animal and vegetable "souls," as it were) as of fundamental cultural importance. Such a view of man was prominent in the rites of the ancient mystery religions, and the Eleusinian mysteries are, appropriately enough, the subject of the next lines. Pound himself can be called upon to provide us with an excellent commentary applicable to the passage I have just explicated and to that which follows:

> I offer for Mr Eliot's reflection the thesis that our time has overshadowed the mysteries by an over-emphasis on the individual. . . . Eleusis did not distort truth by exaggerating the individual, neither could it have violated the individual spirit. . . . Romantic poetry, on the other hand, almost requires the concept of reincarnation as part of its mechanism.[14]

Part III A is the climax of the Nekuia imagery. Light dissipates the darkness; Odysseus-Pound experiences mystical illumination in the sacred act of coitus that guarantees the rebirth of plant life. One recalls from Canto 36, "Sacrum, sacrum,

13. *Ezra Pound: Poet as Sculptor* (New York, 1964), p. 156.
14. *Guide to Kulchur*, p. 299.

inluminatio coitu." The voyager, finally achieving the insight
for which all else in the poem has been preparing him, accepts
not only intellectually, but feels on his very pulse his vital connection with the entire organic world:

> The light has entered the cave. Io! Io!
> The light has gone down into the cave,
> Splendour on splendour!
> By prong have I entered these hills:
> That the grass grow from my body,
> That I hear the roots speaking together,
> The air is new on my leaf,
> The forked boughs shake with the wind.
>
> . . .
>
> By this door have I entered the hill.

In his moment of ecstasy Odysseus becomes identified with the
whole process of nature, whose continued fruitfulness his sacral
act is intended to promote and, of course, does actually promote. In commenting on the line "Whores for Eleusis" in
Canto 45, Pound emphasizes the religious significance of copulation at Eleusis:

> "Eleusis" is very elliptical. It means that in place of the sacra-
> mental——in the Mysteries, you 'ave the 4 and six-penny 'ore.
> . . . the degradation of the sacrament (which is the coition
> and *not* the going to a fatbuttocked priest or registry office) has
> been completely debased largely *by* Xtianity, or misunderstand-
> ing of that Ersatz religion.[15]

The opening images of the previous section (II C), which anticipated the identification of man with nature in the multiple
ambiguities of the "forked shadow," are now fulfilled in the
"forked boughs" of Odysseus, who has transcended the limitations of his Ego and has entered like a god into the almond
tree.

15. *Letters*, p. 303.

The "door" of sex unites man with the hill of nature, measuring now not only his mortality but his immortality as well. Odysseus-Pound, who has experienced a god-like ecstasy, understands that he himself is the immortal Adonis who, in sexually "dying," rises to new life in the fruit that grows from his seed. Such is the meaning of the return to the Adonis theme now in III B, which I have prefaced with the transitional last line of III A:

> By this door have I entered the hill.
> Falleth,
> Adonis falleth.
> Fruit cometh after. The small lights drift out with the tide,
> sea's claw has gathered them outward,
> Four banners to every flower
> The sea's claw draws the lamps outward.

With the voice of his guides now absorbed in his own, Odysseus-Pound repeats the instructions of Hesiod to remind Western man of the second source of his life, the foundation of his civilization in agriculture, and the dependence of agriculture on precise regard for "the times and seasons." The canto ends on the note of rebirth:

> When the almond bough puts forth its flame,
> When the new shoots are brought to the altar,
> > Τυ Διώνα, Και Μοῖραι
> > TU DIONA, KAI MOIRAI
> Και Μοῖραι᾽ Ἄδονιν
> KAI MOIRAI᾽ ADONIN
> > that hath the gift of healing,
> that hath the power over wild beasts.

Adonis, symbolizing seasonal renewal, has "the gift of healing" in the dual sense that he both comes back to life himself and in the process heals nature and man. The last line, which concentrates all previous themes into a triumphant conclusion, is the true climax of the canto. "Wild beasts" have appeared in the canto in several forms. First there were the "drugged beasts" of Circe, men transformed because of immoderate self-surrender to appetite, as we saw in Canto 39. Secondly, Scylla's dogs threatened Odysseus with destruction. Third was the bull who "runs blind on the sword." Finally, of course, there is the wild boar that slew Adonis. All these "wild beasts" are blind natural forces, the instinctive life in man that corresponds with the rest of the unconscious organic world external to him. Pound has attempted to show that man's survival as a species and his development of civilization has depended not on any rejection of nature, which is the prime characteristic of Usura, but on holistic acceptance of instinct combined with the ability to harness its blind potencies to the service of ever more spiritual ends. The key to the development of civilization, to "the power over wild beasts," is the intelligence of man that could measure the rhythms of organic time (by the stars and other regular natural occurrences) and raise man from will-less subjection to them to creative accord with them. Pound celebrates physical procreation not as an end in itself, but as the necessary basis and source of energy for cultural creation. He celebrates agriculture as the first great creative conquest of nature by the mind of man and the basis of all later and intellectually more sophisticated cultural achievements, such as, in the West, religion and the arts.

Light imagery reinforces the general thematic movement. The canto begins "in the dark" and proceeds to show light continually descending. The lamps of Adonis drift out, like the dying god, toward the lower world, "The red flame going seaward"; "the Pleiades go down to their rest"; "the small stars . . . fall from the olive branch"; and the "light has gone down into the cave." All this is cumulatively symbolic of the light of the intelligence seeking its ultimate roots, the mind in search of the sources of its strength, and finally discovering them. The last image of light is one of triumphant ascent: "the almond bough puts forth its flame." Analysis is succeeded by synthesis, and knowledge bears fruit in action.

One of the most fascinating possibilities to explore is the idea that the form of Canto 47 epitomizes the form taken and to be taken by the *Cantos* as a whole. I have felt this to be the case for the Sirens-Circe-Aphrodite sequence introduced at the end of Canto 1, and I feel quite strongly that this is equally the case for the whole of the present canto, which recognizably completes a circle and "returns" to the beginning to inaugurate a new phase of poetic effort.

I find it illuminating to view parts I, II, and III of the canto as miniatures, respectively, of the three large-scale movements—an *Inferno*, *Purgatorio*, and *Paradiso*—that make up the *Cantos* as a whole. Pound's *Inferno* is resumed in the first part of Canto 47. Here, the predominant themes are the descent into hell of Odysseus and the death of the life-force, which is symbolized by the disappearance into the underworld of Adonis, whose presence among men is necessary for agricultural (and cultural) renewal. In Cantos 1–30, also, as I have tried to show, the life-force is seen in retreat in all spheres of life and the modern world appears a wasteland.

Part II of the canto certainly epitomizes the *Purgatorio* of which the whole of the canto is actually a part. The essence of Pound's *Purgatorio*, as I see it, is the presentation of the rhythms of organic time as the cosmic basis of Confucian "order within" and, consequently, of order in society. Man's relation to natural forces and to the earth itself is the subject matter of this second part of the canto. Hesiod's plowing directions embody the ideal relationship between man and nature, a creative accord based on the precise adjustment of man's elemental activities to the appropriate times and seasons.

The *Paradiso* of the *Cantos*, which is characterized in my introduction as the poet's attainment of "cosmic consciousness," the mystical identification of the Self with the immortal "process" of nature, is foreshadowed in the visional episode of part III. Just as in the first section of Pound's *Paradiso* (*The Pisan Cantos*) Pound uses himself dramatically as the first-person subject, here, too, in a corresponding position, the mystical experience of unity with nature is projected by a first-person narrator (as opposed to the consistent use of second-person narration in all the rest of the canto). The theme of the triumph of light which dominates Pound's *Paradiso* is here prefigured in the rapture of "The light has entered the cave. Io! Io!" and, finally, in the "flame" of the flowering almond bough.

CHAPTER VIII

The Dimension of Stillness

HUGH KENNER describes Canto 49 as "one of the pivots of the poem: the emotional still point of the *Cantos*." [1] "Stillness" is literally, of course, one of its major themes. In reading the canto, one is left with the general impression of static, symmetrical balance, and the structure of its imagery appears largely to confirm such an impression. As indicated in the previous chapter, Canto 49 is a twin to Canto 47. There are important structural and thematic reasons for the relationship. The narrator, as we shall see, is an Odysseus chastened by his new insights, which he now transposes into a Confucian vision of social order, thereby adding a further dimension to his knowledge, "the dimension of stillness."

Pound's preoccupation with the theme of time, central to Canto 47, is equally central to Canto 49, where the theme serves as a counterpoint to the complementary theme of stillness. Although much smaller in size, the canto is also similar structurally to Canto 47. There are three main parts, and once again each of these parts is divisible into three subsections (but the divisions are not necessarily indicated by the line-spacings between stanzas). If we consider the structure from a dynamic point of view, the canto reveals a pattern of progressive abstraction. Pure lyricism, concreteness of imagery, and complete absence of abstract, evaluative statement characterize the first part; overt social criticism mingles with the lyrical base that continues through part two; and pure abstraction on a meta-

1. *The Poetry of Ezra Pound*, p. 326.

physical plane joins with a final lyrical statement in part three.
The form of the canto is, moreover, one of progressive self-
analysis. The concrete images of part one undergo socio-
economic analysis in part two, and that analysis is in turn sub-
jected to a final metaphysical analysis in part three, where,
appropriately enough, the abstract theme of time, implicit
throughout the canto, emerges explicitly.

Part one, as I read it, takes up thirty-two of the canto's forty-
seven lines, or the first four stanzas (up to "A light moves on
the south sky line."). The source of this whole section is a
"series" [2] of Chinese and Japanese poems forming a small
book in Pound's possession.[3] The cover page reads, in Pound's
own hand, "Source of 7 Lakes Canto." The whole manuscript consists of fourteen poems, each one on an individual
page, and seven delicate drawings illustrating the poems, also
on individual pages. Seven of the poems are in Japanese, apparently all written in the same hand. The other seven are in
Chinese, composed in different calligraphies and possibly by
different authors.[4]

The seven Chinese poems are much more easy to read, even
for a literate Japanese, than the other seven, since those in
Japanese are in an archaic calligraphy and their complete deci-
pherment requires a specialist. Pound, therefore, could not have
read some of the material, but he may have heard a rough translation read by a friend of his father's from the Orient (Homer
Pound originally owned the manuscript). The poems are connected by the seasonal themes of autumn and winter; some in-

2. Pound's answer, when I asked him whether the source was a
single poem.

3. I am indebted to Mary de Rachewiltz for showing me a set of
photographs of the book.

4. I owe this and the following discussion of the "source" of Canto
49 to the kindness of Professor Sanehide Kodama of Doshisha Women's
College, Kyoto. He has provided me with his own translation of the
Chinese and Japanese poems, a translation made from photographs of the
manuscript that were sent to him by Princess Mary de Rachewiltz.

clude a sunset; and four of the chief images in them are of wild
geese, snow, boats, and reeds. These elements are recognizable
in Canto 49, but that is about as far as the resemblance goes
between the source and the canto. Structurally, there is no similarity between the two. Not only does Pound omit passages
from the original, but he picks up images from these poems
with no regard for the sequence in which they originally appear,
combining images from disparate poems at will. In other words,
avoiding mechanical adherence to the original, Pound is creat-
ing in the first thirty-two lines of his canto a sequence of images
organic to his own thematic and structural purposes.[5] The
images he chooses to "translate" are organized to express the
Confucian theme of the whole canto and to harmonize structurally with the following stanzas, which also consist mostly of
translated—and even transliterated—poems (these, however,
from the Fenollosa manuscripts from which he once quarried
his *Cathay*). Once the problem of sources is disposed of, one
can proceed to examine the canto as a unit of poetry obeying its
own internal laws of development.

Stanza one begins:

> For the seven lakes, and by no man these verses:
> Rain; empty river; a voyage.

"No man" (Pound thought all the manuscript poems anonymous) is the name Odysseus gives when asked by the drunken
Cyclops to identify himself. Throughout the *Cantos* Pound is,
in a sense, addressing a modern world inhabited by Cyclopes, "a
violent and lawless tribe" who "neither plant nor plow," each
caring nothing for his neighbors.[6] In addition, "no man" is a
completely impersonalized Odysseus, one who has come to

5. The "Donna mi prega" portion of Canto 36 is an excellent example of Pound's treatment of a non-English poem so as to bring it into
conformity with his thematic and structural purposes.

6. Homer, *The Odyssey*, trans. W. H. D. Rouse, Mentor Classic
(New York, 1937), p. 102 (Bk IX).

realize the relative unimportance of Ego after experiencing the transpersonal dimension of his relationship to mankind and to nature, a dimension of being which transcends the spatio-temporal limitations of the Ego. If Odysseus-Pound has come to identify himself with common humanity, then perhaps the "voyage" he is describing is, more generally, that of man. In any case, the "twilight" mood of the voyage described is one of storm, disorder, and lamentation:

> For the seven lakes, and by no man these verses:
> Rain; empty river; a voyage,
> Fire from frozen cloud, heavy rain in the twilight
> Under the cabin roof was one lantern.
> The reeds are heavy; bent;
> and the bamboos speak as if weeping.

The single use of the past tense, there *was* "one lantern," contrasts noticeably with the present tense of the last two lines, which end with "weeping." Is Pound referring to some *one light* that once unified civilization, but does so no longer? In this case, "the cabin roof" of the ship making the voyage suggests the pilothouse of the proverbial "ship of state," which is in sad condition, apparently in a battle with the elements. It will become more evident later on, when Pound subjects these images to social analysis, that he is indeed writing about the ship of state.

The next stanza contrasts markedly in tone and imagery with the first. There is now almost no motion and almost no sound, and whatever there is of sound and motion serves only to intensify the prevailing impression of stillness. All things are bathed in light and ultimately lose their individual identity in a blaze of pure light:

> Autumn moon; hills rise about lakes
> against sunset
> Evening is like a curtain of cloud,

a blurr above ripples; and through it
sharp long spikes of the cinnamon,
a cold tune amid reeds.
Behind hill the monk's bell
borne on the wind.
Sail passed here in April; may return in October
Boat fades in silver; slowly;
Sun blaze alone on the river.

The picture is almost entirely static. It is impersonal, completely detached from the quotidian doings of men. The "monk's bell" lifts this panoramic view of man's natural setting almost to the level of a religious vision. One notices that the stanza describes a scene imbued with the light of both moon and sun. The mind's eye travels from the opening image of the moon 180 degrees around to the "sun blaze" illuminating the river below the opposite sky line. If we turn to Pound's *Confucius* we discover, in his list of significant Confucian symbols, the ideogram made up of the signs for the moon and sun, which together comprise "the total light process, the radiation, reception and reflection of light; hence the intelligence. Bright, brightness, shining." [7] For Pound, the Confucian symbol reinforces the Neoplatonic association of light with *nous*, or Mind in general as opposed to any individual mind.

We can already see that the two stanzas discussed so far set up a contrast between darkness and light, disorder and order, and they seem now also to suggest a contrast between mindlessness and impersonal or transpersonal intelligence. These are old themes and old images of Pound's now being transposed into an entirely Confucian key. What is the meaning of "Sail passed here in April; may return in October"? One feels that in such a setting of stillness and self-sufficiency a "sail" entering from some distant port is a sort of intrusion, unless it has some accepted function in the whole picture. The comings and goings of this particular sail are rare and predictable, and it appears

7. *Confucius*, p. 20.

likely that it is representative of the distant central government
that ideally, in Pound's view, intrudes little and only for benevolent reasons in the local self-determination of the people. This
"ship of state" passes at significant times: in April, the beginning of the agricultural cycle, and October, at its harvest end—
perhaps to collect taxes in due season. In any case, if it is the
ship of state, it functions in harmony with the seasons and
appears relatively insignificant in the "total light process" of
nature, into which it harmoniously "fades." The probability of
such an interpretation is considerably strengthened by the last
line of the "Sun up" poem near the end of the canto. The voice
of the common man, who lives in harmony with nature, says:
"Imperial power is? and to us what is it?" Pound reminds us, in
Jefferson and/or Mussolini, that " 'The best government is that
which governs least,' remarked Mr. Jefferson." [8] However,
"Shallow interpretation puts all the emphasis on the adverb
'Least' and slides gaily over the verb 'to govern.' " [9] Pound's
point is that for Jefferson the best government is that which
exercises the least *direct authority* and makes the beneficent influence of its internal order and wisdom felt indirectly in the
land at large, by osmosis, as it were. If one places the emphasis
on "least," one gets the impression that no government at all is
the best government, but such a view would be totally errone-
ous from Pound's standpoint, as well as from that of Confucius.
The ideal, indirect effect of government is described by Confucius' great disciple, Mencius:

> under the rule of the *wang* [true king], the people show deep
> contentment. When he puts them to death, they show no re-
> sentment. When he benefits them, they never think of his
> merit. From day to day they make progress toward goodness,
> without knowing who makes them progress. . . . His influ-

8. *Jefferson and/or Mussolini,* p. 11.
9. Ibid. p. 15.

ence, exerting far and wide, can be comparable to that of Heaven and Earth.[10]

If I am correct in my interpretation so far, then the fading of boat into sun at the end of the stanza suggests the identity of good government with the light or intelligence of heaven, which exerts a beneficent influence "far and wide."

The significance of this stanza will emerge more clearly by comparison with the group of images in the two stanzas that form a unit extending from line 18 to line 32. The fact that the two stanzas are unitary emerges from their content, but is curiously confirmed by a bit of external evidence as well. Although the New Directions edition of the *Cantos* separates lines 18–19 from lines 20–32 by a line-space, the later Faber and Faber edition joins lines 18–19 to the following group and puts the break at line 24, a conveniently symmetrical midpoint between lines 18–32 that not only improves the visual appearance of the page but more importantly, isolates lines 18–19 from possible direct association with the second stanza. It would appear that Pound must have regarded lines 18–32 as a single thematic group because at one point or another they have been joined together stanzaically.

The lines amount to a description of the same landscape, the same autumn sunset outlined in the previous stanza, but from a new point of view. The human detail is now filled in, and the social-political tendency of the canto begins to appear:

> Where wine flag catches the sunset
> Sparse chimneys smoke in the cross light.

The flag is a symbol of statal unity, and its color is always in some sense symbolic of the idea on which the state is founded. Wine suggests prosperity, joy, the rich result of the gathered

10. "The Works of Mencius," *The Humanist Way in Ancient China*, ed. and trans. Ch'u Chai and Winberg Chai, Bantam Matrix edition (New York, 1965), p. 111 (Ch. VIIA–13).

harvest; and it suggests Bacchus, the god of fertility as the patron divinity of the state. In some lines further on in the canto
the idea of a prosperous, peaceful society is advanced literally:
"And at San Yin/ they are a people of leisure." The scene described is of the river and a "small boat" floating there "like a
lanthorn," a fishing vessel and birds in flight:

> Wild geese swoop to the sand-bar
> Clouds gather about the hole of the window
> Broad water; geese line out with the autumn
> Rooks clatter over the fishermen's lanthorns.[11]

The fishermen represent man in productive harmony with nature, making possible the leisure at San Yin. The final lines of
the stanza emphasize this creative harmony between man and
nature and introduce the idea of wise government as its sustaining cause:

> A light moves on the north sky line;
> where the young boys prod stones for shrimp.
> In seventeen hundred came Tsing to these hill lakes.
> A light moves on the south sky line.

The lights that surround this picture so symmetrically seem
clearly to be the moon and sun that stand in the same positions
in stanza two. Now these heavenly lights are brought down to
earth, so to speak. They are associated with the intelligence of
the emperor Tsing, who obviously put things in order and
whose wisdom still shines, like moon and sun, in the economic
prosperity he made possible by promoting harmony between

---

11. The present "lanthorns" as opposed to the "lantern" of the first
stanza most probably has no Cabbalistic significance. The *Cantos* does not
reveal any great solicitude on Pound's part for uniform spelling. In any
case, Pound's translation of Enrico Pea's short novel *Moscardino* (Schei-
weller: Milan, 1956) contains, like Canto 49, one instance of "lanthorns"
(p. 35) and one of "lanterns" (p. 72), the difference being purely arbitrary.

man and nature. Tsing is either the wise Yong Tching of Canto 61 or his equally wise father, Kang Hi, both of whom brought prosperity to China by governing according to Confucian principles. (Both were *Ch'ing* dynasty emperors: the spelling of the same Chinese names often varies even *within* the Chinese history cantos.)

We have established, I think, three different movements in part one. The first stanza suggests social disorder, the absence of guiding intelligence in the affairs of state. The second stanza suggests the abstract principle of order itself, as it appears in the perfect harmony of nature, the accord between heaven and earth. The musical sounds that enter this image of timeless perfection seem to have the meaning assigned to music in the *Li Ki*, the "Book of Rites," which Pound translates in part in Canto 52: "Music," says the *Li Ki*, "expresses the harmony of Heaven and Earth." [12] The next two stanzas show this underlying principle of order in action in human affairs, harmonizing the activities of man in time (the year 1700) with nature's timelessness so that peace and prosperity are the social result.

Part two, consisting of lines 33–45, clarifies the social and economic meaning of the images of part one. Corresponding to the images of disorder in stanza one is the first half of stanza five (ll. 33–4):

> State by creating riches shd. thereby get into debt?
> This is infamy; this is Geryon.

The principle of governmental intelligence needed to destroy Geryon (Dante's monster representing fraud, "twin with usura" in Canto 51) appears in the following two lines and is eulogized in the Japanese translation of a Chinese poem that follows:

> This canal goes still to TenShi
> though the old king built it for pleasure.

12. E. R. Hughes, ed. and trans., *Chinese Philosophy in Classical Times* (London, 1960), p. 278.

Jefferson, too, had a canal-building project, if we remember Canto 31. A canal is of benefit to the whole people, and if the king's personal "pleasure" redounds to the good of his people, then that king has attained the summit of order within, the point at which one's inmost desires are never antisocial. "At seventy," says Confucius, describing the final step of his spiritual development, "I could follow the desires of my mind without overstepping the boundaries [of what is right]." (*Analects*, II, 4.) [13]

The poem which follows gives the appearance of perfect symmetrical order—and for most English-speaking readers is literally a mystery. But this is exactly the effect which Pound wishes to create. The principle of order at the core of things is an unanalyzable mystery; it is the mystery of "the dimension of stillness" that is finally named at the end of the canto. The poem in translation appears almost as mysterious as it does in Japanese:

> The clouds are aglow with splendor
> Twirling and whirling (like winding silk)
> The light of sun and moon
> (May it shine) dawn after dawn.

In its impersonal "sun and moon" imagery, the poem stands in clear parallel with stanza two. For the Chinese, the poem has special symbolic significance. Angela Jung tells us that it "is a eulogy traditionally accredited to the period of Shun Emperor, whose illustrious reign is compared in the poem to the light of the sun and the moon, which brightens and gives life to the surrounding air and clouds (symbol for the people in the collective sense)." [14]

13. Fung Yu-Lan, *A Short History of Chinese Philosophy* (New York, 1948), p. 46. Bracketed material is part of the quotation.

14. The poem and commentary on this and the "Sun up" poem are quoted from Angela Chih-Ying Jung, "Ezra Pound and China" (Ph.D. dissertation: University of Washington, 1955), p. 109.

If the present poem symbolizes the wisdom of the Emperor in the imagery of heavenly light, the "Sun up" poem that follows it (all five lines are a translation by Pound) focuses on the concrete effect of such wisdom in securing the contentment of the people, who are permitted to live in harmony with nature and to enjoy the fruits of their labor. The good king establishes and maintains the conditions for such harmony, and his beneficent influence is especially active when his subjects are least aware of his existence. Miss Jung says that the poem "is supposed to belong to the period of the legendary Emperor Yao who ruled a hundred years earlier than Shun. . . . it shows . . . contentment with the simple agrarian life, unoppressed by taxes or any other form of tyranny."

The identification of lines 33–45, therefore, as another main segment of the canto, is based on the discovery that these lines comprise another distinctive sequence of images following the tripartite pattern of (1) social disorder; (2) the principle of order itself, symbolized by the "light" of heavenly intelligence (now literally embodied in the image of the wise ruler, whose presence personifies this principle just as Geryon now personifies disorder); and (3) this principle of heavenly order seen in social action in the productive harmony between man and nature. The third and highly elliptical final part of the canto subjects the two previous image-sequences to a metaphysical analysis. Part three consists of only two lines, but the first line is divisible into two contrasting themes:

> The fourth; the dimension of stillness.
> And the power over wild beasts.

For Pound, the fourth dimension is that of "stillness," and not that of "time," with which "the dimension of stillness" is here elliptically contrasted. The fourth dimension is inevitably associated with Einstein's theory of relativity, and the question arises as to what, precisely, Pound means by his seemingly presumptuous criticism of a highly involved mathematical-physical theory which he, no more than any other layman, can profess to understand beyond the level of its presentation by popularizers. It is clear, however, from the structure of the canto, that Pound is attacking not a mathematical theory, as such, but its philosophical implications, which on the social plane appear in his eyes to promote disorder.

Time ("The fourth;"), in this canto, is an image structurally parallel to, and therefore identified with, previous imagery of social disorder. The concept of mechanical time as representing social disorder, established as the "evil" in the first thirty cantos, re-emerges now in a new guise. Pound is not attacking Einstein's theory of relativity, but rather the conception it has given rise to in the minds of laymen and many philosophers alike that "everything is relative" and there are no absolute standards by which men ought to guide their behavior and determine their moral responsibility. It is evident that Pound, being a Confucian and concerned with the establishment of individual and social order, is a moral absolutist and can not abide anarchical formulations, such as concepts of "moral relativity." He can least abide such notions when they are widespread, seem to have unfortunate social consequences, and, further, are presented as sanctioned by a scientific authority so unimpeachable as Einstein.

Pound's own statements about Einstein are few, but very revealing if brought to bear on Canto 49. The following passage from Pound's *Antheil* (1927) appears to contain an almost direct commentary on the passage under discussion:

Antheil is supremely sensitive to the existence of music in time-space. The use of the term "fourth dimension" is probably as confusing in Einstein as in Antheil. I believe that Einstein is capable of conceiving the factor time as affecting space relations. He does this in a mode hitherto little used, and with certain quirks that had not been used by engineers before him;

though the time element enters into engineering computations.[15]

The main point for us here is Pound's belief that Einstein's use of the term "fourth dimension" was "confusing." In the paragraph that immediately follows, Pound goes on to suggest that mathematical concepts such as Einstein's are not only confusing, but irrelevant:

> The x, y, and z axes of analytics would appear to me to provide for what Antheil calls the fourth dimension of music, the "oblique," but technical mathematical language is almost as obscure as Antheil's. The first of his piano sonatas shows perfectly clearly what he means. And a gang of African savages would probably illustrate what he means by the "hole in time-space." [16]

The technical concept of the fourth dimension is unnecessary and irrelevant, Pound is saying, to the concrete *experience* of art. It serves to confuse and complicate rather than illuminate. The misapplication of Einstein's purely mathematical-physical concepts by philosophers draws Pound's comment more than a decade later, at about the time Canto 49 was itself being written:

> In our time Al Einstein scandalized the professing philosophists by saying, with truth, that his theories of relativity had no philosophic bearing.[17]

Evidently Pound, like Wyndham Lewis before him, was disturbed at the debased currency the so-called "philosophy of relativity" was enjoying in the twentieth century. Pound would have agreed with much that Lewis said in 1927 about the "time-

15. *Antheil and the Treatise on Harmony with Supplementary Notes* (Chicago, 1927), p. 56.
16. Ibid.
17. *Guide to Kulchur*, p. 34.

philosophy" that was undermining Western culture; and, indeed, Lewis's thinking on Einstein is so close to Pound's that
one can to some extent use Lewis as a helpful gloss on the present canto. Lewis said, "What I am concerned with here . . . is
not whether the great *time-philosophy* that overshadows all
contemporary thought is viable as a system of abstract truth,
but if in its application it helps or destroys our human arts." [18]
Lewis, like Pound, is concerned with the effect of Einstein in
the philosophical domain:

> A great many *effects*, a whole string of highly characteristic
> disturbances, *come out of* einsteinian physics. . . . And those
> I am thoroughly competent to observe, and it is those with
> which I have set out to deal: the physics themselves can re-
> main for us in the region at most of hypothesis, a vague *some-
> thing* that produces, in the observable field of philosophy, a
> chain of *effects*, or of mysterious happenings.[19]

Lewis notes particularly the political interpretation of relativity.
He describes

> the way in which Einstein's Boswell [Moszkowski] regards his
> master's discoveries. He brings to them, perhaps, a peculiarly
> political eye: he sees them as a rooting out from the Cosmos,
> by means of a kind of mathematical guillotine, of the principle
> of *the Absolute*.[20]

The concept of mechanical time, introduced into the poem
as early as Canto 5 as the root of all sorts of social disorder, has
progressively expanded to include the disordered Christian sensibility, the practice of usury fostered by Protestantism, and
now the regnant time-philosophy in the West regarded as an attack on the existence of an absolute principle of order. Pound's
concept of order, however, has also undergone development. At

18. *Time and Western Man*, p. 112.
19. Ibid. p. 142.
20. Ibid. p. 145.

first, the idea of order was suggested by certain myths, various gods and goddesses, works of art, an idealized image of Venice, and various heroes of social order such as Malatesta, the Confucius of Canto 13, and Jefferson. In cantos 30 to 39, the concept of order underwent progressive "analysis," or conceptual clarification, and became psychologized into an ideal state of dynamic equilibrium among our various physical and mental drives. Finally, the idea of order became explicitly associated with organic time as the objective, cosmic basis of order to which man must attune himself.

Now, in Canto 49, Pound is interested in a further, metaphysical analysis of the concept of order, the statement of a first principle that should stand in place of the debased concept of relativity that Pound sees as a symbol of the Cyclopian individualism and concomitant loss of values in the West. "Stillness," a suggestive image in Cantos 2 and 17, was first introduced in a philosophical context in Canto 36, where the nature of Love in the abstract was indicated in the following line: "He himself moveth not, drawing all to his stillness." Love's stillness is here strongly suggestive of the Unmoved Mover, and "stillness" thereby assumes conceptual status as a sort of metaphysical Absolute. It is associated throughout the whole canzone with the Neoplatonic imagery of light.

"Stillness" in Canto 49 emerges as a principle of order connected with the light of sun and moon. The phrase, "the dimension of stillness," corresponds to the second section of each main part of the canto. Stanza two is literally an image of stillness. It has a religious suggestiveness that embraces the whole panorama of nature. In part two the second section further elaborates the principle of order, giving it a specifically social context. "This canal goes still to TenShi" carefully employs the word *still* to prepare for its final conceptual development in "the dimension of stillness." *Still*, in this case, has double meaning. In the temporal sense it means "without ever having ceased" and gives the impression of permanence. In the spatial sense, the canal is "still," unmoving in itself, but facilitating movement. The qualities of permanence and immobility are both involved in the "dimension of stillness," and the conception of an immobility that "causes" movement ("*goes* still" involves the paradox of a stillness causing motion) is highly suggestive of the Unmoved Mover. The idea of stillness, as developed in Canto 36, seems re-enlisted now as a key concept in Canto 49.

But surely, in a canto so heavily Confucian as this, there must be a Confucian possibility of interpreting the concept of stillness. One seeks a Confucian Absolute in answer to the relativity of the Western "philosophists," and the closest equivalent to the Unmoved Mover in Confucianism (at any rate, in Pound's view of Confucianism) is the Chung Yung, which Pound has translated as the "Unwobbling Pivot." Although the usual translation of Chung Yung as "Just Mean" represents a primarily ethical principle, something like the Golden Mean, Pound has been at pains to regard it rather as a metaphysical concept with ethical implications. In a "Note" to his translation of "The Unwobbling Pivot" he says:

> The second of the Four Classics, Chung Yung, THE UN-WOBBLING PIVOT, contains what is usually supposed not to exist, namely the Confucian metaphysics. It is divided into three parts: the axis; the process; and sincerity, the perfect word, or the precise word.[21]

The "axis," the Unwobbling Pivot itself, is what presently concerns us, and Pound defines this (in a highly imagistic, yet at the same time almost pedantic translation) in a way completely harmonious with the concept of stillness (italics mine):

> What exists plumb in the middle is the just process of the universe and that which never wavers or wobbles is *the calm principle* operant in its mode of action.[22]

21. *Confucius*, p. 95.
22. Ibid. p. 97.

It is important to distinguish between this calm "axis" itself and the "process," or the visible harmony it produces:

> Happiness, rage, grief, delight. To be unmoved by these emotions is to stand in the axis, in the center; being moved by these passions each in due degree constitutes being in harmony.
>
> That axis in the center is the great root of the universe; that harmony is the universe's outspread process [of existence]. From this root and in this harmony, heaven and earth are established in their precise modalities, and the multitudes of all creatures persist, nourished on their meridians.[23]

The "process," Pound's translation of the *Tao*, is represented in the third section of each part of the canto, in which man is pictured in creative accord with nature. If the "axis," the Chung Yung, is the "dimension of stillness," then the "process," the outspread harmony, is "the power over wild beasts." The "dimension of stillness" comes to symbolize the Confucian system in general, which for Pound contains the metaphysical, political, and ethical principles needed to maintain social order and give men "the power over wild beasts." "Wild beasts" in Canto 47 signified the forces of nature which man, by attuning himself to the times and seasons, brings under his control. In the present canto, however, with its emphasis on social order, "wild beasts" seems particularly to connote the untamed forces in man himself which can be disruptive of social order. The first such wild beast implied in this canto is the cannabalistic Cyclops, which "no man" defeats through intelligence rather than brute force. The Cyclops is superseded, however, by the as yet undefeated monster Geryon, usury, the society-destroying beast that Pound is attempting to root out of its lair as one of the aims of the *Cantos*.

Of course there is no direct relationship intended between usury and Einstein, but Einstein does nevertheless become a

23. Ibid. pp. 101–3.

convenient "symbol" for all that is wrong in the West. His name, or talk of "relativity," or of the "fourth dimension," has a charismatic effect in our culture. Millions of us stand in awe of Einstein without ever understanding an iota of what he has accomplished. He becomes a symbol of our blindly abstract orientation to reality, and we accord his name a worship which we no longer give to the founders of our religions. I think it is in part, at least, this "meaning" of Einstein which Pound is attacking. Our orientation toward the abstract is, in Pound's view, not balanced by equivalent attention to the concrete, everyday matters of government, economics, and social ethics which affect us most intimately. Pound believes that Confucius, who spoke in concrete terms about everyday living, the ultimate laboratory of his ideas, offers a practicable guide to conduct and a sorely needed corrective to the philosophical and moral confusion of the West.

CHAPTER IX

The Dynastic Cantos

IF IN THE first thirty cantos history was presented primarily as a
process of decay, succeeding cantos concerning the American
Revolution and Italian banking practice have emphasized the
creative possibilities of history, history as a process under the
control of man's intelligence and productive of the kind of social order that is compatable with human freedom and dignity. I
have tried to show that Pound ultimately compresses his perception of history as disorder and decay into the concept of
mechanical time, which aptly symbolizes the violent imposition
by the Western consciousness of abstract and unrealistic patterns upon nature. Conversely, history as creative order is developed in terms of the concept of organic time, which involves a
consciousness of "the times and seasons" of things, a concrete
appreciation of reality that Pound finds deteriorating in the
West, even though such an "organic time-consciousness" is essential to creative action in any sphere.

The dynastic cantos, 52–71, are intended to elaborate on a
grand scale the idea that harmony with the rhythms of organic
time is the basis of social order. The Chinese history cantos
(52–61) provide the necessary historical evidence to support
Pound's thesis that Confucianism is and has been an idea capable of going into action, as opposed to the abstract and sterile
philosophizing of the West that has no fruitful connection with
social reality and thereby contributes ultimately to the triumph
of disorder. The consequent need to present Chinese history *at
length* arises from a thesis which requires substantiation:

namely, that Confucianism is not a philosophy that went into practical effect only once or twice in history, revealing itself to be perhaps as limited in applicability as any other stop-gap system to the local peculiarities of a certain favorable time and place, but that the Confucian philosophy, founded in the essential nature of things, is universally applicable to the social condition of man regardless of time and place. The Chinese history cantos show the repeated resurgence of social order over a period of millennia, whenever Confucian ideas were put into practice. Social order, for Pound, is never the result of innovation but of renovation, the renewal in practice of principles fallen into disuse. "THE LESSON of Chinese history?" he asks —and answers:

> As I can have no pretence to "potting" it here, might nevertheless be of two kinds. By implication, we might more despise and suspect the kind of education which we (my generation) received, and we might acquire some balance in NOT mistaking recurrence for innovation.[1]

"For 2,500 years," he claims, "whenever there has been order in China or in any part of China, you can look for a Confucian at the root of it." [2] He has given the following account of Chinese history, which serves equally well as a brief summary of the Chinese history cantos:

> The dynasties Han, Tang, Sung, Ming rose on the Confucian idea; it is inscribed in the lives of the great emperors, Tai Tsong, Kao Tseu, Hong Vou, another Tai Tsong, and Kang Hi. When the idea was not held to, decadence supervened.[3]

The question arises, why does a group of cantos (62–71) concerned with the career of John Adams succeed the Chinese

1. *Guide to Kulchur*, p. 274.
2. *Jefferson and/or Mussolini*, p. 113.
3. *Confucius*, p. 189.

history cantos? There are several answers. First, since the purpose of the Chinese history cantos is to point up a lesson for the West, especially for the United States, and since John Adams has already been sketched in as a sort of Confucian statesman in earlier cantos, it does not seem totally arbitrary that Pound should choose for display the career of John Adams, who functions as an example of Confucianism in practice in the West. Second, there is a coincidental link between Adams and the preceding Chinese cantos. Clark Emery points out the chronological continuity between the birth of John Adams in 1735 and the death in the same year of the great emperor Yong Tching [4] (Canto 61), at which point Pound alludes to "the rise of the Adamses" (p. 85). It is this latter phrase which gives us the essential reason for the selection of John Adams as a type of Western successor to a line of Chinese emperors. For Pound, the career of Adams was the only logical choice for extended treatment at this juncture (as opposed, for example, to that of Jefferson) because John Adams embodied the closest thing in American history to the idea of dynasty stressed in the Chinese cantos. In this regard, Pound writes that

> John Adams believed in heredity. Jefferson left no sons. Adams left the only line of descendants who have steadily and without a break felt their responsibility and persistently participated in American government throughout its 160 years.[5]

The idea of dynasty implies the belief, whether conscious or unconscious, that social responsibility extends beyond an individual lifetime. It implies the belief that the social effectiveness of an individual is capable of indefinite extension in time and in spite of time. The dynastic cantos would therefore appear to be a refutation of the popular philosophy of "social relativity," which denies the real persistence, in substance rather than in name only, of social ideals and institutions from generation to

4. *Ideas into Action*, p. 43.
5. *Jefferson and/or Mussolini*, p. 19.

generation. Pound has asserted (in Canto 49) that his "fourth" dimenison is the "dimension of stillness," the belief in a permanent core of order in the universe existing behind all processes of change, which are only superficial. The "dimension of stillness" in the social sphere is the persistence of a fundamental "formula" for social order, an unchanging pattern capable of going into action in spite of time and place. The "dimension of stillness," or Unwobbling Pivot, makes possible the recurrence of social order, the renewal in the social sphere of an equity springing from the metaphysical heart of things.

The constant resurgence of Confucianist dynasties in China and the rise of a similarly Confucianist Adams clan, devoted through the generations to the maintenance of social order, are intended by Pound to reveal that the achievement of order is not automatically subject to dissolution by time. One of the most important themes of Canto 47, Pound's criticism of the West for investing the Ego with undue importance and his allied attempt to reveal dimensions of the Self that are unlimited by space and time, now appears as an "idea in action," not a mere metaphysical quibble but an idea important for the guidance of men's conduct in society. The history of Confucian dynasties is adduced by Pound as evidence that men have been able to look beyond the interests of their limited egos to the vaster interests of an unlimited Self that extends horizontally in space to include one's contemporaries and vertically in time to include posterity. The feeling of social responsibility is, for Pound, the necessary outgrowth of a truly enlightened Selfishness.

All this is meant as no defense of the poetic *quality* of the dynastic cantos. However, if their structural and thematic relevance goes unperceived, whatever quality they do have as poetry must also to some extent fail to be appreciated. I am assuming, I suppose, a distinction between two kinds of poetic intensity. There is the intensity possessed by individual lines or passages of poetry whose local density of language renders them eminently quotable out of context. There is also, however, the kind of poetic intensity that results from the cumulative effect of a total structure, a context which may give great power to passages unexceptional in texture by conditioning our emotional responses to them. Pound has discussed this method of achieving poetic intensity, but not in direct relation to poetry. Nevertheless, his remarks do cast light, I think, on the way the *Cantos* are constructed and must be read:

> "Neither prose nor drama can attain poetic intensity save by construction, almost by scenario; by so arranging the circumstance that some perfectly simple speech, perception, dogmatic statement appears in abnormal vigour." [6]

The *Cantos* appears to me to be such a close-knit work structurally that much of the poetic effect of individual passages and even of whole sections, like these dynastic cantos, is conferred upon them by their position in a climactic sequence of theme development. I regard this process of theme development as essentially dramatic. The dynastic cantos rise as a fully articulated counter-myth, clothed in concrete, historical detail, to challenge the myth of Western decay that was presented in equally full historical costume in the first thirty cantos, and as usury in the transitional cantos that followed. Only when full allowance is made for the structural effect of these cantos can there be, I believe, a just appreciation of both their poetic merits and defects.

After Canto 49 the conflict of major forces in the poem is represented more and more insistently in terms of a contrast, on various planes, between the Confucian "master man" whose activities are in harmony with the rhythms of nature and the "mean man" who acts contrary to the nature of things. This conflict between the organic and mechanical time-consciousness is given world-historical significance in the Chinese cantos and

6. Quoted by Donald Davie in *Ezra Pound: Poet as Sculptor*, p. 237.

in large measure determines their dramatic structure. Preparation for the dynastic section continues in Canto 50, which vehemently denounces the triumph of usury in the Napoleonic era. The climax of the canto is Pound's analysis of Napoleon's defeat, due not to the intrinsic superiority of the usury-ridden nations ranged against him but to Napoleon's own failure to pay attention to the times and seasons:

> 'Not'
>   said Napoleon 'because of that league of lice
>   but for opposing the Zeitgeist! That was my ruin,
>   That I ran against my own time, turning backward'.

Canto 51, the last of "The Fifth Decad of Cantos" (42–51), establishes the connection between usury and the theme of time more clearly and emphatically than at any previous point. The canto divides at the break into two main parts, each of which is further divisible into two contrasting subsections. The first part consists of a slightly condensed and slightly modified repetition of Canto 45, the famed "Usura Canto," followed by a list of minutely detailed instructions for making and using certain flies for trout-fishing. Usury is described as the destroyer of arts, crafts, life, and love. Usury, says Pound, reminding us of the evil effects of Pity in Canto 30,

> breaks short the young man's courting
> Usury brings age into youth; it lies between the bride
> and the bridegroom
> Usury is against Nature's increase.

W. M. Frohock says that the passage of "precisely detailed directions for tying the Blue Dun and Grannom trout flies" presents an image of the skill and precision that usury is out to destroy. Pound, he says,

> displays two examples of perfectly disinterested creative effort.
> For neither the Blue Dun nor the Grannom is anything but

a lovely piece of work to contemplate. They are both note-worthily useless, even for catching fish.[7]

Frohock's analysis is interesting but does not account for a major element in the passage which has nothing to do with actually *making* the flies. What Pound emphasizes at the beginning, middle, and end of the passage is the precise *times* these flies may be used, as the following lines indicate:

> Blue dun; number 2 in most rivers
> for dark days, when it is cold
> A starling's wing will give you the colour
>
> . . .
>
> 12th of March to 2nd of April
> Hen pheasant's feather does for a fly,
>
> . . .
>
> bright lower body; about the size of pin
> the head should be. can be fished from seven a.m.
> till eleven; at which time the brown marsh fly comes on.
> As long as the brown continues, no fish will take Granham.

There is no doubt that Pound is setting up the ideal of skillful precision against the blight of usury, but the skill here presented is that of the fisherman, who depends for his success on close observation of nature, of the forms and colors of natural objects and of the "times and seasons" that ultimately limit the effectiveness of his fly-casting, no matter how skillfully his flies are constructed.[8]

The skill of the fisherman depends finally on extreme patience, whether in constructing his intricate flies or in awaiting the proper times for their use. In the second part of the canto

7. "The Revolt of Ezra Pound," in *Ezra Pound*, ed. Sutton, pp. 89–90.

8. Mary de Rachewiltz has informed me of the source of this fly-fishing passage: Bowlker's "Art of Angling," Enlarged and Improved Edition by Charles Bowlker, of Ludlow. Proctor & Jones, 1829, London.

the time-sense of the usurers is very carefully characterized as just the opposite to that of the fisherman:

> circling in eddying air; in a hurry;
> the 12: close eyed in the oily wind
> these were the regents.[9]

Usurers are "in a hurry"; they have no patience to tolerate a natural rate of production and so they cause an unnatural speed-up which destroys the integrity of the producer and the quality of the product. With usura, Pound says in Canto 45, pictures are "made to sell and sell quickly" but not "to endure," and in Canto 51 he says that usury destroys "the craftsman, destroying craft." "Slowness is beauty," Pound was to write many years later, in the *Rock-Drill* cantos. But we need look no further than Canto 49, whose theme is that harmony, order, or beauty arises out of "the dimension of stillness."

The latter part of Canto 51 begins with a celebration of "the light of the doer," the mind that intends its ideas to be put into action. (In *Polite Essays* Pound says, " 'The light of the DOER, as it were a form cleaving to it' meant an ACTIVE pattern, a pattern that set things in motion." [10] After a quotation in German on the subject of achieving peace,[11] the rest of the canto deals with the theme of usury. The victims of usury are the passive, the will-less, the non-doers, "You who have lived in a stage set," to whom Geryon addresses himself at the end of the canto:

9. Ezra Pound has told me that the regents are "bankers." I cannot more specifically identify them.

10. Page 51.

11. The allusion to the man in Königsberg speaking on the subject of "a modus vivendi" being achieved between peoples is not to Kant, as the *Annotated Index* misleadingly implies, but to either Adolf Hitler or Rudolf Hess. Mary de Rachewiltz remembers Pound telling her it was "Adolf," but she tells me that Eva Hesse researched the matter and found it to be a quotation from Rudolf Hess.

sang Geryone; [12] I am the help of the aged;
I pay men to talk peace;
Mistress of many tongues; merchant of chalcedony
I am Geryon twin with usura,
You who have lived in a stage set.
A thousand were dead in his folds;
in the eel-fishers basket
Time was of the League of Cambrai:

After the colon, the canto ends with the Confucian "Ch'ing Ming" ideogram, which Pound construes to mean the precise definition of terms. In *Guide to Kulchur* Pound says, "The art of not being exploited begins with 'Ch'ing Ming'!" [13]

The image of the fisherman, introduced in Canto 49 as a symbol of creative accord between man and nature, is intensively employed in Canto 51 to illustrate the ideal adjustment of man to organic time. Such an adjustment is, for Pound, the basis of a healthy economic order. It is only precise knowledge of the environment that enables men to thrive, and usury, in Pound's view, is dedicated to the destruction of such precise awareness. If men depend on precise terminology to communicate exactly their perceptions, then precise definition is usury's greatest enemy. Usury, says Pound, in a passage which amounts almost to direct commentary on Canto 51,

> is not merely in opposition to nature's increase, it is antithetic to discrimination by the senses. Discrimination by the senses is dangerous to avarice. It is dangerous because any perception or any high development of the perceptive faculties may lead to knowledge. The money-changer only thrives on ignorance.[14]

The final two lines seem to sum up the theme of all fifty-one cantos. The serpent Geryon, who contrasts sharply with the eels

12. The Faber and Faber edition has a colon.
13. Page 244.
14. Ibid. p. 281.

in the "eel-fishers basket," is identified finally with "Time," [15] and "Time" in this context is time-as-history, time as a process of destruction due to the anti-social perversion of the will. The ahistorical disposition of the eel-fisher, whose time-consciousness is based on the cyclic motions of the tides, will in Pound's view prevail against the forces of history:

> in the eel-fishers basket
> Time was of the League of Cambrai.

The League of Cambrai was a short-lived association of states against Venice lasting from December 1508 to February 1510. Envying Venetian power, Maximilian and Louis XII formed an alliance at Cambrai against Venice in December, 1508, and the republic was excommunicated in April, 1509, by Pope Julius II, the promoter of the alliance. Several nations, including England and Spain, joined this league against Venice and devoted all their energies to crushing her. Within a few months, their design was very nearly accomplished. Soon afterward, however, because of a turn in the fickle political tide, the Venetians reasserted their power, recaptured most of the territories they had lost to their greedy neighbors, and on February 24, 1510, were even absolved from Pope Julius's censure.[16]

Pound's point in these last lines is that time-as-history, or the pressures of mechanical time, can achieve no more than a temporary victory over the man whose sense of reality is condi-

15. Pound's practice in the last part of this canto (after the break) is not to begin with a capital any line run on as a continuation of the preceding line. The last line of the canto, to be consistent with this practice, should not begin with "Time" capitalized unless Pound is stressing it as a philosophical abstraction, or as a personification of an abstraction, like Geryon, or both. It seems to me that "Time" is now being given as an all-inclusive proper name for usury (Geryon) and the record of historical evils generally.

16. Luigi Salvatorelli, *A Concise History of Italy: From Prehistoric Times to Our Own Day*, trans. Bernard Miall (New York, 1939), pp. 375–76.

tioned by immediate and continual contact with nature. The eel-fisher, like the trout-fisherman, must be finely attuned to nature's changing tones and times if his efforts are to meet with success. Pound implies that the eel-fisher, whose senses must be highly developed, is not likely to mistake a serpent for an eel and allow Geryon to remain for very long in his basket.

In this final canto of Pound's "Fifth Decad," as in Canto 30, the clash between two antagonistic views of reality is presented in terms of two conflicting time-systems. In Canto 30, mechanical time appeared to prevail against order and sanity, but now, in Canto 51, Pound is confident that as long as men continue to live in harmony with organic time, social and economic sanity is capable of reasserting itself in a world befogged by usury. Pound has had the problem of offering a constructive solution to the ills of the world in terms as poetically powerful as he employed in his dissection of the world's evils in the first thirty cantos. He seems finally to achieve this necessary "balance of power" in the Fifth Decad" and particularly in Cantos 45, 47, and 49. Pound gave an estimate of his achievement when, in the fifties, in reply to some student visitors as to how the Cantos were progressing, he said, "It takes a while till you get your bearings—like a detective story—and see how it's going to go. I hit my stride in the *Fifth Decad of Cantos.*" [17]

In this second phase of the *Cantos* another type of hero rises to take up a position of prominence equal to that of the great Confucian statesman and artist—the Noble Savage, whether camel-driver, farmer, or fisherman. One is reminded of Yeats's admiration of peasants and aristocrats, and his scorn of the middle classes for their indifference or positive antagonism to culture. Pound, too, scorns the middle classes, not only because of their cultural insensitivity, but because it is they, most of all, who in his opinion have lost contact with reality and have consequently become the slaves and henchmen of the usurers.

17. Charles Norman, *Ezra Pound* (New York, 1960), p. 444.

The basic theme of the dynastic cantos is set forth at the beginning in Canto 52, most of which, except for an ugly Jew-baiting tirade against usury, consists of a translation of a portion of the *Li Ki* (Pound's translation is from a French version by Father Couvreur, S.J.[18]). Miss Jung informs us that

> Pound reproduces by paraphrase the "Yüeh Ling" (monthly command) chapter from Chapter 5 of the Li Chi [same as Li Ki] (Book of Rites), one of the five Confucian canons. In this chapter each of the four seasons is divided into three months. Each season (and each month of the season) has its characteristic functions in the natural process. To harmonize with nature, man must act in tune with the spirit of the four seasons and the five elements of nature [metal, wood, water, fire, earth]. . . . In Pound's paraphrase of the "Yüeh Ling" summer alone receives a lengthy treatment as in the original.[19]

Throughout these Chinese cantos, Confucian order is based on harmony with organic time, whereas intervening periods of disorder are connected with the mechanical time-consciousness, that is, the imposition of laws which are unjust because they are out of step with nature. It is in the sphere of economic justice that the conflict between the two time-views is most significant for society, so that Pound is centrally concerned with translating the theme of the *Li Ki* into economic terms. Two basically opposed economic policies recur repeatedly in these cantos, the policy of those rulers who impose a fixed tax, and the policy of those who exact a tithe.[20] The Confucian idea held to the justice of the tithe system, which is obviously an elastic measure that recognizes nature's variable rhythms of productivity from

18. Noted by Achilles Fang in *The Pound Newsletter*, ed. John Edwards, No. 9 (January 1956), p. 4.

19. Angela Chih-Ying Jung, "Ezra Pound and China" (Ph.D. dissertation: University of Washington, 1955), pp. 114–15.

20. Henry Swabey, "Towards an A.B.C. of History," *An Examination of Ezra Pound*, ed. Peter Russell, p. 187.

year to year, whereas the fixed tax system is a rigidly mechanical
measure which in a bad year can reduce a people to utter pov-
erty.

At the basis of the *Li Ki* is the philosophy of the *Yin* and
Yang, and if either of these two cosmic principles is suppressed
—for example, by failure on the king's part to perform the activities appropriate to a particular season—abnormal natural
phenomena occur, such as earthquakes.[21] In the *Li Ki* portion
of Canto 52 Pound includes definite reference to the *Yin-Yang*
(darkness-light) philosophy, as we see in the directions for the
month of June (italics mine):

> Then goes the sun into Gemini
> Virgo in mid heaven at sunset
>   indigo must not be cut
> No wood burnt into charcoal
>   gates are all open, no tax on the booths.
>
>   . . .
>   Month of the longest days
> Life and death are now equal
>   *Strife is between light and darkness*
> Wise man stays in his house.

Throughout the China cantos, whenever the sovereign disobeys
the "Monthly Commands" and throws his people out of harmony with the seasons, natural anomalies abound, as in the following instance from Canto 53 (p. 17):

> The Lady Pao Sse brought earthquakes. TCHEOU falleth,
>   folly, folly, false fires no true alarm
>   Mount Ki-chan is broken.
> Ki-chan is crumbled in the 10th moon of the 6th year of
>   Yeou Ouang
> Sun darkened, the rivers were frozen. . . .

Pound continually reminds us in this manner of the need
for government to pay heed to the times and seasons. The good

21. Fung Yu-Lan, A *Short History of Chinese Philosophy*, p. 138.

Confucian ruler, like the seventh-century Emperor Tai Tsong, is an observer of the seasons in all that he performs:

> TAI TSONG was no friend to taozers hochangs and foés.[22]
> Was observer of seasons, saying:
> > Take not men from the plough
> Let judges fast for three days before passing capital sentence

And his counselor, Ouei-Tching,

> Said: in war time we want men of ability
> > in peace we want also character
> 300 were unjailed to do their spring ploughing
> > and they all came back in October.
> > > (Canto 54, pp. 31–32.)

The Mongol dynasty (A.D. 1206–1368) ended with the dissolute Emperor Chun-Ti, who was so steeped in useless luxury that when he was being swamped with rebellion he could not rise to the measures the times called for. Pound associates him with the image of the clock, symbol of the mechanical time-consciousness out of touch with reality:

> Tienouan beat the rebels, Taipou was killed by rebels
> > Singki respected
> and the lamas put on a ballet for CHUNTI
> > in ivory headgear
> castagnettes crinkling and clacking, and a Tang dance
> > without fancy clothes
> Kongpei said to Toto: Don't open dispatches,
> > Dragon barge drifted with music
> Statue poured water amidship
> Spirits struck the night watches
> > they say CHUNTI invented this clockwork
> The Red Caps called their candidate Ming Ouan.

22. "Taozers" are Taoists; "hochangs" and "foés" are Buddhists.

The *Annotated Index* tells us that Toto, honest minister of state under Chun-Ti, tried to quell the rebellion but was hindered by court intrigue. The Red Caps were a group of rebels (the White Lily Society) who rose against Chun-Ti.

The image of the clock is to mark what I consider the climactic episode of the Chinese history cantos, the first meeting between East and West, Confucianism and Christianity, as described in Canto 58. Christianity will represent the culminating intrusion of disorder in China and will conflict philosophically with the Confucian concept of time. To prepare for this meeting, Pound selects his materials in the manner of a dramatist or novelist. As steps in the development of this philosophical conflict, he introduces the bad effects on China of the Taoists, Buddhists, and the government-employed eunuchs. In Canto 54 (p. 27) the disorders with which they are associated are crisply suggested:

> war, taxes, oppression
> backsheesh, taoists, bhuddists
> wars, taxes, oppressions
>
> .   .   .
>
> HAN HUON was run by eunuchs
> HAN LING was governed by eunuchs
>   wars, murders and crime news.

For Pound, what the Taoists, Buddhists, and Eunuchs have in common is a selfish, anti-social philosophy and behavior. Taoism stresses mysticism and passive contemplation as opposed to the practical activism and socially oriented ethic of Confucianism. In addition, the spiritually profound message of Lao Tzu was quickly corrupted in China by a superstitious, devil-hunting "Taoist" priesthood. Buddhism, founded on the doctrine that all earthly existence is evil, is equally incompatible with a Confucian sense of social values. Once again on page 27, Pound gives the gist of Buddhist or Taoist doctrine as "emptiness is the beginning of all things," and he is continually at pains to attack the underlying dualism of such doctrines. He quotes, for example, the anti-Buddhist intellectual Tan Tchin [Fan Tchin] as saying, in an attempt to refute the dualistic distinction between body and mind, "Thought is to body as its edge to a sword" (pp. 29–30).

Taoists and Buddhists are never mentioned in these cantos except with scorn and derision for the obvious reason that they are at the opposite extreme philosophically from Confucianism. Pound is often vulgar or near-vulgar, calling them "goddam bhuddists," "taozers," and "shave-heads." For Donald Davie, Pound's "strident language" in condemning these religious sects "recalls fisticuffs in the schoolyard and brutal and contemptible rabble-rousing. There is no alternative to writing off this whole section of Pound's poem as pathological and sterile." [23] If the critic were to apply this criterion consistently, he would have to write off the *Cantos* as a whole: as far back as the Malatesta cantos Pound introduces this low style in calling Pope Pius II an "s.o.b." I find it more likely that Pound, indulging in none of the "ambiguity" frequently desiderated by modern critics, is identifying himself in the dramatic sense strictly with the Confucian point of view. Such an approach tends to degenerate into slapstick, and I am convinced that such low-comedy relief is precisely the effect Pound is after. (Perhaps this comic effect, the serio-comic effect of whipping an historically dead horse, is the desired "ambiguity," after all.) When Pound is loading invective against the modern usurers and their presumed associates, however, no slapstick effect is intended, for his material is not historically distanced; his enemies are still very much alive and dangerous. The one-sided tone of these cantos derives also from the one-sided tone of their historical source, De Mailla's massive *Histoire générale de la Chine*, translated from the Chinese between 1777–85. Achilles Fang writes that "there is not a

23. Davie, *Ezra Pound: Poet as Sculptor*, p. 161.

kind word about either Taoists or Buddhists in De Mailla, nor, since Pound followed his source, in the *Cantos*." [24]

The following passage (p. 34) is typical of the dramatic identification of Pound's own voice with that of the Confucian who is relating events:

> and we were sad that the north cities, Chépoutching
> and Ngan-yong were in hands of the tartars
> > (*Tou-san*) [25]
> And there came a taozer babbling of the elixir
> that wd/ make men live without end
> and the taozer died very soon after that.

Pound attacks what he regards as an egocentric Taoist refusal to recognize the natural order and the limits of the individual within that order. At the beginning of Canto 56 the unrealistic (or, at least, un-Confucian) Taoists are again presented as charlatans (" 'There is', said the Taozers,/ 'A medicine that gives immortality.' "), and at the end of the canto Pound reports that the great Confucian emperor, Hong Vou, "declined a treatise on Immortality/ offered by Taozers." In Canto 57 various emperors are pictured as succumbing to Taoist illusions. Forgetting their social responsibilities, they go "seeking elixir" or indulge in magic and alchemy. Finally, in Canto 58, the Ming dynasty is sent headlong toward ruin by the Emperor Chin Tsong (reigned 1573–1620), who fell completely under the influence of the court eunuchs. At this point, when the Ming dynasty is caving in from a lack of internal order combined with the military incursions of the Japanese and the tartars, the Christian theme is introduced:

> and Père Ricci brought a clock to the Emperor
> that was set in a tower

. . .

24. "Notes on China and the Cantos," *The Pound Newsletter*, No. 9 (January 1956), p. 3.
25. *Tou-san* means "tartars."

> And the eunuchs of Tientsin brought Père Mathieu to court
> > where the Rites answered:
> > Europe has no bonds with our empire
> and never receives our law
> As to these images, pictures of god above and a virgin
> they have little intrinsic worth. Do gods rise boneless to heaven
> that we shd/ believe your bag of their bones?
> The Han Yu tribunal therefore considers it useless
> to bring such novelties into the PALACE,
> we consider it ill advised, and are contrary
> to receiving either these bones or père Mathieu.
> > The emperor CHIN TSONG received him.

The symbol of the Christian West is of course the clock, which represents Western success in imposing an abstract, mechanical order on the social existence of men. But the mathematical-technical know-how of the Christians eventually comes to be regarded by the Chinese as a double-edged sword. It turns out that what the Chinese are most grateful to the missionaries for is "reforming our mathematics" and "making us cannon" (Canto 60, p. 77). However, fear of *Christian* cannon finally turns the great Ch'ing emperor, Kang Hi, against the spread of Christianity within Chinese borders (p. 77):

> their vessels stand any wind and carry a hundred cannon
> if ten of 'em get into Canton
> > who knows what cd/ happen.

"All I know," continues the petition of "Tching Mao, a sea captain," to the Emperor, "is they refuged in Manilla/ And now they are top dog in Manilla."

The clock, therefore, ultimately has the ominous significance of a death-symbol, the threat posed by the abstract, mechanical time-consciousness of the West against the integrity of Confucian civilization. It is worth a slight digression to indicate the extremely concrete, organic way in which the Chinese actually did tell time before the missionaries came:

The most integral and involving time sense imaginable is that expressed in the Chinese and Japanese cultures. Until the coming of the missionaries in the seventeenth century, and the introduction of the mechanical clocks, the Chinese and Japanese had for thousands of years measured time by graduations of incense. Not only the hours and days, but the seasons and zodiacal signs were simultaneously indicated by a succession of carefully ordered scents. . . . The sense of smell is not only the most subtle and delicate of the human senses; it is, also, the most iconic in that it involves the entire human sensorium more fully than any other sense. . . . Societies that measured time scents would tend to be so cohesive and so profoundly unified as to resist every kind of change.[26]

The corrupt Chin Tsong accepted the Jesuit missionary Père Mathieu Ricci (and his clock) against the advice of the Tribunal of "Rites" who in 1601 were expressly commissioned by him to judge of the merits of Christianity. Their rejection of Christianity seems to me to be the thematic climax of the Chinese history cantos. It is notably the eunuchs who lead Père Ricci to court. The similarity implied between eunuch and Catholic priest—their truncated relationship to reality—is central to the meaning of what the Rites find to criticize about Christianity. In the holistic Confucian view of the Tribunal, Christianity is founded on an unnatural approach to reality, the disparagement of body in favor of some abstract, spiritual entity that is considered capable of a separate existence apart from the body: "Do gods rise boneless to heaven," say the Tribunal, "that we should believe your bag of their bones?" Christian dualism, a threat to the first principles of the Confucian world-view, necessarily appears a threat to social order as well. In Confucianism, the man who lacks order within can spread only disorder about him. The Tribunal has no choice but to recommend that Père Ricci return to Europe.

The rest of Canto 58 is a rapid, impressionistic account of

26. Marshall McLuhan, *Understanding Media*, p. 136.

the downfall of the Ming dynasty and the rise of the Manchu (Ch'ing dynasty). The Christians are now listed among the elements of disorder leading to the Ming downfall:

> Against order, lao, bhud and lamas,
> night clubs, empresses' relatives, and hoang miao,
> poisoning life with mirages, ruining order; TO KALON.

("Hoang miao," or "Hong-mao," as is clear from Canto 60, p. 75, means "red-heads," i.e., at first Dutch and English traders, but finally, Europeans or Christians in general.)

The Manchu dynasty, which replaced the corrupt Ming, is founded in Confucian order. Pound develops this idea not only through his description in Canto 58 of the wisdom of Tai Tsong, second Manchu emperor, but also at the beginning of Canto 59, which pays eloquent tribute to Chun Tchi, the son of Tai Tsong. Chun Tchi revered the *Chi-King* or Book of Odes (presumably collected and edited by Confucius himself) and wrote a preface to them in which he reveals his deep understanding of their significance:

> less a work of the mind than of affects
> brought forth from the inner nature
> here sung in these odes.
> Urbanity in externals, virtu in internals
> some in a high style for the rites
> some in humble;
> for Emperors; for the people.
>
> (Canto 59, p. 70)

Chun Tchi has respect for the "affects/ brought forth from the inner nature" which, in the Odes, are a perpetual mine of wisdom for the guidance of life. The Odes are not a mere "work of the mind," by which Chun Tchi seems clearly to mean the abstract or superficial intelligence out of touch with the nature of things, devoid of either *virtu* (generative power) at its base, or

of urbanity in action. This quotation from the Emperor's preface is Pound's comment on the nature and function of his own
book of "odes," or cantos, which have equally developed from
"the inner nature" and should, if based on order within, offer
its precise vision of realities as a guide to the attainment of integrity, or wholeness, "for Emperors; for the people."

The philosophical climax of these cantos, the Tribunal's rejection of Christianity in principle, is complemented by its
dramatic sequel in the last of the China cantos, when the
Christians are expelled physically. Yong Tching, son of Kang
Hi,

> putt out Xtianity
> chinese found it so immoral
> his mandarins found this sect so immoral
>
> . . .
>
> Xtians being such sliders and liars.
>
> . . .
>
> Xtians are disturbing good customs
> seeking to uproot Kung's laws
> seeking to break up Kung's teaching.
>
> (Canto 61, p. 80)

A final comment on Christian dualism by a court mandarin re-
emphasizes the metaphysical incompatibility of Christianity
and Confucianism:

> 'You Christers wanna have foot on two boats
>   and when them boats pulls apart
> you will d/n well git a wettin' ' said a court mandarin
> tellin' 'em.
>
> (Canto 61, p. 82)

Earlier in this chapter I discussed the Adams Cantos as a
continuation of the dynastic theme of the Chinese cantos. Although the Adams Cantos are logically called for in the scheme
of the poem, I feel that Pound has treated the subject in exces-

232

sive detail and at disproportionate length, so that after the Chinese cantos the Adams section figures as an anti-climactic bulge which even the relatively open form of the *Cantos* can ill assimilate. If I could see any significantly new thematic development in the Adams Cantos worthy of such lengthy treatment, my opinion would be different, but I find only the repetition and expansion of previously developed themes.

The general failure of these cantos to achieve poetic intensity is hardly disputable. Didacticism now prevails, and little is left of the sense of humor which so often enlivens the Chinese history cantos. Pound is concerned, in the late 1930's, to keep America out of the coming European war, and he makes certain to stress Adams's similar policy of preserving American neutrality. In Canto 65, for example, a dark vertical line in the right-hand margin (p. 123) sets off this particular passage for special note:

> For my part thought that Americans
> Had been embroiled in European wars long enough
> > easy to see that
> France and England wd/ try to embroil us OBvious
> that all powers of Europe will be continually at manoeuvre
> to work us into their real or imaginary balances
> > of power. . . .

Aside from all consideration of poetic value, the Adams Cantos nevertheless do have an orderly structure, and whatever is "repeatedly arbitrary" in the method probably results from a lack of proportion rather than from a lack of definite structural outline. William Vasse, in an essay called "American History and the *Cantos*," sees this structure in terms of Pound's own early remark that the form of the *Cantos* is based on a division between "the permanent, the recurrent, the casual":[27]

> The structure of these cantos is based upon a counterpointing of permanent, recurrent, and casual themes. . . . John Adams

27. *Letters*, p. 239.

is the permanent theme. . . . Much of the material is casual; it is stated once and never repeated, but it serves as the background, a panorama of minor personalities, events, ideas, and interests against which are placed Adams' most important actions, which are made recurrent. . . . In the same manner those events which, in Pound's consideration, were the most important to the nation are emphasized by repetition: the Stamp Act, the writs of assistance, the Boston Massacre, the Continental Congresses, the Paris Treaty Conference.[28]

The recurrence of critical historical events seems to be the clue to the patterning of imagery in these cantos. There appears to be no consistent chronological structure determining the general design, but one notes, for example, that Canto 63 deals primarily with the education of the youthful Adams, Canto 64 concentrates on the period from 1761 to 1773 (including major events from the Writs of Assistance to the Boston Tea Party), and that Canto 70 deals with Adams near the end of his term as President. In the last of these cantos (71), Adams is glancing in retrospect over his entire career. No clear chronological pattern emerges, however, from the intervening cantos. William Vasse observes that the Adams Cantos not only consist of excerpts from the ten-volume edition of the *Works of John Adams* (ed. Charles Francis Adams), but that these cantos follow the *order* of this edition volume by volume.[29] The volumes are arranged according to types of documents (a diary, political writings, state papers, etc.) and so did not furnish Pound with an inherent narrative structure. Part of the strength of the Chinese cantos derives from Pound's faithfulness to the *chronological* ordering of De Mailla's account of Chinese history.

The principle of "precise definition," stressed repeatedly by the presence of the Ch'ing Ming ideogram, is at the root of Adams's varied intellectual interests and profound knowledge of government systems, law, and economics. Pound considers

28. *The Pound Newsletter*, No. 5 (January 1955), p. 17.
29. Ibid. p. 18.

Adams's implementation of the Ch'ing Ming the instrument which preserved the American Revolution in the early years of struggle. The poet presents Adams in the continual process of "making it new," giving permanent form to the American ideal of freedom, steering the new-sprung nation through the Scylla and Charybdis (France and England) of a European policy which strove to deplete the resources of the infant nation by entangling it in foreign wars.

Fundamental to Adams's respect for precise terms is his scrupulous attention to the times and seasons, his Confucian "discretion in perceiving the when." In Canto 62 he criticizes England as "always too late (*sero*)/ Britain never in season" (p. 91). Soon afterwards, Pound quotes the principle which is the basis of Adams's entire political career—"fundamentals in critical moments" (p. 93). In the last of the Adams Cantos Pound makes clear, in another brief excerpt, the relation between the principle of precise definition and the need to observe the times and seasons of things (Pound's italics):

> to elucidate the meaning of words *at that time*
> and then determine intentions.[30]

30. One can do no more than speculate about the plans Pound had for the next section of the poem until the missing Cantos 72 and 73 are printed. They were the only ones written during the war years, and there is conjecture that they have been suppressed because of libelous content concerning politicians who are still alive. According to Mary de Rachewiltz, however, who knows these cantos and was with her father during the years they were composed, they contain nothing libelous. They were written in Italian, and the fact is hardly surprising when one considers Pound's isolation from the English-speaking world during the early war years. The Princess de Rachewiltz further informs me that these cantos deal with Pound's friends, and that their style is prelusive of the *Pisan Cantos*.

PART THREE

Paradiso

❌❌❌❌❌❌❌❌❌❌❌❌❌❌❌❌❌❌

TIME AS LOVE

❌❌❌❌❌❌❌❌❌❌❌❌❌❌❌❌❌❌

CHAPTER X

The Pisan Cantos

PARADISAL MOTIFS, intimations of ideal order, have mingled with infernal and purgatorial elements throughout the *Cantos* in accordance with the general contrapuntal texture of the poem. At the same time, however, the *Cantos* has displayed a progressive or linear structure in passing from a predominantly infernal phase through a purgatorial section. Now, with *The Pisan Cantos*, the paradisal state of consciousness achieves dominance, and all the materials of the poem are once again thrown into a new perspective.

The paradisal vision is not suddenly thrust upon the reader like a blinding light but is circuitously, arduously, and suspensefully approached. It is prepared for by the parallel development of images, feelings, and insights which merge into successive stages of synthesis. These partial syntheses, difficult to maintain, are themselves occasionally subject to disintegration, but spiritual synthesis always manages to reassert itself against the pressure of the quotidian. Finally, the sensibility of the poet achieves a breakthrough into the realm of the permanent; a culminating vision is vouchsafed him that is not subject to dissolution, but, on the contrary, becomes his permanent possession and the basis of the future articulation of the poem. The strength it gives him is great enough even to reconcile him to the menacing possibility of approaching death. The experience can perhaps best be described as mystical, for the poet-voyager emerges from it in a mood of tranquility that can be likened to "the peace that passeth understanding." Canto 47, it is true, also involves a mystical experience, one which provides the spiritual basis for the cantos that follow it, but the mystical vision we are now to be concerned with takes place on a higher level of spiritual sophistication.

The transitional stages that prepare for this moment of vision amount to a process of purgatorial cleansing in the Dantesque sense, and this long, involved effort by the poet at self-purification takes up nearly ninety-eight out of the 118 pages of *The Pisan Cantos*. The bulk of these cantos consists of memories, largely of Pound's London days. They are actually cycles of memories, a sifting and resifting of the past that follows an associational rather than chronological order. The materials that in previous sections of cantos were for the most part literary are now autobiographical, and the emphasis is less on books than on the men behind the books, less on the public, achieved tradition than on the personalities through whom the tradition was given new life.

His pipe dream of a fascist millennium shattered, Pound retrieves bit by bit, through an inventory of memory, the viable, indestructible fragments of himself, the atoms that have not been split by Time, from which he reconstructs a new self invulnerable to Time. One can not help recalling these words from Hemingway's *A Farewell to Arms*, words which Pound may have recalled in composing the Pisan sequence: "The world breaks every one and afterward many are strong at the broken places." [1] Although Pound mentions Hemingway only once in the *Pisan Cantos* (Canto 74, p. 5), he seems to have used his famous image of the burned and broken ants who, in the last chapter of *A Farewell*, when Frederick's fortunes have reached their lowest ebb, symbolize mankind as they swarm confusedly over a burning log and fall into the fire. Like the surviving but broken hero of the novel himself, "Some got out,

1. *A Farewell to Arms*, Scribner Library edition (New York, 1962), pp. 258–59.

their bodies burnt and flattened, and went off not knowing where they were going." [2] In Canto 76 (p. 36), Pound writes:

> As a lone ant from a broken ant-hill
> from the wreckage of Europe, ego scriptor.

Shortly after the moment of paradisal vision, insect imagery comes strikingly into play once more, but now to signify spiritual reintegration and rebirth: "and Brother Wasp is building a very neat house," from which there soon emerges "an infant, green as new grass," who soon descends into the grass "to carry our news/ . . . to them that dwell under the earth" (Canto 83, pp. 110–11).

The basic metaphor of a voyage is insisted upon, now more than ever before in the *Cantos,* through the repeated use of the term "periplum." The word implies not only a voyage of discovery, like Hanno's, but in the case of a poet, a voyage of spiritual discovery. As a narrative device, the "periplum" image binds the disparate elements of the *Pisan Cantos* into a pattern of continuity. We have come to expect that sequences of images embody "successive discoveries breaking upon the consciousness of the voyager," [3] but we are not necessarily helped in this manner to understand the nature of these discoveries.

The basic step in analysis, it would seem, is recognition that the persona of the poet is traversing several different orders or categories of experience. Forrest Read, in an excellent article on the *Pisan Cantos,* says that "The periplum of the persona passes through three general areas of experience. First, that of Pound's own past and present"; second, "that of the natural world which surrounds the [army detention] camp"; and third, "that

2. Ibid. p. 338.
3. M. L. Rosenthal, *A Primer of Ezra Pound* (New York, 1960), p. 44.

of ancient wisdom: folk, classical, Christian, and Confucian."
Pound seeks a synthesis of these three realms.[4] The poet's

> persona is making a journey among the experiences out of which
> the consciousness is being formed, and is seeking a new order-
> ing of the three realms: of self (as prisoner of time, infernal);
> of nature (as time redeemed in its harmony with the process,
> purgatorial); and of ancient wisdom (as revelation of the pro-
> cess in the human mind, paradisal).[5]

Within this threefold category, as outlined by Read, some
further distinctions, which will prove very helpful as our analysis progresses, can be made. The persona experiences, as it turns
out, three different orders of time and one of timelessness. The
poet's own past and present are dramatized as two fundamentally opposed time-realms. The flow of images out of the poet's
past offsets the brutal, strident counterflow of images of the
prison camp, which constitutes the narrative present. The third
time-realm is the order of non-human nature present within
and beyond the camp confines, and symbolized especially by the
movements of sun and moon. The realm of timelessness is, as
Read says, "that of ancient wisdom," but the most significant
embodiment of that wisdom for the *Pisan Cantos* is non-
rational and non-discursive—the element of myth, especially
the gods and goddesses, and chief among those, Aphrodite.

The movement of the poet's consciousness towards reintegration has as its symbolic goal the vision of Aphrodite. The
character of this movement is twofold: "Simultaneous with the
movement of purification is a movement of affection, an expansion from what often seems in Pound a too-intellectual and little urgent sensibility." [6] Pound's reconstructed self is cemented
by affection, love, *humanitas*, or, in Confucian terms, *jen*. We

4. "The Pattern of the *Pisan Cantos*," *Sewanee Review* LXV (Summer 1957), 405–6.
5. Ibid. p. 416.
6. Ibid. p. 409.

have already seen that in the middle phase of the *Cantos* Pound expanded his sympathies to include the common man, but he did so out of emphathy with the economic plight of the masses and seems to have been motivated more by hatred of usury than by love of man. Conversely, in the *Pisan Cantos* it is love which prompts Pound's occasional outpourings of hatred. Love is recognized as the self-sufficient reason for being, and the key phrase of these cantos and those to come is "Amo ergo sum" (Canto 80).

The re-ordering of the self which is the primary "action" of these cantos involves the fusion and reconciliation, in the mind of the poet, of the disparate realms of experience. The first major fusion or identification that takes place is that of the self with the "process," the Confucian *Tao* or harmony of the natural order. Such a fusion did, in fact, take place in Canto 47, but the identification there was that of the biological self with the rhythms of nature. The ego, limited in time and space, was de-emphasized in order to stress the vaster importance of the relatively immortal species, and man and nature were pictured as an organic continuum through Pound's exploitation of such a multiple animal-vegetable rebirth image as "seed." The problem of effecting a fusion of self and process in the *Pisan Cantos* is much more difficult because Pound is now attempting identification of the ego itself, of his own personality (albeit dramatized) as Ezra Pound, with the great impersonal process.

The fusion attempted is that of the spirit with nature, and common ground is happily discovered in the phenomenon of memory. Personal memory, like the rhythms of nature, is marked by recurrence. Moreover, again like nature, memory has a creative role. Just as nature guarantees rebirth and continuity in the plant and animal kingdoms, the human memory infuses with new life whatever was truly alive in the cultural past and carries on the "live tradition." That which is of lasting value, therefore, in the individual human memory, transcends the limitations of time and space. Memory, like "the process," contains

its own sort of "seeds" and is equally capable of self-regenera-
tion and self-perpetuation. The process itself is a manifestation
of a sort of undying cosmic memory, and the individual human
memory not only corresponds to it analogically but is conceived
of as an actual extension or counterpart of the process on a
different plane of being. Memory and "the process" emerge in
these cantos as two complementary aspects of a "superpro-
cess."

Apart from such metaphysical intuitions as these, which I
believe Pound is quite clearly expressing, he makes a parallel
moral discovery of even greater significance. He realizes that
whatever is lasting in memory is alive because formed there by
love:

> nothing matters but the quality
> of the affection—
> in the end—that has carved the trace in the mind
> dove sta memoria.
>
> (Canto 76, p. 35)

This initial insight is the basis for the climactic vision, which
occurs in Canto 80. Love, already established as the ground of
the permanently valuable in memory, comes at last to be recognized also as the hub of the great process of the universe itself.
The recurrent patterns in the personal memory, in the impersonal, cultural memory (the "tradition"), and in the process of
nature itself, are regarded as the temporal manifestations of Absolute Love. To put it more precisely, in the world of the *Pisan
Cantos*, cyclical or organic time is the fundamental *form* of
love. In accordance with the holistic tendency of the *Cantos*,
abstract or Absolute Love does not really exist for Pound apart
from its form. When I speak of Absolute Love with respect to
the *Cantos*, the idea intended is that of "the concrete universal" as explained in Chapter 4. Just as Dante's supreme vision
of the divine takes the concrete form of a rose, so Pound's culminating vision of love takes the form of Aphrodite.

These cantos begin in despair and end in triumph, and it is the function of the very long first canto of the sequence to effect a major transition between despair and renewed hope. "If the canto open[s] in chaos," says Emery, "it closes in recognition of the potential of order—the ordering possible through memory." [7] It is desirable to trace at least the main lines by which such a change in outlook occurs.

The first line of the canto, "The enormous tragedy of the dream in the peasant's bent shoulders," concentrates the three states of the soul, infernal, purgatorial, and paradisal, that interact throughout this section of the poem and have counterpointed each other through the *Cantos* as a whole. The *Pisan Cantos* open in "enormous tragedy," but their entire movement is toward a re-assertion of the viable elements in the "dream." Pound transforms infernal tragedy into divine comedy. "The peasant's bent shoulders" is the purgatorial motif of the line. In what I have designated as Phase Two of the *Cantos*, the peasant has emerged in the role of indestructible cultural minimum, the immemorial survivor of historical tragedy because of a simple wisdom which consists in his remaining in harmony with "the process." The peasant, and the whole world of nature in the *Pisan Cantos*, is emblematic of "the process," and consciousness of "the process" is the heart of Pound's Purgatorio. Restatement of the "enormous tragedy" follows in the reference to Mussolini's death; "the dream" is then presented as the ideal "city of Dioce"; and next, the image of the peasant is transposed into a passage concerning "the process."

The following lines (19–21), recalling the periplum of Hanno in Canto 40, give the first intimation of the union that the poet-voyager desires to establish once more with "the process": " 'the great periplum brings in the stars to our shore.' " Pound projects his own spiritual journey on to the motions of stars and planets, which more and more come to symbolize the poet's progress toward self-renewal. There follow in swift suc-

7. *Ideas into Action*, p. 135.

cession three images of profound importance to the development of the Pisan sequence:

> if the suave air give way to scirocco
> ΟΥ ΤΙΣ, ΟΥ ΤΙΣ? [8] Odysseus
> > the name of my family.
> the wind also of the process,
> > > sorella la luna

The air, or wind can either be destructive or gentle, can either bring tragedy or foster the dream. Potentialities for both creation and destruction, the Yang and the Yin, are "of the process," or inherent in the nature of things and are, therefore, neither moral nor immoral. Pound, however, as a Confucian moralist, is "led to construct ethics upon fundamentally amoral material. . . . Confucianism . . . places the responsibility for action on the individual. Man's efforts are to be directed toward furthering the creative phase [of the process, the Yang] . . . and impeding the progress of the destructive [Yin]." [9] Historical tragedy, for Pound, is the result of society's loss of harmony with the process, and in the course of the *Pisan Cantos* Pound will not only share the collective guilt of Western man but will also experience the ordeal of self-purgation that he believes society as a whole ought to undergo if it is to step back into harmony with nature. The theme of Odysseus tricking the Cyclops by giving his name as "no man" sets forth the poet-voyager's hope that will and intelligence will ultimately prevail against the brutal circumstances of history. Finally, the moon ("sister moon") becomes the most important single image in the *Pisan Cantos* because it eventually comes to gather up the whole complex of feelings and intuitions out of which the poet's climactic vision of love emerges. Here the moon is "sister" of the

8. "Ou tis" means "no man."

9. Edgar F. Racey, Jr., "Pound's *Cantos*: the Structure of a Modern Epic" (Ph.D. dissertation: Claremont Graduate School, 1963), pp. 4–5.

process, of the wind, of Odysseus-Pound; and as sister of the poet, she already is suggestive of the bond of affection that is eventually to unite the poet with the cosmic process on a higher spiritual level than he has as yet been able to achieve.

The "tragedy of the dream" soon finds its objective correlative in a major pair of contrasting images from the narrative present of the poet, the opposition of the prison camp to Mt. Taishan, a holy place of sacrifice and the name Pound gives to the imperturbable mountain seen in the distance beyond the camp:

> from the death cells in sight of Mt. Taishan @ Pisa
> as Fujiyama at Gardone
> when the cat walked the top bar of the railing
> and the water was still on the West side
> flowing toward the Villa Catullo
> where with sound ever moving
>   in diminutive poluphloisboios
> in the stillness outlasting all wars.
>
> (Canto 74, p. 5)

In this passage, Taishan is associated with the theme of "stillness," a theme which has already become powerfully connected with the theme of love through the *Canzone d'Amore* of Cavalcanti (Canto 36). This canzone, it should be noted, is the seed from which the major themes of love and memory in the Pisan sequence are derived. Mt. Taishan is the still point around which the broken world of Europe, symbolized by the prison camp, whirls out of harmony with the process in strident, mechanical, militaristic rhythms—the world of time-as-history beating out of phase with the rhythms of nature.

The major symbol of mechanical time in the Pisans is the military band of the camp, especially the drum, which suggests the inhuman linear movements of the troops that march to its beat:

> the voiceless with bumm drum and banners,
>   and the ideogram of the guard roosts
> el triste pensier si volge
>   ad Ussel. A Ventadour
>   va il consire, el tempo rivolge.
>
>   (Canto 74, p. 6)

Pound, like Thoreau, responds to the sound of a different drummer. His "sad thought goes to Ussel. To Ventadour goes his counsel, *time returns.*" Memory, in which time is recoverable or cyclical, turns back in time against the linear and unidirectional logic of the drum beat. Not only memory, but nature, too, is solace against the apparent victory of the "bumm drum" [10]: the rain brings out the smell of mint, and "A lizard," says Pound, "upheld me."

Against the pressure of physical imprisonment and social injustice, Pound asserts the principle of attention to the times and seasons: "Tempus tacendi, tempus loquendi" (p. 7).[11] The principle of timeliness introduced the whole second movement of the *Cantos*, which surged upward out of an *inferno* of despair into a *purgatorio* of hope. Rising against the note of hope, the theme of death ("Till was hung yesterday") and the growing mood of personal defeat, stressed by Pound's repeated description of himself as "a man on whom the sun has gone down," lead to anxiety-ridden introspection and awareness that the forces of mechanical time are not alone in threatening his extinction. Not only rebirth, but death, too, is of the process, and the moon and sun remind him of both:

---

10. The spelling "bumm" stresses the continuous rumbling of the musically incompetent (bum) drumming that reminds also of the military "music" in Canto XXI (l. 139) of Dante's *Inferno,* in which the captain of the squad of devils "made a trumpet of his rear."

11. The elements of the Latin phrase appear in reverse order in Canto 31. The reason for the present sequence will be discussed at a better opportunity.

> as the light sucks up vapor
>   and the tides follow Lucina [12]
> that had been a hard man in some ways
>   a day as a thousand years.

One recalls "wave falls and the hand falls" from Canto 42, but now the inevitability of death reaches Pound as a deeply personal matter. The meaning of "a hard man" intended in the present context becomes fairly clear if one looks ahead to Canto 80, where Pound says, "I have been hard as youth sixty years." The illusion of youth shattered, Pound sees himself as subject to the diurnal rhythms of moon and sun, and realizes that he has paid scant attention to the barely perceptible running out of his own life in his concentration on the optimistic, transpersonal import of the rhythms of the process. He has mistakenly regarded his limited number of days as if each were "a thousand years." The emotional force of this insight leads him shortly to the elegiac theme from "The Seafarer":

> Lordly men are to earth o'ergiven
>   these the companions: [13]
>   (Canto 74, p. 10)

Nostalgic memories of Ford, Yeats, Joyce, James, Plarr,[14] and others, companions recalled with affection, rapidly succeed one

12. Lucina is the Roman title of Juno (which was later applied also to the moon-goddess Diana) as goddess of light and childbirth.

13. Pound is also underlining the fulfillment of Tiresias's prophecy in Canto 1: " 'Odysseus/ 'Shalt return through spiteful Neptune, over dark seas,/ 'Lose all companions.' " The identification of Pound's personal odyssey with the mythic one of Odysseus, here made explicit, now achieves the dimension of tragedy.

14. Victor Plarr, a minor poet of the nineties and librarian of England's Royal College of Surgeons, appears as Monsieur Verog in *Hugh Selwyn Mauberley*. Mention of Plarr is one of many links in this canto and throughout the Pisan sequence with the material of *Mauberley*, material which is particularly important, as I intend to show, in forming the climax of Canto 74.

another: "où sont les heurs of that year?" Pound asks, his allusion to Villon serving to dignify his personal nostalgia and pain.
Only now does he feel the full impact of his loss, because only
now does he fully realize the depth of love he bore those "lordly
men" and those golden hours—the best years of his life. Dormant love, stirred out of the past into renewed action by the
power of memory, begins its redeeming work in the infernal
present of the prison compound and leaps out to one of
Pound's new "companions," Mr. Edwards

> of the Baluba mask: "doan you tell no one
> I made you that table".

The "greatest" virtue, Pound says,

> is charity
> to be found among those who have not observed
> regulations.
> (Canto 74, p. 12)

The theme of love is soon transposed into terms of myth.
Allusion is made to Aphrodite, who "by Terracina rose from the
sea Zephyr behind her." The lines following those which allude
to Aphrodite hint at a connection between the sea-born, wind-
borne love-goddess and the process: "The wind is part of the
process/ The rain is part of the process." There follows a short
address to Chthonia Gea, Mater, the womb and tomb of all
things, whose herbs, invoked by Pound as if they constituted a
holy trinity, symbolize the perfection of the process:

> χθόνια γέα, Μάτηρ,
>> by thy herbs menthe thyme and basilicum,
>>> from whom and to whom,
>>> will never be more now than at present.

The hidden puns, such as that on "thyme," become more overt
at a later point in this sequence.

Pound is undergoing the pains of hell, a dark night of the soul ("magna NUX animae" [15]), but the torment is more bearable now than at any time before. Released by love from the more confining of the two prisons, the inner stockade of the isolated ego, Pound has the comfort at least of feeling himself not entirely alone in his misery: "Mr Edwards, Hudson, Henry *comes miseriae*/ Comites Kernes, Green and Tom Wilson" (p. 14). Not as lucky as Odysseus, Pound has been trapped by the Circe of history: "ac ego in harum/ so lay men in Circe's swinesty" (p. 14). This aspect of Circe, identified with usury, is carefully distinguished from the beautiful Circe of creative passion celebrated in Canto 39:

> robbing the public for private individual's gain
> nec benecomata Kirkê, mah! [16]
>
> (Canto 74, p. 15)

Love begins to assert itself against "nox animae magna," and Pound correspondingly gains a deeper understanding of the process:

> filial, fraternal affection is the root of humaneness
> the root of the process
> nor are elaborate speeches and slick alacrity.
> employ men in proper season
> not when they are at harvest.

The principle of the *Li Ki*, that the ruler should act in harmony with the seasons, is now recognized as founded in humaneness rather than simply in reason. We find Pound beginning to adjust his achieved Confucian insights to a deepening spiritual

15. Pound is clearly distinguishing his own dark night of the soul from the purely Christian experience of St. John of the Cross by mixing Greek (*nux* = night) with the Latin. Perhaps he is suggesting the darkness in which the initiate at Eleusis had to spend some time before being granted the vision of the innermost mysteries.

16. "And not the fair-tressed Circe!"

perspective, but the Confucian principle of timeliness will persist as ground bass through the whole development of his higher awareness. *Jen*, in Confucianism roughly equivalent to humaneness, is beginning to gain primacy in Pound's mind over the principle of Order. Pound is beginning to see *jen* as the profounder principle, as the root of order.

After three pages on the theme of usury, the social disorder which "leads to the death cells," Pound reports Aristotle's conviction that

> philosophy is not for young men
> their *Katholou* can not be sufficiently derived from
>   their *hekasta*
> their generalities cannot be born from a sufficient
>   phalanx of particulars
> lord of his work and master of utterance
>   who turneth his word in its season and shapes it.
>   (Canto 74, pp. 19–20)

In these lines Pound is justifying the general poetic method he has employed throughout the *Cantos*, the inductive, intuitional, *ideogrammic* method of trusting to an accumulation of concrete particulars rather than to abstract, logical statement as the way of presenting the truth of things. Pound's respect for the individuality of things, his tolerance for diversity, is frequently expressed in the *Pisan Cantos* in the Biblical phrase "each in the name of its god" (Micah IV, 5). Nevertheless, when Pound does accumulate "a sufficient phalanx of particulars" whose nature permits of accurate generalization, he does not hesitate to rise to the level of abstract statement which seems warranted by the evidence. At various stages in this analysis of the *Cantos*, I have pointed out apices of thematic generalization and I have attempted to show the inductive processes by which these generalizations were made. The development of Pound's conception of "time" is the outstanding example of such a process and always stands at the center of thematic progression in the poem.

As a result of this method of accumulation of particulars followed (ideally) by an appropriate level of generalization, Pound has managed for the most part to keep within the bounds of discretion voiced by Aristotle: he is one "who turneth his word in its season."

Pound's re-introduction on page 7 of the theme which opened the second phase of the *Cantos*, "Tempus loquendi, tempus tacendi," should now appear as a purposeful anticipation of this attitude toward philosophical generalization. But one further peculiarity ought to be noted before we proceed. The Latin phrase, as repeated in this canto, appears with its elements in reverse: "Tempus tacendi, tempus loquendi." The order of phrasing in Canto 31 emphasized, appropriately enough, the "tacendi," the time of silence needed for the accumulation of knowledge and wisdom on which to base effective speech, or action. Accordingly, throughout the second phase of the poem Pound had been developing an understanding of "the process" and of the meaning of organic time in relation to the social organism. He had simultaneously been developing a more precisely focused conception of the evil he desired to expose and attack. In other words, Phase Two of the poem was a time for the selection and the sharpening of the poet's weapons—as though in anticipation of an eventual all-out battle with an enemy who was at last clearly defined. The call for "precise terms" was the call for the sharpening of the axe. Now, in the *Pisan Cantos*, Pound is literally beleaguered by the enemy in as close an approximation to a battle-field as could be desired. One almost feels that if they had not actually happened to him, Pound's experiences in a prison stockade would have had to be invented for the sake of the major formal demands of the poem. It is at last the time for the testing of cherished principles in *action*, and for this reason the Latin phrase is reversed to emphasize the "loquendi," the time for action that must succeed and put to proof the time of silence. The "loquendi" is the *Pisan Cantos* themselves, and the degree to which they succeed as poetry is the sole measure of the effectiveness of the "loquendi." [17]

Struggling as never before against brutalization by the forces of history, Pound is concerned to re-establish order within and to achieve harmony with the process. As a poet, he desires only to turn "his word in its season," but to do so he must feel a force of inspiration powerful enough to offset the stifling pressure of the prison compound. In what I take to be the climactic moment of Canto 74, Pound invokes his Muse. The invocation is much too long to quote in full, but at the cost of losing the rhapsodic "winds" passage, I reproduce it here with the omission of ten lines from the middle:

ΣΕΙΡΗΝΕΣ   had appreciated his conversation
        ΧΑΡΙΤΕΣ   possibly in the soft air
        with the mast held by the left hand
        in this air as of Kuanon
enigma forgetting the times and seasons
but this air brought her ashore a la marina
with the great shell borne on the seawaves
                nautilis biancastra
    By no means an orderly Dantescan rising
but as the winds veer

                .   .   .

        "in the name of its god" "Spiritus veni"
            adveni / not to a schema
                "is not for the young" said Arry, stagirite
    but as grass under Zephyrus
                as the green blade under Apeliota
    Time is not, Time is the evil, beloved
    Beloved the hours βροδοδάκτυλος

17. In Pound's case, imprisonment at Pisa presents us with the paradox of a "Fortunate Fall." His descent into the historical inferno galvanizes all his resources as man and poet and ends in the triumph of a paradisal vision whose solidity is proved by the strength it had to sustain him personally and by the impersonal, enduring power of the poetry which registers and makes a public possession of his private vision.

> as against the half-light of the window
> with the sea beyond making horizon
> le contre-jour the line of the cameo
> profile "to carve Achaia"
> a dream passing over the face in the half-light
> Venere, Cytherea "aut Rhodon"
> vento ligure, veni
> "beauty is difficult" sd/ Mr Beardsley [18]
> beauty is difficult.

(Canto 74, pp. 21–22)

The invocation to Aphrodite, the poet's Muse, proceeds by a series of contrasts or alternations of motif, which achieve synthesis in the explanatory final phrase, "beauty is difficult." Very little direct help toward analysis is offered by the passage immediately preceding the lines quoted. Valuable, perhaps, is Pound's mention of what he sees from his tent, "two red cans labeled 'FIRE,'" which seem to prompt the following Sirens [ΣΕΙΡΗΝΕΣ] image that is soon repeated detachedly at the beginning of the invocation proper. The "Fire" warning that leaps out at Pound seems to suggest simultaneously the flames of hell and of sexual passion, and Circe's warning to Odysseus against the song of the Sirens. Perhaps there is also allusion to actual mechanical sirens in the camp compound whose strident music signals danger or disaster. In any case, the Sirens sum up the wartime inferno and contrast with the gentle Charites, or Graces, who traditionally dwell with the Muses on Olympia and are especially associated with Aphrodite. Pound calls upon the Graces in the same way he might call on the Muses, for in classical times the inspiration of the Charites was considered necessary to the poet, as to the painter, sculptor, or musician.[19]

Assuming that "his conversation" is Pound's,[20] I do not see

18. The Faber and Faber edition omits an eight-line reminiscence here.

19. Seyffert, *Dictionary of Classical Antiquities*.

20. "His conversation" may be that of the German admiral Von Tirpitz (d. 1930), a likely antecedent for "his," but Von Tirpitz seems

clearly the meaning of the first line—unless Pound is alluding ironically to one of the harder conditions of his imprisonment: that no one was permitted to converse with him.[21] Whatever the interpretation, it is clear that Pound has his doubts as to whether his conversation is being "appreciated" by the Charites, for they are only "possibly" in the air, whose softness is suspiciously like the sudden calm that beset the ship of Odysseus when he entered the vicinity of the Sirens. Likening himself to an Odysseus dangerously exposed to Siren-song, loosely holding the mast rather than securely tied to it, Pound expresses his uncertainty as to the meaning of this "air as of Kuanon" (Chinese goddess of mercy). He regards his confusion, his uncertainty as to whether the Graces or the Sirens most influence his poetic labors, as an enigma which puts him in danger of "forgetting the times and seasons." The "tempus loquendi," however, is now or never, and he decides to take this gentle "air"—the mood that has come over him and the music that softly plays in his mind—as the same air that once brought Aphrodite ashore on her "nautilis biancastra" (white-colored shell) in Botticelli's "La Nascita"; the same gentle air, therefore, might now be wafting Aphrodite, goddess of Beauty, towards the hapless Pound.

The second movement of this invocation describes the poetic method of the *Cantos* as a non-linear *veering* in response to the pressure of experience, "as the winds veer and the raft is driven," as Pound says in one of the lines I have omitted. As

---

to me to be another Odysseus-Pound mask, and the clearest antecedent for "his," in my judgment, is "an old man (or oldish) still active/ serving small stones from a lath racquet" (pp. 20–1), that is, Pound again, as he describes himself playing imaginary tennis "in sight of the tower che pende" (p. 21). (Hugh Kenner informs me that Von Tirpitz is warning his daughter against the charm of the English, who are then called "Sirens.")

21. David Park Williams, "The Background of *The Pisan Cantos*," *A Casebook on Ezra Pound*, eds. William Van O'Connor and Edward Stone (New York, 1959), p. 43.

opposed to Dante's Catholic certainty, his "orderly . . . rising," Pound's movement is more perceptibly a non-progressional oscillation among different spiritual states. He has no "Aquinas-map," tends therefore to get lost, and must repeatedly backtrack to find himself again. But in back of the entire metaphor of Pound as Odysseus, tossed on his raft of poetry by shifting wind and wave, is always the fact that Odysseus does finally reach Ithaca. This fundamental metaphor expresses Pound's abiding faith that in spite of his occasional surrender to despair, the *Cantos* will ultimately display a rising line of development. One can meaningfully arrive at a *Paradiso*, that is, by continually taking three steps forward and two back, just as certainly as by progressing lineally in an "orderly Dantescan rising." "Spirit, come," says Pound, "come"—but "not to a schema." A philosophic schema, or system of generalizations, "is not for the young," said Aristotle. If Pound's poetry is to be in harmony with the process, then it is desirable that his Muse visit him like the shifting wind, which is "part of the process," blowing now east, now west, over the flexible grass whose nature is to grow slowly upward though from moment to moment it appears only to sway from side to side.

His confidence in himself now restored by an act of faith in the inscrutable purposefulness of the process, in spite of its seemingly fickle divagations, Pound is now ready for a powerful assertion of his own spiritual values, and the artistic fruit they have borne in the past, against the destructive mechanism of history:

> Time is not, Time is the evil, beloved
> Beloved the hours βροδοδάκτυλος.

In repeating the climactic phrase that generalized the meaning of Western history for the first thirty cantos, Pound is asserting the validity of that earlier conclusion, which has withstood the test of "Time." *The Pisan Cantos*, as I have said before, are the testing-ground for principles developed over a lifetime. Coupled with this moral assertion that Time is evil is the metaphysical assertion that "Time is not." This deeper level of generalization is now possible because Pound, stripped in the prison environment to his bare and essential self—that preserved in mind and memory—has, for the first time, come into conscious possession of that indestructible *essence* of self which reveals Time-as-history to be mere *accident* (in Aristotle's sense). In the Aristotelian environment of this passage, such must be the philosophical intention of the phrase. The coupling, however, of the two phrases, "Time is not, Time is the evil," suggests also the idea that "Evil is a privation of . . . being, and the theory of evil as privation of being [is] derived from Neoplatonism." [22] The poetic seed of this idea is to be found in Canto 7, where the poet describes himself and his vision of the beautiful Nicea as "alone having being," as opposed to the "thin husks" of the "tawdry class" who are "moved by no inner being." Pound fuses Aristotle and Plato in the all-out offensive against Time which he inaugurates in this invocation to his Muse.

Love is the indestructible essence, and that which is "beloved" is infused with this essence, surviving the abstract onslaught of Time in concrete, remembered "hours." "Où sont les heurs," Pound asked earlier, and the whole movement of the *Pisan Cantos* backward in memory, while chronological time concurrently rolls forward, is toward massive Proustian retrieval of the beloved hours in a vindication of the integrity of the Spirit against Time. "What thou lovest well remains," the magnificent lyrical crescendo of these cantos, brings the process to its artistic and metaphysical conclusion.

Hours versus Time: these are the antipodal symbols which generate the whole unfolding drama of the Pisan sequence. If Time is history, then the "hours" are poetry, as is implied by the adjective *brododaktulos*, "rosy-fingered," Homer's epithet for the dawn and Sappho's for the moon. Pound now recalls his

22. Julius R. Weinberg, *A Short History of Medieval Philosophy* (Princeton, 1964), p. 39.

most triumphant hours as a poet, the creative culmination of his London years in *Hugh Selwyn Mauberley*, whose poet-hero, ultimately defeated by his inability to maintain a balance between his own dreaming subjectivity and the march of Time, does nevertheless leave as legacy the minor perfection of his "Medallion" poem. "Medallion" is a tribute to Venus Anadyomene, embodiment of the poet's "dream" of Beauty. The small but perfect diamond Mauberley does leave behind, in spite of his ultimate personal failure to neutralize the forces of Time, becomes in Canto 74 a symbol of hope. *Mauberley*, a minor work compared to the *Cantos*, is achieved beauty, and Mauberley's own minor work, "Medallion," symbolizes Pound's own achievement in the *Mauberley* sequences as a whole. As Pound calls once more for Venus to come to him in the "Ligurian wind," he seems humbly to be hoping for some sort of artistic triumph once again, even if minor, against Time. "Beauty is difficult," said Beardsley, who was very literally a victim of time, and through Mauberley and Beardsley, Pound voices a chastened awareness of his own limitations. In spite of repeated invocation, Aphrodite does not appear; she is "difficult." But she has come before, even if seen only in "the half-light," and it is on this hope that the poem proceeds.

The Mauberley-Beardsley motif echoes through the rest of the canto, which continues its Nekuia into memory to recapture the hours in stubborn opposition to Time:

> Came Madame Lucrezia [23]
> and on the back of the door in Cesena
> are, or were, still the initials
> joli quart d'heure, (nella Malatestiana)
>   Torquato where art thou?
> to the click of hooves on the cobbles by Tevere
> and "my fondest knight lie dead" . . or la Stuarda
> "ghosts move about me" "patched with histories".

23. Not Borgia, as in Canto 30, but the daughter of Sigismundo Malatesta.

The "joli quart *d'heure*" is contrasted with "the click of hooves" associated with the murder of Giovanni Borgia in Canto 5.[24] That murder and that "click" first introduced the theme of mechanical time (the "clock-tick") into the *Cantos*.

The desolation of Time-as-history continues to be stressed in this canto with the allusion to "la Stuarda," Mary Stuart, Queen of Scots, whose chief advisor, David Rizzio, was also the victim of a brutal political murder. The most interesting of the lines quoted is the last, in which Pound recalls that the theme of Time-as-history had been central to his conception of the *Cantos* from the very start. The line is from the rejected first version of Canto 1, in which Pound is addressing Browning with regard to the historical anachronisms in his *Sordello,* only to realize that history is mere accident, and that the main thing is to get one's own "intensest life" breathed into the figures one would resurrect through poetry:

> And half your dates are out, you mix your eras;
>
> . . .
>
> Does it matter?
>   Not in the least. Ghosts move about me
> Patched with histories. You had your business:
> To set out so much thought, so much emotion;
> To paint, more real than any dead Sordello,
> The half or third of your intensest life
> And call that third *Sordello*.[25]

The last few pages of Canto 74 are concerned with the theme of memory's resistance to Time:

> funge la purezza,[26]
> and that certain images be formed in the mind

24. Recalling the beauty of the Tempio Malatestiano, Pound naturally thinks of his old friend, a former librarian of the Malatestiano and author of the *Eccelinide*, Manlio Torquato Dazzi, to whom Pound dedicated his *Cavalcanti*. (I am indebted to Mary de Rachewiltz for this identification.)

25. Poetry X (June 1917), 114.

26. "Purity *acts*."

> to remain there
> > *formato locho*
> Arachne mi porta fortuna
> to remain there, resurgent ΕΙΚΟΝΕΣ.
>
> > > > (p. 24)

Snatches from the Cavalcanti canzone reinforce and generalize upon the permanence of images in the memory, images Pound calls "resurgent," stressing their undiminished power to *act* whenever needed and to strengthen the Time-embattled spirit. The resurgent quality of memory images relates them to organic time, the recurrence of the seasons, of vegetation, the "eternal return" of sun, moon, and stars, but the connection is not to be made consciously and deliberately until Canto 80, where several major syntheses of thought and feeling finally take place in preparation for the vision of paradise's reality vouchsafed Pound in Canto 81. The Baudelairian leitmotif introduced on page 16, "Le Paradis n'est pas artificiel," is an expression of faith that paradise is objectively real and is not to be confused with any of the numerous fictions invented by man to console himself for an irredeemable state of perdition.

Canto 74 ends with a lyrical comparison of memory to a fountain and in the intimation that there is a "rose," a living form yet to emerge that shall transform the "steel dust" of war and the "swansdown" of the beloved hours of memory into the "diamond clearness" of art, harder and purer than either of its contrasting elements. Noteworthy also is the recapitulation of mountain and wind imagery which suggests, without as yet conceptualizing, a connection between memory and "the process":

> Serenely in the crystal jet
> > as the bright ball that the fountain tosses
> (Verlaine) as diamond clearness
> > > How soft the wind under Taishan
> > > > where the sea is remembered
> > > out of hell, the pit
> > > out of the dust and glare evil

             Zephyrus / Apeliota
        This liquid is certainly a
                property of the mind
        nec accidens est   but an element
                            in the mind's make-up
        est agens and functions   dust to a fountain pan otherwise
                Hast'ou seen the rose in the steel dust
                            (or swansdown ever?)
        so light is the urging, so ordered the dark petals of iron
        we who have passed over Lethe.

Canto 74 is an expression of faith that art corresponds to a permanent order in reality beyond Time or "accident." It is equally
an expression of faith in art as the key to both the vision and
possession of that hyper-reality which so far has been imagined,
intuited, but not directly perceived by the poet. Having "passed
over Lethe," as did Dante upon leaving hell, the poet has now
entered into the purgatorial state of hope. In spite of continued
pain, he now has the ineradicable hope of achieving the final
vision.

For the sake of economy I shall treat in much less elaborate
detail the cantos that follow. As it happens, however, the treatment of Canto 74 at length became necessary in order to establish the main axes of reference for the further study of the Pisan
sequence. The theme of memory as an active force surviving
time, as the cultural tradition, conservative and yet essential to
the creative process, is presented in musical terms in Canto 75:
"Janequin's Birds," says Pound, "out of Arnaut (possibly), out
of immemorial and unknown, takes a new life on Francesco da
Milano's lute," and he goes on to mention "Münch's Janequin," the latest metamorphosis of the same theme.[27] Canto
75, says Emery, "comments upon . . . the durability (recurrent vigor) of the excellent, the substance of which maintains
its validity regardless of a change in its accidents." [28] As an

27. *Guide to Kulchur*, pp. 250–51.
28. *Ideas into Action*, p. 137.

image of artistic rebirth, the bird canzone is an elaboration of the idea represented by the rose-symbol (p. 27) and an intimation of the artistic synthesis Pound's contrapuntal oscillations are yet to achieve.

Pound makes thematic advances in Canto 76 along three lines of development traceable throughout the whole of the *Pisan Cantos*. These three lines of development correspond to the three levels on which awareness operates in the *Cantos* as a whole: the moral-emotional, the rational-intellectual, and the aesthetic-visionary. Insight on one level is not necessarily accompanied by simultaneous insight on any other. Experience of a moral-emotional sort, however, does seem to generate developments in the other two dimensions of awareness. There is action and reaction among the different levels, levels which sometimes combine and lack distinctness, but if we keep in mind such a three-dimensional pattern, certain problems of structural analysis will be eliminated.

Canto 76 opens on the aesthetic-visionary level, a level usually recognizable by the illusive, wished-for, or real appearance of gods and goddesses:

> But on the high cliff Alcmene,
>> Dryas, Hamadryas ac Heliades
>> flowered branch and sleeve moving
>> Dirce et Ixotta e che fu chiamata Primavera
>>> in the timeless air.

The "high cliff" is literally the sun-lit "cloud ridge" objectively described a few lines earlier. In these cloud formations Pound sees certain legendary and historically beloved women mingled with nymphs. It seems to Pound that they "suddenly stand in my room here," but the illusion is explained, apparently by the clouds themselves, who

>> answered: the sun in his great periplum
> leads in his fleet here

> sotto le nostre scoglie
> under our craggy cliffs.

Pound's memory and imagination have for the moment fused
with nature to create an illusion that is the precursor of the ultimate vision. Fusion of Pound's subjectivity with the objective
process takes place, in the final vision, on a profoundly mystical
plane. But a long process of self-purification on the moral-
emotional level must take place before the poet is ready for
such an act of communion.

The illusion subsiding, Pound turns to sad irony in thinking
of extinct friends and places. "B[itc]h your progress," [29] he
says, contrasting the tragic historical illusion of Western "progress" to "the timeless air over the sea-cliffs." It is with pain,
however, that he gives up his moment of optical self-deception,
for he is soon to murmur in the midst of a series of nostalgic
memories, "but all the vair and fair women" (p. 33). Insight
does soon take place, however, on the rational-intellectual
plane, where examination into the nature of memory gives conscious formulation to what he had discovered only on the moral-
emotional plane in Canto 74:

> nothing matters but the quality
> of the affection—
> in the end—that has carved the trace in the mind
> dove sta memoria.
>
> (Canto 76, p. 35)

It is important, from the structural point of view, to distinguish
the intellectual realization of the centrality of love from the
later, climactic vision of love, because if the two are confused,
the visionary climax must appear in some sense anticlimactic or

29. Pound's "B . . . . h" would indicate four missing letters, but
the presence of invective here seems clearly called for, and I can not discover anything more fitting in tone than "bitch."

repetitious. Visionary synthesis lags far behind the emotional and intellectual. In this canto, for example, simultaneous with the rational formulation about love, effort takes place on the far less developed visionary plane for a breakthrough into union with the process. Pound thinks of Aphrodite as a real form and potency in the air apart from the forms suggested by the clouds:

> Cythera potens, Κύθηρα δεινά
> no cloud, but the crystal body
> the tangent formed in the hand's cup
> as live wind in the beech grove
> as strong air amid cypress.[30]
>
> (pp. 34–35)

But in spite of the forms he sees in the air "before sunset," he admits to not having attained mystical union as yet with "the process." He refers to this union by the Arabic term *atasal:*

> spiriti questi? personae?
> tangibility by no means *atasal.*[31]
>
> (p. 37)

In frustration he cries out to a "white-chested martin" to "carry a message,/ say to La Cara: [32] amo." He then begins to weep [δακρύων], realizing in a moment of moral-emotional awareness a further sense in which he has been a "hard man," namely, that he has not always exercised as much charity as he might have:

30. It is worth noting that Pound's method of variable line-indentation in the *Pisan Cantos* frequently mimics the shifting of the winds.

31. The lines admit of another likely interpretation, complementary to that given above, namely, that the mystic communion Pound wishes to attain is not formlessly abstract, as Arabic *atasal* might imply, but concrete, form-filled: spirit, for Pound, has form, is tangible.

32. Possibly Pound's wife.

> J'ai eu pitié des autres
> probablement pas assez, and at moments that suited my
> own convenience.[33]
>
> (p. 38)

Recalling the beginning of his career, his uncertainty as to whether he ought to publish *A Lume Spento*, he enters upon a string of early memories which end in full awareness of what Confucius meant when he said, in the *Great Digest*: "things have ends and beginnings" (p. 40). The phrase is a justification for the process of self-examination and purgation that is to continue at length through the *Pisan Cantos* as an element in the poet's progress toward self-renewal.

Canto 76 approaches its mournful end in an elliptical quotation from Sappho's "Hymn to Aphrodite," but the immortal ['AΘANATA] goddess is "saeva" (cruel), and Pound is left with no vision in the timeless air, confronting once more the banalities of Time, "the sound of the bumm drum" (p. 41). He has arrived at the conscious formulation that love is what gives memory its active force, enabling the mind thus to exert counterpressure against hostile circumstance, but he has far to go before achieving a complete triumph, artistically and spiritually, over Time.

Canto 77 consists largely of memories, a spate of economic criticism, and prison camp images. The most significant event in the narrative present is the news that "the war was over." But for Pound, who ironically recalls Frazer's description of the brutal method of combat by which chief traditionally succeeded chief at Nemi, "With drawn sword as at Nemi/ day comes after day" (p. 45); nothing has changed with respect to the ascendancy of usury: "we are not yet out of *that* chapter" (p. 46). If external circumstances have not essentially changed, the state of

33. Pound distances the emotional poignancy of his tears and painful confessions of guilt by expressing them in Greek, Latin, or French, languages which give classical grace to what might otherwise smack of self-pity or sentimentality in English.

Pound's soul has: the ideal city, which in Canto 74 was "now in the mind indestructible" (p. 8), is "now in the heart indestructible" (p. 43). Canto 77 consolidates emotional and conceptual gains made earlier, but on the visionary plane, there is only the further attempt to focus on the intuited but as yet unseen paradise:

> the wind mad as Cassandra
> who was as sane as the lot of 'em

> Sorella, mia sorella,
> che ballava sobr' un zecchin'

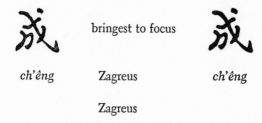

ch'êng   Zagreus   ch'êng

Zagreus

The "Sorella" passage seems to be, at least on one level, a muted address to Terpsichore (Muse of the dance, coupled on page 23 with Clio, Muse of history—the pair representing the alternating lyrical and profane moods of these cantos). The Muse's ability to perform an exquisite feat of tightrope balance (over a *zecchin'*: a gold coin) symbolizes the ideal of artistic-visionary focus.[34]

Canto 78 is primarily a polemic against usury, but it nears its end with a premonition of the vision to come. Beginning with

---

34. Pound's Muse dancing over a gold coin suggests also the peculiarly economic concern of his verse as well as the ideal of economic *balance*. The final "focus" image consists of a horizontal and vertical pair of terms —images seen as in a rangefinder—not yet visually brought into focus. For the poet, this final image suggests that under the healing guidance of his Muse the moon, symbolic of "the process," the shattered elements of himself—Confucian intellect and Dionysian power—are becoming reunited.

satirical commentary on the peace negotiations then in progress, it counterpoints Pound's present with cherished recollections from the past. An initial series of such memory fragments ends on "Gaudier's word not blacked out/ nor old Hulme's, nor Wyndham's" (p. 57). One pauses here to take in the full significance of this image, for it is an allusion to Canto 7's "Time blacked out with the rubber," and it asserts the faith that art blacks out Time, not Time art. The point is explored in the following lines, where Pound, his consciousness once more assaulted by the camp environment, reasserts his conviction that Time is unable to black out the Ch'ing Ming:

> "definition can not be shut down under a box lid"
> but if the gelatine be effaced whereon is the record?
> "wherein is no responsible person
>   having a front name, a hind name and an address"
> "not a right but a duty"
>   those words still stand uncancelled,
>   "Presente!"

In Pound's ensuing attack on usury he contrasts images of mechanical and organic time: the "fixed charge" against the policy of the wise ruler who keeps in harmony with the seasons by employing the tithe system:

> **nothing worse than fixed charge**
>   several years' average
> Mencius III, 1. T'ang Wan Kung
>   Chapter 3 and verse 7
> Be welcome, O cricket my grillo, but you must not
>   sing after taps.

There is an amusing correlation of the "fixed charge" system with the martial music of taps that Pound regards as presumptuously setting curfew on the cricket: both images, the economic and musical, are instances of Western man's violation of natural rhythms. "Aram vult nemus," Pound says (p. 59), "the grove needs an altar": men must return to a reverence for nature.

The significant difference between Pound's present tirades against usury and his economic verse of the 'thirties is sounded by the Cassandra motif near the beginning and end of the canto. Allusions to the *Agamemnon* and the doomed House of Atreus recur frequently in the *Cantos*, always suggesting the tragedy of the human spirit trapped in the toils of time. Pound's use here of Cassandra symbolizes, as I see it, the poet's final recognition that his own prophetic voice is doomed, like that of the captive prophetess, to have no reformative effect on the immediate post-war social environment. The "heroic," optimistic note of his polemical verse of the 'thirties is now significantly modulated to "tragic":

> Cassandra, your eyes are like tigers,
>   with no word written in them
> You also have I carried to nowhere
>   to an ill house and there is
>   no end to the journey.
>   (p. 55)

The canto nears its end, however, in more hopeful anticipation of the vision to come than we have yet seen:

> Cunizza's shade al triedro and that presage
>   in the air
> which means that nothing will happen that will
>   be visible to the sargeants
> Tre donne intorno alla mia mente.

The three Graces are now definitely, not merely "possibly," smiling upon him. The canto ends with a summarizing juxtaposition of mechanical and organic time images:

> The shadow of the tent's peak treads on its corner peg
> marking the hour. The moon split, no cloud nearer than Lucca
> In the spring and autumn

In "The Spring and Autumn"
there
are
no
righteous
wars

The tent, concrete embodiment of his imprisonment by Time, turns into a clock marking the empty hour. The split moon, literally in a phase less than full, recalls one of the leitmotifs of the *Pisan Cantos* which emerges in Canto 76 (p. 31) as

la scalza: Io son' la luna
and they have broken my house.

(The broken moon as *la scalza*, "the barefoot" Artemis, re-calls the forlorn goddess of Canto 30.) The final Confucian apothegm opposes the organic time-consciousness to that of the clock. The visual hieroglyph formed by "there are no righteous wars" is that of an amphora and suggests the wine and oil that reward the peaceful pursuit of agriculture in "the spring and autumn." It is clear that Pound is not pacifistically condemn-ing all war but only the kind of war waged by those who have no reverence for the times and seasons.

Canto 79, bursting into the lyricism of the lynx-song, takes a giant stride toward the achievement of the paradisal vision. The first movement is full of the sense of loss and the strident sounds of the stockade, but the second movement builds up a new sense of hope and replaces the outer stridency with a music generated from within. The canto moves from darkness to light, from night to day; the first word is *Moon*, the last, *Helios*.

The major theme is presented at the outset in a variation upon Lovelace's "To Althea from Prison":

Moon, cloud, tower, a patch of the battistero
all of a whiteness,

dirt pile as per the Del Cossa inset [35]
think not that you wd/gain if their least caress
were faded from my mind
I had not loved thee half so well
Loved I not womankind."

The canto is a celebration of woman, earth-goddess or "female principle," as the source of man's aesthetic appreciation of nature and love for the arts—woman as the inspiration of his creativity. The motif, "So Salzburg reopens," introduces the musical imagery that pervades the whole canto, as in the repeated glimpses of birds on the fence wires like notes on a staff. "[S]ome minds take pleasure in counterpoint," Pound says, and a few lines later he introduces the major contrapuntal image of the first movement:

can that be the papal major sweatin' it out to the bumm drum?
what castrum romanum, what
          "went into winter quarters"
is under us?
as the young horse whinnies against the tubas
          in contending for certain values
(Janequin per esempio, and Orazio Vechii or Bronzino).
                              (p. 63)

The mechanical "bumm drum" and tuba combo plays against the organic whinnying of the horse, who is comically presented as both musician (like the cricket) and music critic aware of the profounder "values" of music that stems from the observation of nature, as does Janequin's Bird canzone, for example. The image is soon re-introduced in juxtaposition with an earlier motif:

as from the breasts of Helen, a cup of white gold
2 cups for three altars. Tellus γέα feconda

35. An allusion to the damaged portions of the Schifanoja frescoes in the Este palace at Ferrara.

    "each one in the name of its god"
    mint, thyme and basilicum,
the young horse whinnies against the sound of the bumm band.

An extensive range of ideas is suggested in these lines. Helen is the ambiguous beauty of the first thirty cantos, the blameless cause of destruction, who has become Helen-Tellus, "Mother Earth—ambivalent," says George Dekker, "as the earth is ambivalent." [36] The "ambiguity" of the life-death rhythm of the earth is a theme that receives undoubted stress as the Pisan sequence continues, but the passage is not really as distinctive for this Yin-Yang theme, already fairly well explored in the previous phase of the poem, so much as for a subtle development which particularly marks this new phase of the *Cantos*. The relationship between nature and *art*, between the creative potentialities of the process and those of the artist, is the primary metaphysical concern of the *Pisan Cantos*, and its importance begins to emerge in this canto and in such a passage as this, which connects the form of a gold cup with that of "the breasts of Helen."

In the middle phase of the poem, Helen and all other mythical females became rationalized into an impersonal sort of Dame Nature, a conservative but kindly old matron who was likely to be quite bountiful if shown the proper respect. She had no direct relationship to the art-process as such, but she provided the economic abundance that makes possible all the higher activities of man. Nature was considered largely in the light of Pound's polemical need to present a rational, workable ideal of social order. Pound's failure in his role as social prophet, however, induced in the *Pisan Cantos* an examination of his direct connection as *artist*, not as *Homo economicus*, with the process of nature.

If the perfect order of Mother Nature could be taken as

36. *The Cantos of Ezra Pound*, p. 102.

model for the perfect social order, then by extrapolation the forms inherent in nature could be regarded as pre-existent models for forms produced by the artist. The fundamental Platonism of such an idea is obvious. A corollary to such a conception would be the critical theory that any artistic form not ultimately modeled on some natural form is aesthetically worthless. This is precisely the idea that unites the horse's whinnying and Helen's breast-cups against the "bumm band" in the present instance.

Anticipating the development of this aesthetic theory is a phrase in Canto 74, "stone knowing the form which the carver imparts" (p. 8), where stone is then associated with female figures such as Cythera and Isotta degli Atti. Dekker says that "The stone cooperates, as the woman cooperates in the sexual act. . . . the attitude Pound takes toward the female part of the world is that she yearns for the form which the male alone can give her." [37] Dekker's estimate, as I see it, might be revised to state that the male (artist) does not give form to nature but recognizes the forms inherent in her and "imitates" them in the Platonic sense. It does *not* follow, however, that Pound, like Plato, would evaluate as inferior such artistic "imitations." [38] Nevertheless, we have here in the Pisan sequence a considerable reversal of the metaphysical ground of Pound's aesthetic when we compare it to the earlier statement in Canto 29 of woman, or nature, as a formless "chaos" and merely "Our mulberry leaf." In the *Pisan Cantos* we are witnessing the continuation of that process of ego-humbling begun in the middle cantos and extending onto the moral-emotional plane (Pound's sense of guilt and contrition) as well as onto the aesthetic plane. Pound's aesthetic theory might now be stated in part as follows: Nature, earlier conceived of as matter, as mere "accident" with respect to the art-process, is now conceived of as "essence," an

37. *The Cantos of Ezra Pound*, p. 43.
38. See *Guide to Kulchur*, p. 128.

armory of forms which the "accidental" activity of the artist releases or imitates. The radiant center of intelligence in Pound's universe undergoes a shift from man to nature.[39]

The form of the "cup of white gold" is not originally in the mind of man but is suggested by "the breasts of Helen." The "three altars" recall, of course, "the grove needs an altar," and imply again the need for man to show reverence for nature, but they look forward as well to the mystical characterization of Aphrodite at the end of the canto as "Κόρη καὶ Δήλια καὶ Μαῖα/ trine as praeludio." Dekker says that "It is not clear why Maia, mother of Hermes, is chosen as the representative of motherhood to set beside Delia the virgin and Kore the daughter, but the implication of 'trine as praeludio' appears to be that Aphrodite is 'three goddesses in one'—the Poundian Trinity." [40] The "Poundian Trinity" is now a restatement, in mythic terms, of the *"concret Allgemeine"* announced as early as Canto 8: the holistic reconciliation of the concept of the One with the experience of the Many is at the heart of both formulations. Pound's trinitarian goddess with three altars to match are of course a slap at Christianity, the assertion of a nature-oriented mysticism to replace Christian transcendental mysticism. The three altars are particularly an image of the polytheis-

39. Seen from this new point of view, Pound's *Inferno* might now be characterized as the state of mind of the poet himself at that period when he considered the artist as the isolated intelligence working against the inertia of dumb nature. Such an attitude is itself, through ignorance, a violation of nature parallel to the range of consciously presented evils in the early cantos. The blindness of ego, operating in dissonance with reality, is an adequate generalization, it would seem, for all the individual moral evils presented in those cantos (and ultimately subsumed under the concept of mechanical time). What Pound has said in an interview with regard to *Thrones* is applicable to the whole movement of the poem after the *Inferno*: "The thrones in the *Cantos* are an attempt to move out from egoism and to establish some definition of an order possible or at any rate conceivable on earth." See Donald Hall, "Ezra Pound: An Interview," *The Paris Review* 28 (Summer-Fall 1962), p. 49.

40. *The Cantos of Ezra Pound*, p. 73.

tic tolerance to be expected of a Gemisto-like religion founded in nature. Dekker's uncertainty as to what each of the component goddesses represents may perhaps be relieved if we follow up the "three-in-one" idea and ask in what way all these goddesses are identical and in what significant way or ways they retain their individuality. Kore (Persephone), Delia (Artemis), and Maia (mother of Hermes) are identical in that they were all worshiped as life-fostering goddesses of nature whose festivals were particularly associated with spring. Their individuality is expressed, however, by the fact that each is symbolic of a different natural province: Kore is an earth-goddess; Artemis is goddess of the moon, and Maia is the "eldest and most beautiful" of the nymphs who became the Pleiades.[41] The three goddesses together, then, represent the whole visible world of nature whose three realms—earth, moon, and stars—were sung so magnificently in Canto 47.[42]

The cups molded on Helen's breasts Pound would set as chalices upon the three altars to symbolize the relationship he now perceives between art and nature. (There are only two cups for three altars, but perhaps Pound means two cups—a pair of breasts, those of a priestess of Aphrodite and devotee of natural beauty—to serve at each of the three altars. In general, Pound's entire game with number-pairs throughout this canto stems from the theme of "pleasure in counterpoint" announced on page 63.) "[E]ach one in the name of its god" suggests, of

41. See Seyffert, *Dictionary of Classical Antiquities*.

42. The significant omission of the sun (unless one is to consider it a star in this context) is connected with the dramatic role of Helios (who hardly squares well, in any case, with a female trinity) as killjoy. His sharp light brings into relief the ugliness of the prison environment and awakens its inmates to their oppressive daily round. At the end of the canto he emerges to cut short the "praeludio" leading to vision. Underlying all this cosmic mythology, as we shall see, is the fact that throughout the Pisan sequence Pound is appealing to all the female goddesses, epitomized in Aphrodite and the moon, to act as merciful *intercessor(s)* between himself and the sun.

course, the polytheistic tolerance of the three altars. In gold cups on these altars Pound would set the aromatic herbs "mint, thyme and basilicum," those representatives of nature's abundance which Pound previously swore by (p. 13). ("Thyme" looks to me more and more like a punning reference to organic time, especially in such close proximity to the organic-mechanical time symbolism of the horse's whinny against the "bumm band." We have not yet seen the last of these herbs.)

The beautiful lynx-song, invoking the whole gamut of fertility deities, is primarily an invocation to "Kuthera," Aphrodite, who is slow to respond. The apparition of roses in the underbrush suggests the forthcoming presence of Aphrodite, to whom roses were sacred. At one pathetic moment Pound asks the unseen goddess, "Will you trade roses for acorns[?]" (p. 69), alluding to the hard fare eaten by those like himself trapped in Circe's pigsty, and suggesting, even more subtly, the coming ascendancy of the third phase of the poem (the phase of Aphrodite) over the second, purgatorial phase of the poem (the phase of Circe). The "dance of the bassarids" (maenads) announces the imminent arrival of the goddess: "The Graces have brought ᾿Αφροδίτην/ Her cell is drawn by ten leopards" (p. 69), but at the same time the sun is rising: "῞Ηλιος is come to our mountain/ there is a red glow in the carpet of pine spikes" (p. 70), and the goddess, "terrible in resistance," fails to reveal her direct presence. The canto ends in a brief but unanswered plea to Cimbica (stinginess),[43] "servant of Helios," but the vision is denied.

"Amo ergo sum, and in just that proportion," says Pound in line 5 of Canto 80, and on the same page, "senesco/ sed amo." Natural time, the process of aging, is no enemy of love and causes no diminution of essential being. When Pound said "Time is not," he was making a philosophical statement as to the lack of being in Time-as-history, and it is now clear that the non-being of mechanical time is due to the absence of love in

43. Read, "The Pattern of the *Pisan Cantos*," p. 412.

its processes. The length of Canto 80 is due in large part to its
elaboration of "Amo ergo sum" in the particulars of memory,
but there is always the contrapuntal theme of mechanical time
to be reckoned with:

> to each tree its own mouth and savour
> "*Hot   hole   hep   cat*"
> or words of similar volume
> to be recognized by the god-damned
> or man-damned trainee.
>
> (p. 76)

In this example, the infernal regimentation of marching (can
any ex-soldier forget the music of "COWnt cadence,
COWnt!"?) is contrasted with the theme of tolerance for natural variation.

Shortly afterwards, the soldiers' rendition of the "Battle
Hymn of the Republic" is occasion for irony to the musically
sensitive Pound, who admits that "there is a good deal to be
seen" of the glory of the Lord but finds that glory difficult to
perceive in the march-like cadence of the trainees:

> well in contrast to the *god*-damned crooning
> put me down for temporis acti
> OY TIΣ
> ἄχρονος
> now there are no more days
> οὔ τις
> ἄχρονος
>
> (p. 77)

The myth of Odysseus, the wily "no man," is impervious to
Time [achronos]. Pound is not. Quoting scraps from Dante
(*Inf.* V, 1, 86), he says:

> così discesi per l'aer maligno
> on doit le temps ainsi prendre qu'il vient.
>
> (p. 77)

("Thus I descended through the spiteful air/ one must take the weather as it comes.") French gives Pound a convenient phrase for linking the weather of hell to Time, which he must endure as well as he can.

The main movement of the canto, beginning after the break on page 78, opens and closes emphatically on the theme of time. Pound returns in memory to the beginning of his European odyssey ("so that leaving America I brought with me $80"), then enters upon a complicated series of images whose center is the moon and whose main point is that just as things have organic beginnings, so also do they have natural endings: "Death's seeds move in the year." The passage is, as a matter of fact, an intentional variation upon the major themes of Canto 30, a new exposition of the conflict between Artemis and Pity. It begins with a passage in Italian describing a little boy stretched out on the earth in the form of a cross, looking pitiful ("di pietosa sembianza") and saying,[44] with his feet on a silver scythe, "I am the moon," apparently a vision of Pound's and not traceable to any literary or other source. There follows the "young Dumas" weeping without clear cause (Dumas said, "Je pleure parce que j'ai des larmes." [45]):

> The young Dumas weeps because the young Dumas
> has tears
> > Death's seeds move in the year
> > > > semina motuum
> > > falling back into the trough of the sea
> > > the moon's arse been chewed off by this time
> semina motuum
> > > "With us there is no deceit"
> > > > said the moon nymph   immacolata
> > > > > Give back my cloak, *hagoromo*.
> > > > > had I the clouds of heaven

44. The text (p. 78) should read "disse," not "diss'io," according to the table of "Author's Errata" printed on page 2 of the New Directions editions of the *Cantos*, sixth printing.

45. Mr. Kenner has kindly supplied me with the Dumas quotation.

          as the nautile borne ashore
       in their holocaust
          as wistaria floating shoreward
with the sea gone the colour of copper
       and emerald dark in the offing
the young Dumas has tears thus far from the year's end
At Ephesus she had compassion on silversmiths
       revealing the paraclete
standing in the cusp
       of the moon et in Monte Gioiosa
       as the larks rise at Allegre
                    Cythera egoista
       But for Actaeon
       of the eternal moods has fallen away.
                    (Canto 80, pp. 78–79)

Taken in the context of the exaggeratedly pitiful crucifixion vision, Dumas's tears underscore a theme of emotional self-indulgence, of romantically disproportionate response to circumstance. Dumas's tears represent for Pound the typical Christian reaction to death, undiscriminating and unbalanced. The crucifixion of Christ is an event of moral significance and properly evokes pity, but for Pound there is no connection between death as a murderous violation of nature (the Crucifixion) and death as a phase in the fulfillment of nature's cyclical course (the waning of the moon). Dumas's tears indicate uncritical confusion of the two. He weeps only because he "has tears"—and for no better reason than that he is a sentimentalist. Christian "Pity" is equally condemned in Canto 30. There, its uncritical equation of the two types of death is bewailed by Artemis as throwing nature (and the relations between man and nature) into confusion. What Dumas fails to realize is that "Death's seeds move in the year"; they are "seeds of movement," *semina motuum,* "the inner impulses of the tree," as Pound says in his *Confucius* (p. 59). "Death's seeds" is an oxymoron which stresses the inseparability of life and death, the Yin and the Yang, emphasizing the indivisibility of the "process." Death in nature is not permanent; the process is essentially a comedy, albeit a dark comedy, and the proper attitude towards natural death is gaiety rather than tears: "falling back into the trough of the sea/ the moon's arse been chewed off by this time." When, several lines later, Pound writes, "the young Dumas has tears thus far from the year's end," one is struck by the ambiguity. One sense of the line is that Dumas has tears so far because the year comes to an end, and it this sense which directly supports the reading I have given of Dumas's sentimentalization of nature. Another sense of the line is that Dumas thus has tears well before the year's end, that is, unseasonably, and this sense expresses Pound's conviction that the Christian West has lost harmony with the seasons. Either sense of the line comments on the failure, due to sentimentality, of nineteenth-century romantic literature.

The "moon nymph" from the Noh play *Hagoromo* does not deceive the priest who finds her magic "feather-mantle." An artist at heart, he returns her cloak on condition that she teach him her dance, which is symbolic of the moon's daily changes, and she fulfills her promise to do so.[46] In "immacolata" Pound conflates her with the Virgin Mary for her purity, but the Virgin is soon to be recalled for her mercy instead. In the lines that follow, Aphrodite is linked to Artemis, the moon-goddess. The juxtaposition prepares for the significant merging of Aphrodite with the moon later in the canto. Artemis has so far been symbolic of the strict justice of the process, as we saw in Canto 30. In this case, however, Pound refers to the Artemis of Ephesus, an Artemis who shows compassion to artists—and compassion is a higher spiritual quality than the business-like equity shown by the moon nymph to the priest. She embodies the character of the Virgin as merciful intercessor ("paraclete") more completely than does the moon nymph, for she tempers justice with mercy—indeed, with love.

In effect, what Pound is doing is again invoking Aphrodite,

46. See Ezra Pound and Ernest Fenollosa, *The Classic Noh Theatre of Japan* (New York, 1959), pp. 98–104.

"Cythera egoista," the proud Cytherean, asking her to reveal herself to him in her loving and compassionate aspect—much as she revealed herself, once, to the mortal Anchises, and to Botticelli. He wants his Muse to look upon him with mercy. So far she has been "terrible in resistance." Only if and when she smiles upon his efforts will the poet be able to burst into full song. But she "of the eternal moods has fallen away," [47] and Pound falls once more into a "lower" style, continuing the process of self-purgation through the instrumentality of memory.

Although the moon has become the chief symbol of "the process," Artemis is no longer, as in Canto 30, its adequate embodiment. Reason and justice no longer suffice as the metaphysical ground of Pound's universe. What he desires is the knowledge and the certainty that love, which he has discovered to be the center of his own being, is equally at the core of "the process." What he desires is a knowledge beyond attestation by the reason. He is already intellectually convinced of the centrality of love in the universe. But though such knowledge may suffice for a philosopher, it is not enough for a poet. The certainty he desires can only be attained on a mystic, visionary level. When he attains this certainty, a fusion of emotion and reason, a reintegration of his Time-shattered, dissociated sensibility will have occurred.

The theme of Pound's memories, as they continue in profusion through the canto, is "remember that I have remembered,/ mia pargoletta,/ and pass on the tradition" (p. 84), and when the *ubi sunt* theme arises once more it is answered triumphantly, though almost inconspicuously:

> Nancy [48] where art thou?
> Whither go all the vair and the cisclatons
> and the wave pattern runs in the stone

47. A quotation from Yeats's "The Moods."
48. I cannot identify the "Nancy" referred to, nor do I think it important to do so, since the name functions symbolically as *concret Allgemeine* and metonymic representation of the object of Pound's nostalgia

> on the high parapet (Excideuil)
> Mt Segur and the city of Dioce
> Que tous les mois avons nouvelle lune.
>
> (p. 88)

The "resurgent" images of memory are seen at last as identical in nature with the pattern of endless recurrence observable in the objective process. Just as no season and no phase of the moon is ever permanently lost in the ever self-renewing process, so nothing once loved is ever essentially destroyed, but returns in original splendor: "tous les mois avons nouvelle lune." Memory and the process are of a like conservative and re-creative nature and have become intuitively equated.

Concurrent with this analogical, aesthetic discovery of equivalence between the inner and outer realms, there appears a new accession of insight, or grace, achieved on the visionary plane. It is registered with surprise, parenthetically—but the parenthesis does not close on grace: [49]

> (Cythera, in the moon's barge whither?
>   how hast thou the crescent for car?
>
> (p. 88)

Cythera is now visible in the barge-like crescent moon, responding more and more to Pound's call for her to reveal herself. The entrance of Aphrodite into the moon signifies the approach of the visionary realization of that which the poet already knows intellectually: that love is the root of the process and is the Concrete Universal which fuses the subjective and objective worlds into unity. Even now, however, Aphrodite is the dread,

---

as of his paradisal quest. It remains generally true that if Pound does not bother to identify or enlarge upon a name or event, then such identification is inessential and beside the point.

49. The parenthesis serves also as a pictogram for the crescent moon, which itself seems to link with Arabic *atasal*.

the terrible [deina], revealing herself still with the cold reserve of Artemis:

> with the veil of faint cloud before her
> Κύθηρα δεινὰ as a leaf borne in the current
> pale eyes as if without fire.[50]
>
> (p. 89)

Pound now reaches the end of his ordeal of self-purgation. Uttering the "Introibo" in preparation for communion with *"toh pan,* the all" (p. 89), he calls for the compassion of the Virgin, "Immaculata Regina," who is equally the moon-embarked Aphrodite, as he sounds the note of contrition to its depths:

> repos donnez à cils
>   senza termine funge Immaculata Regina
>   Les larmes que j'ai créées m'inondent
> Tard, très tard je t'ai connue, la Tristesse,
> I have been hard as youth sixty years.
>
> (p. 91)

The goddess may not yet have responded fully to his pleas for grace, but the following morning the poet awakens with a new, expanded sense of compassion. It includes all those fellow-prisoners on sick-call, for whom he feels the love that Odysseus had for his ill-fated crewmen, and even includes "England now that Winston's out," that England from which Pound had permanently and contemptuously parted in 1920. Now, after having sounded contrition to the depths, he has achieved an intermediate level of grace that translates itself into the fine lyrical

---

50. When we consider the preceding allusion (p. 89) to the "B-J" (Burne-Jones) "cartons" praised in *Mauberley* for doing justice to the eyes ("Thin like brook-water") of Elizabeth Siddal, it seems probable that Pound is superimposing Burne-Jones and Botticelli to get his picture of the "pale eyes" of dread Aphrodite.

mood of the "rose" lyric. These stanzas, based as they are on the stanzaic form of the *Rubaiyat*,[51] do in artistic fact accomplish that reinvigoration of tradition which has become programmatic in the *Pisan Cantos*:

> Tudor indeed is gone and every rose,
> Blood-red, blanch-white that in the sunset glows
> Cries: "Blood, Blood, Blood!" against the gothic stone
> Of England, as the Howard or Boleyn knows.

> Nor seeks the carmine petal to infer;
> Nor is the white bud Time's inquisitor
> Probing to know if its new-gnarled root
> Twists from York's head or belly of Lancaster;

> Or if a rational soul should stir, perchance,
> Within the stem or summer shoot to advance
> Contrition's utmost throw, seeking in thee
> But oblivion, not thy forgiveness, FRANCE.

A statement as to the structure of the lyric is necessary before its theme can be clearly discerned. The first stanza, it is obvious, presents the rose as suggestive, through color-symbolism, of the horrors of English history. The next two stanzas, however, consider the rose as a rose, suggestive only of the continuously self-renewing process of nature which exists without any relationship whatsoever to Time-as-history. The first stanza, as I see it, presents an attitude that past historical wrong is still painfully present in the consciousness of a new era, so that the present (the rose) cannot be enjoyed for itself but is constantly reminiscent of past evil. The rose as a symbol of nature cannot, in this view, be regarded for itself alone but is sentimentalized into suggesting the bloody past. Such is the view of the "young Dumas," who finds the waning moon an adequate symbol of the Crucifixion (and vice-versa). But Pound regards nature, or

51. John J. Espey, *Ezra Pound's* Mauberley: A *Study in Composition* (Berkeley, 1955), p. 108.

the process, as independent of history, as transcending Time-as-history and ultimately casting it into oblivion.

The next stanzas correct or oppose the picture given in the first by expressing absolute faith in self-renewal and in the ultimate non-entity of Time-as-history. The living present, the "white bud," is in Pound's view unrelated to past evil because the self-renewing "process" by which both external nature and the spirit of man are reborn operates without relevance to the moral order. Self-renewal, Pound is saying, is not achieved within any moral framework; the ordeal of contrition which he has undergone is not to be interpreted in the Christian sense of seeking forgiveness; it is to be interpreted in the amoral sense of the achievement of oblivion, the passing over of Lethe.

Time, capitalized in this lyric, is Time-as-history, as evil, and "Time is not." The evils of history, the evils any man commits, are ultimately buried by the life-restorative operation of the process. In the process, that which is deficient in essential being, and as such is evil, is never revived; only that which is full of being can come into being again. Pound's contrition has been an enactment of the death and burial of the old self, making way for the new. The "white bud" of Pound's new spiritual condition does not carry into its unfolding any contrition-laden, Time-oriented "rational soul," as Pound clearly states in the logically evolved syntax of the latter two stanzas.

On another level of interpretation, the "white bud" is England come to life again after the long period of self-decimation in the Wars of the Roses and after many wars with France. The rebirth of England is accomplished by the loss of historical bitterness—on the part both of the new England and the new France—and her ability to co-exist with France in complete "oblivion" of past wrong. Pound's personal experience of self-renewal is applied to the spiritual rebirth of nations, and his personal experience of the nullity of Time-as-history is extended into a symbolic expression of faith that not only in the past, but even now, after the blood-bath of World War II, a true European peace will be accomplished by a natural process of spiritual rebirth and burial of the old, guilt-laden self. The bitterness engendered by Time, lacking in true being, has not the strength to sustain itself against the onslaught of the process.

The last line of the canto is "sunset grand couturier." Nature is recognized as the great artist-dressmaker, and Pound, by implication, places himself in a lesser, dependent position. Canto 81, the visionary climax of the *Pisan Cantos*, uses the same image in bringing the theme of nature-as-artist to its apex of development. The canto begins with lines prelusive of the mystic union that is shortly to take place between Pound and nature conceived of as love:

> Zeus lies in Ceres' bosom
> Taishan is attended of loves
> > under Cythera, before sunrise.

Cythera is in the moon; Cythera is the moon. The moon, the major symbol of organic time, has come to be the unifying focus of time as subjectively experienced (in memory) and time as objectively experienced (in nature), and it is now fully identified with the major symbol of love, Aphrodite. Their imaginative fusion needing only the completion of mystical certitude, the vision proper soon begins. It is announced by the sudden onset of song. Dramatically speaking, it is not Pound who is singing, but Aphrodite who is singing to Pound:

> Yet
> Ere the season died a-cold
> Borne upon a zephyr's shoulder
> I rose through the aureate sky
> > *Lawes and Jenkyns guard thy rest*
> > *Dolmetsch ever be thy guest.*
> > > (p. 97)

The vision itself occurs when "there came new subtlety of eyes into my tent, whether of spirit or hypostasis,/ . . . nor

any pair showed anger." Pound sees and experiences the love
that is at the center of the universe, and he bursts into a song of
affirmation:

> What thou lovest well remains,
> > the rest is dross
> What thou lov'st well shall not be reft from thee
> What thou lov'st well is thy true heritage
> Whose world, or mine or theirs
> > or is it of none?
> First came the seen, then thus the palpable
> > Elysium, though it were in the halls of hell,
> What thou lovest well is thy true heritage.

The opening of this song, "What thou lovest well remains,/ the
rest is dross," announces the grand resolution of the conflict between Time and the beloved hours that generated the entire
dramatic movement of the Pisan sequence. Time-as-history,
mechanical time, is "dross."

It is not man, but nature who made order and grace, says
Pound:

> Pull down thy vanity, I say pull down.
> Learn of the green world what can be thy place
> In scaled invention or true artistry,
> Pull down thy vanity,
> > Paquin pull down!
> The green casque has outdone your elegance.

Paquin, the Parisian dress-designer, is a happy choice of symbol
for Western egotism, and especially for the egocentricity of the
Western artist, whom Pound chides for foolishly imagining that
he can do nature, "grand couturier," one better, so ignorant is
he of his proper place in relation to the natural world.

Canto 82 brings to an intense resolution the theme of death,
obverse of the theme of rebirth that has culminated in Pound's

mystical vision of love. The full vision of love completes itself in
this "death" canto, which is the second half of a climactic diptych of the sort Pound employs throughout the whole poem. If
we remember that "Death's seeds move in the year," that death
implies new life just as life implies death, we can have no difficulty in apprehending Pound's attitude toward physical death
in the present canto. Calling upon Whitman's great "Out of
the Cradle" lyric, in which the speaker realizes that the most
loving and soothing of all words is *death*, Pound enlarges upon
the same theme,[52] knowing now in his inmost being that love,
which is the heart of the process, is the central experience of
both life and death. Dying becomes an act of love (in a metaphysical sense, not simply as in light Elizabethan usage) by
which the dying lover becomes "connubium terrae":

> How drawn, O GEA TERRA,
>> what draws as thou drawest
>>> till one sink into thee by an arm's width
>> embracing thee. Drawest,
>>> truly thou drawest.
>> Wisdom lies next thee,
>>> simply, past metaphor.
> Where I lie let the thyme rise
>> and basilicum
>> let the herbs rise in April abundant.

When Pound says, "Where I lie let the thyme rise," the
suggestion is stronger than ever of the punning use of *thyme* to
mean organic time, that is, the process, which would reconsti-
tute the atoms of Pound's corpse into new life through the
vegetative cycle. *Basilicum* seems to be a punning reference to
the temple or altar which the grove still needs, suggesting a new
religious sensibility founded on reverence for nature. When

52. See an interesting discussion of this canto in Roy Harvey Pearce,
"Pound, Whitman, and the American Epic," *Ezra Pound*, ed. Sutton, pp.
164–67.

Pound now says, "let the herbs rise in April abundant," the pun on *urbs* completes an ingenious trio that compresses his whole world-view and its underlying comedy—the *hilaritas* of the poet's genial response to life (see Canto 83, p. 106) as well as the "happy ending" implicit in a *Paradiso*. The *urbs* Pound wishes to see rise is the city of Dioce, a *social* paradise on earth consonant with the paradisal vision of reality Pound has just experienced privately. Since Pound is certain that paradise exists in the here and now, the city that should be founded upon it, though it seem to rise from "the halls of hell," is more of a real possibility in his eyes now than ever before. The "rose" lyric, I think, expresses best the social optimism of the Pisan sequence. In the next canto the theme of "let the herbs rise" is restated in another image that similarly compresses the idea of the "city" with vegetation. The passage lends final support to my identification of the "herbs" pun:

> The roots go down to the river's edge
> and the hidden city moves upward
> white ivory under the bark.
>
> (p. 108)

In Canto 83 we have the tranquil aftermath of Pound's vision of the relation of love to the full process of life and death. He has attained, of course, complete certainty that

> Le Paradis n'est pas artificiel
> and Uncle William dawdling around Notre Dame
> in search of whatever
>   paused to admire the symbol
> with Notre Dame standing inside it.
>
> (p. 106)

After enjoying this bit of gentle fun at Yeats's incorrigible dualism, he returns to awareness of his own spiritual condition:

in the drenched tent there is quiet
sered eyes are at rest
(p. 107)

Water is finally connected with peace ("HUDOR et Pax"),
the peace that passes understanding. At the beginning of the
Pisan Cantos, however, Pound wished to be protected from the
rain:

and they digged a ditch round about me
lest the damp gnaw thru my bones.
(p. 7)

At the end of that first canto he had compared his memory to a
fountain, and the diamond-clear water within arose to counter-
balance the miserable rain that afflicted him from without. Finally, in Canto 83, Pound is at peace in his "drenched tent,"
the water within having merged with the water without: the
fountain of memory, and the rain (which is "of the process")
have become interfused.[53] They are both as one, and the
dualism of the basic subject-object relation, one of the central
problems of philosophy, is resolved in holistic synthesis. The
resolution is, of course, suprarational, but the problem of the
subject-object relationship is the philosophical center of the
Pisan sequence, announced as such in the poem on page 89, just
after Cythera appears "in the moon barge" to symbolize the
fusion that is to take place:

"This alone, leather and bones between you and τὸ πᾶν,"
[*toh pan,* the all] [54]

"You" (subject) and "the all" (object) finally merge. The beloved hours achieve transpersonal hypostasis in the indestructi-

53. Read discusses water imagery from a different but complementary
point of view ("The Pattern of the *Pisan Cantos,*" pp. 408–9).
54. The brackets surrounding this last phrase are Pound's.

bility of the process, and Time-as-history—indeed, the whole
time-space continuum in which the subject-object dichotomy is
a reality—is nullified.

This attainment of union, or *atasal*, as Pound has called it, is
most fully realized poetically in this later passage from Canto
83, which attempts to express the confused sense of self and
non-self that the vision has left in its wake:

> A fat moon rises lop-sided over the mountain
> The eyes, this time my world,
>> But pass and look *from* mine
>> between my lids
>>> sea, sky, and pool
>>> alternate
>>> pool, sky, sea

> morning moon against sunrise

> like a bit of the best antient greek coinage.
>   (p. 113)

The mystic experience Emerson records of becoming a "trans-
parent eye-ball" is exactly analogous to this experience of
Pound's, the different philosophical positions of the respective
authors notwithstanding. (It would seem that in Pound some
of the giants of American transcendentalism, Whitman, Emerson, and perhaps Thoreau—as naturalist-observer of ants,
wasps, and such—are worthily incorporated and brought down
to earth unsullied in a twentieth-century synthesis.[55]) In the

55. The conventionally recognized American literary tradition, as
treated by F. O. Matthiessen, for example, was consciously junked by
Pound in favor of the Jefferson-Adams-Van Buren corpus in the middle
cantos. Now, in the *Pisan Cantos*, the force of the American transcen-
dentalist tradition emerges as a profound influence on the whole spirit of
the sequence—most influential when Pound is (or seems to be) least
aware of its presence—and both the idealist-transcendentalist and prac-
tical-political strains of our literary heritage rest comfortably together in
a great poetic synthesis. But the influence of the former strain seems to
me the deeper of the two in the profoundly visionary Pisan sequence.

lines quoted, subject and object change places, fuse, share total vision unhampered by the limiting distinction of self and non-self. The last image, combining moon and sun in one field of vision, recalls the Confucian *Ming* ideogram for the "total light process" or intelligence, seen previously on page 117.

Fusion of sun and moon in the *Ming* ideogram is, as a matter of fact, the end or goal of the whole symbolic process involving the moon-goddesses, with Aphrodite at their head, as intercessors between the poet and the sun. The moon, as reflector of the sun's light and as the gentle, feminine counterpart of Helios, has become the half-way point at which the poet's subjectivity is finally merged with the objective process. Throughout the *Pisan Cantos*, both the successful invocation of Aphrodite and the whole course of mystic fusion occur before sunrise, that is, before the distinctions between subject and object are sharply marked by the light of day, which revives the painful sights and sounds of the camp enclosure. The poet never revels in the full light of the sun until after the intercessor, like the moon nymph in *Hagoromo*, reveals her most guarded secrets to her devoted priest and grants him the culminating vision. Full of the certitude of his revelation, the poet can then become reconciled with the sun, which is the light of *reason* in the cosmic symbology of these cantos.

Having achieved spiritual reintegration through a vision far more penetrating than any clarity of physical vision that takes place in the sun, Pound can then face Helios with tranquil reassurance, knowing that the light of day, the light of dissective reason that reveals "the process" in its objective character alone, fails to reveal the whole truth. Helios is, of course, himself an image of "the process," as is the moon, but he is the chief symbol of the process as manifest in the *object*-world, in appearance unrelated to the subject-world of the poet. But the moon, immemorially an image of the "feminine" and "poetic" elements of human consciousness, is in her double nature—her "real" and "imaginative" aspects, a perfect dramatic object in which the two aspects can achieve synthesis.

Now, in Canto 83, the poet's strained sensibilities can relax into peaceful accommodation with the light of the sun; Helios can no longer disturb, as he did at the end of the lynx song, the delicate process of spiritual rebirth that has now been irrevocably achieved:

There is September sun on the pools

Plura diafana
     Heliads lift the mist from the young willows.
                     (p. 108)

And now the ants seem to stagger
         as the dawn sun has trapped their shadows,

             .   .   .

the sun as a golden eye
     between dark cloud and the mountain.
                   (p. 109)

Suddenly, after describing the infant wasp who has descended "to carry our news/ . . . to them that dwell under the earth," Pound exclaims: "Cristo Re, Dio Sole." Christ, wasp, and sun become a striking "metaphysical" image. Just as the Virgin became identified with the moon-goddess, Christ is converted to the sun god, whom Pound can now address directly, with no more need of an intercessor. In the last of the series, Canto 84, Pound offers formal devotion to Apollo, god of the sun:

     Incense to Apollo
               Carrara
                     snow on the marble
   snow-white
          against stone-white
   on the mountain.
                   (p. 116)

But the moon remains still the most intimate and all-encompassing image of the process, the process as the love that

moves all things in harmony, mediating between the inner
world of spirit and the outer world of nature:

> Under white clouds, cielo di Pisa 4.5
> out of all this beauty something must come,
>
> O moon my pin-up,
>   chronometer.
>
> (p. 117)

This beautiful last image of the moon (before its Confucian
presentation in the *Ming* ideogram) would need little comment
except that it forces home the thesis underlying this entire
chapter, that the theme of time provides the structural and
metaphysical key to the understanding of the *Pisan Cantos*.
Just as the clock of history, mechanical time, loses meaning for
the G.I. contemplating his pin-up, so does it lose all reality for
Pound as he contemplates the moon, time-as-nature, time-as-
love, the sole chronometer that would have authority in his city
of Dioce.

Conclusion

I HAVE HAD to reserve for consideration in this final section one of the most interesting of Pound's early comments on the overall design he intended for his vast poem. In "A Packet for Ezra Pound," written in 1928 and published together with A Vision, Yeats reports what Pound had recently told him about the form of that "immense poem" of which twenty-seven cantos had by then been published. Yeats gives us at length a kind of structural outline Pound gave him for the *Cantos*, an outline which begins with sequences of letters of the alphabet and ends with an analogy of the poem to a Renaissance fresco:

> He has scribbled on the back of an envelope certain sets of letters that represent emotions or archetypal events—I cannot find any adequate definition—ABCD and then JKLM, and then each set of letters repeated, and then ABCD inverted and this repeated, and then a new element XYZ, then certain letters that never recur, and then all sorts of combinations of XYZ and JKLM and ABCD and DCBA, and all set whirling together. He has shown me upon the wall a photograph of a Cosimo Tura decoration in three compartments, in the upper the Triumph of Love and the Triumph of Chastity, in the middle Zodiacal signs, and in the lower certain events in Cosimo Tura's day. The Descent and the Metamorphosis—ABCD and JKLM—his fixed elements, took the place of the Zodiac, the archetypal persons—XYZ—that of the Triumphs, and certain modern events—his letters that do not recur—that of those events in Cosimo Tura's day.[1]

1. William Butler Yeats, A Vision, rev. ed. (New York, 1956), pp. 4–5.

It would be fruitless to try to pinpoint the exact material in the *Cantos* represented by the above "sets of letters." It is clear that Yeats is not transcribing all that Pound actually scribbled down for him; and, in any case, we are not at all certain that Pound jotted down on that envelope anything more than a very general outline of his fugal procedure. What is most interesting in Yeats's report is Pound's comparison of the thematic levels of his poem to the "three compartments" of the Cosimo Tura painting. Together with Francesco del Cossa, Cosimo Tura covered the four walls of the Room of the Months in the Schifanoja, the palace of the Estes at Ferrara, with frescoes representing the history of Ferrara under Duke Borso. The photograph Pound showed Yeats is of the east wall. Guy Davenport, in his unpublished dissertation on the first thirty cantos, has done an exhaustive scholarly analysis of the Tura-Del Cossa paintings. He states that "their theme is the order and variety of an ideal life; their form, like that of many long works, is cyclic, the pace of times and seasons; their spirit inheres in the hundreds of portraits of real people." [2]

My own concern will be to show that in the three levels of the Cosimo Tura fresco we have an analogy to the three-phase linear ordering of Cantos 1–84. Did Pound have in mind a similar analogy between painting and poem? Probably no one could ever say with certainty that he did. The closest we can get to "proof" for such an assumption is to establish that there are clear parallels between the three phases of the *Cantos*, as elucidated in this study, and the three divisions of the fresco.

According to Yeats, the events of Tura's day, depicted on the lowest level of the fresco, are represented by letters that do not recur. These events and faces signify the quotidian, the impermanent things of time. Although Tura painted the events of Borso's reign to glorify the Duke, Pound himself negatively regarded such events of history, as indicated by his treatment of Western history throughout the *Cantos* and especially in the

2. "A Reading of I–XXX of the Cantos of Ezra Pound" (Ph.D. dissertation, Harvard, 1961), p. 158.

first phase of the poem, where the failure of Borso to "keep the peace" is a recurrent theme. "Time as Disorder" seems to be the theme, as Pound saw it, both of the lower level of the fresco and of the first phase of the *Cantos*.

Yeats says that the "fixed elements," represented by the letters ABCD and JKLM in various combinations, stand for the two main themes of the poem, the Descent into Hades and the Metamorphosis, and he points out that these themes are identified in Pound's mind with the zodiacal signs in the middle of the fresco. The zodiac stands for the progression of the months and seasons and, of course, for their eternal recurrence. If the historical section of the painting became associated for Pound with "Time as Disorder," then the zodiacal portion stands for "Time as Order," or what I have treated as the theme of organic time. This purgatorial theme, the theme of hope and the vision of an ideal social order based on the rational order of the cosmic process, is the keynote of the second phase of the *Cantos*. The themes of the Descent and the Metamorphosis are symbolic of the disappearance of vegetation, the "descent" of the year into winter, and of the reappearance of plant life, the resurgence of the year into the new life of spring. In my analysis of Canto 47 I brought out, among other things, this relation between the Adonis-vegetation myth (Adonis' descent and metamorphosis into the anemone) and the myth of the Nekuia, the descent of Odysseus into Hades followed by his re-emergence after undergoing spiritual transformation through exposure to the wisdom of Tiresias. The letters ABCD and JKLM, which Pound used to represent these two complementary themes of descent and metamorphosis, appear to be significant also because they are groups of four—the number which Pound particularly ascribes to the "process," as we discover if we read on into *Rock-Drill* and come upon passages such as these, concerning the "4/ seasons" (p. 49), the "tuan [virtues], there are four of them" (p. 61), and "the whole creation concerned with 'FOUR'" (p. 76).

Finally, the letters XYZ stand for the archetypal persons,

the gods and goddesses ceremonially represented in the upper divisions of the frescoes, and specifically Venus in connection with the Triumph of Love. After their disappearance in the middle cantos, the goddesses re-emerge in the Pisan section as embodiments of the paradisal theme. In this third phase of his poem, which I have called "Time as Love," Venus and Diana merge for Pound into two inseparable aspects of the unitary "process"—organic time newly apprehended as the outward form or manifestation of that inner principle of the universe which Pound had previously conceived of as "stillness" and now identifies with Love. If Pound significantly chose groups of *four* letters to represent "the process," in the sketch he gave Yeats, then his choice of *three* letters, XYZ, to symbolize the Triumphs could be equally meaningful. The mystic number three, in the *Pisan Cantos* as in the *Divine Comedy*, stands for the universal principle of Love in its trinitarian aspect. Pound develops, in the *Pisan Cantos*, the conception of a feminine trinity to be worshiped in his ideal city of Dioce at three altars adorned with three aromatic herbs. Just as Beatrice appeared to Dante in the earthly paradise, so Love manifests herself to Pound at Pisa, incarnate in the form of eyes, and his sensibility is "imparadised" even in the midst of hell.

The three panels of the fresco, as Pound discussed them with Yeats, do closely parallel the over-all design of the *Cantos* as this study reveals that design. It is tempting to think that Pound conceived of the design of his poem in direct consequence of his exposure to the frescoes, but "Pound has explicitly said that he came upon the Tura frescoes after the poem was well under way, and found there not a source but a confirmation of his procedures." [3]

Although this analysis of the *Cantos* concludes with Canto 84, I would like nevertheless to quote a passage from the climactic last canto of *Rock-Drill*. The opening lines of Canto 95, which I shall take the liberty to let stand unanalyzed, epito-

3. I quote from an unpublished letter of Hugh Kenner's.

mize, in my estimation, the whole development of the *Cantos* after the Pisan section towards a type of abstract poetry which attempts to formulate, in metaphysical terms, the equation intuited in the *Pisan Cantos* between Love and organic time: [4]

> LOVE, gone as lightning,
> > enduring 5000 years.
> Shall the comet cease moving
> > or the great stars be tied in one place!
> "Consonantium demonstratrix"
> > > > ἔφατ᾽ Beda
>
> Deus est anima mundi,
> > animal optimum
> > > et sempiternum.
> Tempus est ubique,
> > > non motus
> > > > in vesperibus orbis.
> Expergesci thalamis, gravat serpella nimbus
> Mist weighs down the wild thyme plants.

4. The one critic who has concerned himself with the theme of time in the *Cantos* as a whole is George Dekker in *The Cantos of Ezra Pound*. His awareness of the theme is restricted, however, to the consideration of time as one of the dramatic unities. He speaks of Pound's "jumping about in time and place" in the early cantos so that he could "discover and reveal the scope of usura's domain"; "the tyranny of usura is evil," Dekker says, "because it destroys the rhythms, the harmonies, the magnetisms of the temporal order of nature to which man belongs and in which, Pound believes, man must seek his salvation. Therefore, Pound gives up his freedom of movement" and progressively comes "to accept the limitations of time and place" (pp. 178–79). In pointing out the disruptive effects of usury upon "the temporal order of nature," Dekker hits upon the very core of what the *Cantos* are all about, but within the space of a few sentences, unaware of the significance of what he has just said, he remarks: "However, I do not wish to exaggerate the importance of Pound's treatment of time; for it does not provide us with any 'key' to the poem's development" (p. 179).

Appendix A

On the Early Cantos:
From the Letters of Ezra Pound to John Quinn

THE FOLLOWING EXTRACTS from the unpublished letters of Ezra Pound to John Quinn add in small but significant ways to our knowledge of the earliest stages of composition of the *Cantos*. Editorial elisions are marked by three doubled-spaced points (. . .). Pound's own ellipses are represented by thin-spaced points (...). The excerpted letters are typewritten, but little attempt is made here to reproduce peculiarities of spacing.

31 December 1916
Am at work on a long poem. Which last two words have an awful sound when they appear close together.

11 April 1917
A long poem I sent to "Poetry" will feed me during the summer. . . .
. . . It is the three first cantos of an endless affair which will probably, or let us pray I dont [sic] get stuck.... or that I do get stuck..... run to 100.
Both Byron and Swinburn [sic] printed chunks of their long things before they were finished, so there can be no real objection on that ground to including an unfinished opus.

4 July 1917
[Concerning "Three Cantos," which Pound cut from the *Poetry* version of twenty-four pages to eighteen and sent to Quinn for

inclusion in a Knopf book of his poetry, *Quia Pauper Amavi*]

Thanks very much for your trouble with "Three Cantos". It is more than kind of you to have had it copied and gone over it. ALL the punctuation suggestions are improvements. [Pound's underlining]

"Maelids" is correct. They [,] the nymphs of the apple-trees [,] are my one bit of personal property in greek mythology. The professed and professional Hellenists have, I believe, let them alone. I scored with them even on the assiduous Aldington, who had translated the greek as "apple-trees".

6 October 1919

[Canto Four was privately printed October 4, 1919.]
I enclose proofs of my Fourth Canto. . . .

. . .

I have done Canto V. . . . . . somethime [sic] between theatres . . . even tryescript [sic] of it not "dry" yet. .

24 November 1919

I have finished Canto VI.; W.L. [Wyndham Lewis] much distressed by my preoccupation of the XIIth. century; which is I admit very unfortunate from point of view of immediate impact on general public. W. L. does not however offer a better alternative. I cant [sic] knock off a super Madame Bovary in pentameter in a fortnight. Art is not only long but bloody bloody slow.

13 December 1919

[Extract concerns the volume which became *Poems 1918–21*, published by Boni & Liveright in 1921]

. . . Liveright seems disposed to bring out vol. of poems. Same as Quia Pauper Amavi, with cantos 4 to 7 in place of the first three.

. . .

I suspect my "Cantos" are getting too too too abstruse and obscure for human consumption, and I can't follow Yeats into the hopes of a Tuatha Daanaan audience, but am bearing up . . .

24 March 1920
Have now done another small book of verse, I hope an *oeuvre*, and got on with cantos.

24 March 1920 [Pound's enclosure to Thayer of the *Dial*]
Mr. Quinn implies you want my verse, rather than my prose. I send four cantos. Canto IV. is o.k. by itself, Cantos V. VI. VII shd. appear together as the Lorenzacchio [sic] Medici begins in V. and ends the VII. I shouldn't insist on their being all printed together, but it wd. be better. . . . There are not likely to be more than two cantos each year . . . [Canto IV was published in the June 1920 *Dial*; Cantos V-VII in the *Dial* of August 1921.]

9 October 1920 [Extract concerns *Poems 1918–21*]
C. re Liveright. I have sent the rest of copy for "Three Portraits"
It contains the Imperium Romanum (Propertius)
            The Middle Ages (Provence)
            Mauberley (today)
    and cantos IV-VII,
It is all I have done since 1916, and my most important book,
I at any rate think canto VII the best thing I have done;
    If America won't have it, then Tant Pisssss as the French say. . . .
At any rate the three portraits, falling into a Trois Contes scheme, plus the Cantos, which come out of the middle of me and are not a mask, are what I have to say, and the first formed book of poem [sic] I have made.

21 February 1922
    [Extract concerns *The Waste Land* and a new canto which appeared as Canto VIII in the *Dial* of May 1922 but was to become the present Canto 2]
    About enough, Eliot's poem, to make the rest of us shut up shop. I haven't done so; have in fact knocked out another Canto (not in the least à la Eliot, or connected with "modern life"), that also <u>may</u> appear in the Dial.

20 June 1922

Have had busy spring. . . . and have blocked in four cantos
—(Including the "Honest Sailor", which I hope I haven't spoiled).
At work on the "Hell" canto, chiefly devoted to the English. [The
"Honest Sailor" anecdote appears in the present Canto 12.]

4–5 July 1922

. . . having got five cantos blocked out, I am about ready for
the vacation I did not take in Italy.

10 August 1922

[The "Canto IX" of the extract finally became Cantos 8–11]
Am reading up historic background for Canto IX. don't know
that it will in any way improve the draft of the canto as it stands;
shall probably only get more bewildered; but may avoid a few historic idiocies, or impossibilities.

Authorities differ as to whether Sigismund Malatesta raped a
german girl in Verona, with such vigour that she "passed on", or
whether it was an italian in Pesaro, and the pope says he killed her
first and raped her afterwards; also some authorities say it was
Farnese and not Malatesta who raped the bishop of Fano, and in
fact all the <u>minor</u> points that might aid one in forming an historic
rather than a fanciful idea of his character seem "shrouded in
mystery" or rather lies.

I suppose one has to "select". If I find he was TOO bloody
quiet and orderly it will ruin the canto. Which needs a certain
boisterousness and disorder to contrast with his constructive work.

Francesco Sforza, whom I had first cast for the villan [sic] seems
also to have had good reason for etc. etc. At any rate I have had
some interesting hours of research or at least reading; which are
probably of no paractical [sic] use.

I come out rather loke [sic] Ole Man Comley, who used to shoot
his gob, and take a new chaw off the plug, saying "Boys, NEVer
chew terbacca!". No, Mr Quinn, don't you never try to write a
epict, it is too bloody complicated."

. . .

There's one sopt [sic] re/ Malatesta that you may like. He was in Rome toward the end, whole existence of his state depending on negotiations, and he had about made up his mind to murder the pope (Paul II, who however was sly enough not to receive him in private, but surrounded by a gang of <u>cardinals whom he cd. trust.)</u> Malatesta spent most of his time in the papal library, and when they asked the librarian, Platina, what they talked about he said

"We talked about books, and fighting, and unusual intelligence, both in the ancients, and in men of our own time, in short the things one wd. naturally talk about." Hang it all its [sic] a bloody good period,. a town the size of Rimini, with Pier Francesca, Pisanello, Mino da Fiesoli, and Alberti as architect. The pick of the bunch, all working there at one time or another . . .

21 September 1922

I have been plugging on at the cantos, almost without interruption.

17 February 1923

Have blocked in 4 cantos on Malatesta and am now verifying last details (Vatican Library this A.M.), also geographical verification, cross country in wake of S.M. to see how the land lay. . . .

Trust, or rather hope, you'll like my version of the Honest Sailor, which comes in Canto XIII (to follow the Malatesta cantos) . . .

29 May 1923

. . . Have been snowed under, or at least working on my Malatesta Cantos steadily and without let up from middle of Feb. until about five weeks ago . . .

11 August 1923 [Extract concerns the Malatesta Cantos]

Cantos are in Criterion for July. More being prepared for Three Mts, edition de luxe.

Appendix B

The Source of the Seven Lakes Canto

ACCORDING to Mary de Rachewiltz, Canto 49 is one of Pound's favorite cantos. It is, in addition, the pivot of the whole poem, as Hugh Kenner noted two decades ago. Through the kindness of Princess de Rachewiltz and the generosity of Professor Sanehide Kodama of Doshisha Women's College, Kyoto, Japan, the chief source of Canto 49 has recently been made available for publication in this volume. It appears here in its entirety in an English translation of the Chinese and Japanese original, as well as in facsimile reproductions of representative portions. (The contents of this Appendix were obtained too late for inclusion in Chapter VIII, which was already in page proof, so that the following description of the source of Canto 49 considerably supplements and slightly modifies my earlier comments.)

The original manuscript in Pound's possession dates, according to stylistic evidence, from the sixteenth or seventeenth centuries. It could also, of course, be a later copy or imitation of a sequence of poems of that period. Both the Chinese and Japanese poems it contains were composed by a Japanese poet (or poets), since the Chinese poems are clearly in a pseudo-Chinese style following a tradition of imitation that stems from the Hei-an period (A.D. 794). The quality of the poems varies from mediocre to good, and none, whether Chinese or Japanese, is first-rate. Physically, the manuscript is in the form of a book that folds like a screen. Research fails to discover any previous publication of the manuscript poems, and it is safe to assume that the "Source of the Seven Lakes Canto" exists in only the one, unique manuscript copy.

The English translation was made from photographs of the original supplied by Mary de Rachewiltz. Although the manuscript order of the poems was not indicated by the Princess, it can be inferred from internal evidence. Both the Chinese and Japanese poems describe the eight famous scenes in the Sho-Sho area of China, the region where the Rivers Sho and Sho (Hsiang and Hsiang in Chinese) converge. These scenes are always listed in the following order:

I. Wild Geese Plummeting to the Flat Sands
II. Sailboat Returning from Far-off Gulf
III. Mist over a Mountain Town
IV. Evening Snow over the River
V. Autumn Moon on Lake Dōtei
VI. Night Rain in Sho-Sho
VII. Evening Bell of Misty Temple
VIII. Evening Sunlight over a Fishing Village

The scenes as named above are the titles of the two series of poems, Chinese and Japanese, in the manuscript, except that a Chinese poem corresponding to the seventh scene, and a Japanese poem corresponding to the fifth scene, are missing from the photographs supplied by Mary de Rachewiltz. (Whether they are missing from the manuscript itself is a problem discussed in the notes accompanying the translation.)

The reason that Pound calls Canto 49 the "Seven Lakes" Canto is not completely clear. If only seven of the eight scenes actually appear in the manuscript, then the reason for the number seven becomes obvious. (Seven is a mystical number both in the East and the West, and the author or editor of the manuscript may therefore have deliberately omitted one of the eight famous scenes.) Only a few of the poems can be said to refer directly to a lake or lake region, but in composing his verses "For the seven lakes," Pound may be exercising poetic license in order to suggest "the seven seas," or the whole world, which could ideally achieve the condition of Confucian harmony projected in microcosm in the canto.

Pound could undoubtedly read most of the Chinese portion of the manuscript. He could not read the Japanese poems, but a translation of them could have been made for him or read to him. It is clear, however, that that portion of Canto 49 (lines 1–32) based on the source material could derive almost entirely from the Chinese poems alone. I have provided as postscript to the translation of the Chinese poems an outline collating lines 1–32 of Canto 49 with the relevant Chinese materials. The freedom with which Pound selected images and "translated" them becomes immediately evident. The need to study Canto 49 as an integral, self-consistent poetic structure entirely original with Pound is thereby emphasized beyond dispute.

The translations included here were made by Professor Kodama. I have edited those made from the Chinese poems in direct consultation with him, and the resulting tentative versions with accompanying notes are published here with the approval of Mr. Kodama. The translations are as literal as English idiom permits and attempt to capture some of the flavor of the originals. The poems in Chinese consist of four lines each with seven syllables (characters) to a line. The Japanese poems, which appear in the unedited English version of Mr. Kodama, are all in the thirty-one-syllable form known as *tanka*, a form much older than the seventeen-syllable *haiku*. The translations necessarily ignore the metric systems of the originals.

The Chinese Poems

I. Wild Geese Plummeting to the Flat Sands

High across they dot the sky with thin black ink.
In lines the autumn geese fly down to the cold beach.
Reed blossoms and snow look much the same in Kōyō: [1]
Deceived, they thrash [2] frozen feathers at the setting sun.

II. Sailboat Returning from Far-off Gulf

There is a tinge of Autumn on the surrounding blue mountains.

1. More literally, "Reed blossoms deceptively look like snow . . ."
2. The geese shake the unexpected snow off their feathers.

Flat are the silver waves . . . .[1]
The returning mast comes gradually onto ten thousand blossoms.[2]
Home is above the River, toward the setting sun.

III. Mist over a Mountain Town

A wine flag [3] on the pole is in the slanting sun.
Clusters of huts are in the misty mountains on high.
Squatting and drunk, I see the darker peaks and vales.
The peaceful sun . . . .

IV. Evening Snow over the River

The clouds are colorless, the sky is low, and jewel dust is flying.
In a small boat, I fall into a poetic mood.
From an inlet above—the squeaking of an oar.
I imagine another man in rapture, there behind the mountain.

V. Autumn Moon on Lake Dōtei

In the western window first appears the evening mist.
The hazy waves in the vastness bathe the fragrant olive blossoms.
The fishing boat knows not the traveler's gloom.
A wind just wafts its cold silhouette and passes the reed blossoms by.

VI. Night Rain in Sho-Sho

The deserted River simply grieves my soul.
Frozen cloud and clinging rain dampen the twilight.

1. The remainder of the line is obscure in the ms. The same is true for the last line of the following poem.

2. The "ten thousand blossoms" is a metaphor for the sunlight glinting off the waves.

3. The phrase appears in Canto 49, but unrelated to its literal meaning here, which is that of a flag in front of a tavern.

Under a lamp I hear pipes and strings beneath the mugworts.
I can only turn to a bamboo branch and add my teardrops.[1]

VII. Evening Bell of Misty Temple [2]

VIII. Evening Sunlight over a Fishing Village

Twilight bewilders the crows that swarm on the sandy beach.
North of the River and south I hear clamoring fish and shrimp.[3]
I send for a boy to buy wine; I get drunk;
I lie toward the west wind that sets the reed blossoms dancing.[4]

Written by Genryu [5]

---

1. A Chinese legend relates that the Hsiang-chi (Princesses Hsiang), two daughters of the Emperor Yao, wept grievously upon hearing a rumor that their beloved Emperor Shun, who succeeded their father, had passed away. The tears of the Hsiang-chi dyed the bamboo leaves, and dappled bamboos thus came into being. [Lines 2-6 of Canto 49 derive largely from this poem. The interpretation I have given of Pound's lines is that the beginning of the canto introduces the theme of political disorder *via* an image of the ship of state voyaging sadly through a storm. If Pound knew the legend of the sisters Hsiang, he would of course have found in it a perfect justification for giving a political twist to the theme of gloom in "Night Rain in Sho-Sho." In this political connection, it is interesting to note that the two poems which served as sources for Canto 49, lines 37-45, celebrate the legendary reigns of Shun and Yao respectively, the two emperors whose reigns are alluded to in "Night Rain."]

2. This seventh of the eight famous scenes of Sho-Sho seems not to be represented by a separate Chinese poem in the manuscript owned by Pound. In any case, the photographs of the manuscript which Princess de Rachewiltz handed to Professor Kodama contain only seven Chinese poems. However, lines 13-14 of Canto 49, "Behind hill the monk's bell/ borne on the wind," seem clearly derivable from no other poem than the missing "Evening Bell of Misty Temple." Perhaps the photographer, in taking pictures of the manuscript, skipped a page.

3. The poet seems to be saying, elliptically, that he hears the village fishermen shouting as they gather in fish and shrimp.

4. The Chinese verb "to dance," which is used here in a transitive sense, suggests a highly stylized, ritualistic courtly dance executed with plume in hand, especially to petition heaven for rain in time of drought.

5. The poet is otherwise unknown. Nor is it clear whether Genryu wrote only Poem VIII, or several, or all of them.

Collation of lines 1–32 of Canto 49 with their Chinese sources in the "Seven Lakes" manuscript:

Lines in Canto 49	*Corresponding Chinese Sources*
2–6	Poem VI
7–17	Poem II; Poem V (title, and perhaps lines 3–4); perhaps also the missing Poem VII
18–19	Poem III (lines 1–2)
20–24	Poem IV (title, and lines 1–2)
25–27	Poem I (title and lines 1–2)
28	Poem VIII (line 1)
29–30, 32	Poem VIII (lines 2–3).

The Japanese Poems

I. Attracted by their friends on the reedy shore
          feeding first,
    The wild geese flying in the sky
          are also coming down.

II. Seeing the waves of clouds floating
              portending winds and high waves
     The boatman is returning home
          before fishing.

III. Clear are the mountain peaks above the village
              with a tall pine tree:
      Below at the foot are the clouds
          sunk in the storm.

IV. With the deep snow on the reed leaves
     The water near the shore of a deep inlet
          shows the color
              that is not quite the color of the twilight.

V. (No Japanese poem on Lake Dōtei was included in the photographs of the manuscript received from Mary de Rachewiltz.)

VI. By the drops of water
               leaking through the thatch
   I notice the night rain
               voiceless in the waves of the boat coming up.

      VII. At the bells resounding
                  down from the mountain,
        A traveler, too, hurries his way.

    VIII. The color of the waves can still be seen
                 in the track of the setting sun,
       But the shore is dark and home is hidden
            under the trees.

The Manuscript Paintings

PHOTOGRAPHS of six different manuscript paintings were received from Princess de Rachewiltz. Among them, only the scene corresponding to the "Wild Geese" poem is absolutely identifiable by content alone. I succeeded in pairing all the poems and paintings beyond possibility of doubt, however, by matching the mildew stains on each. In the manuscript, which folds like a screen, a poem and painting which face each other show the same mildew marks in reverse. The following reproductions include a selection of paintings and corresponding poems, and it is important to bear in mind that the images of Canto 49 may have been inspired as much by the paintings as by the poems.

A list of the facing pairs of painting and poem reveals more clearly the structure of the manuscript:

1. Chinese Poem I faces Scene (painting) I
2.
3. Chinese Poem III faces Scene III
4. Japanese Poem IV faces Scene IV
5. Chinese Poem V faces Scene V
6. Japanese Poem VI faces Scene VI
7.
8. Japanese Poem VIII faces Scene VIII

No painting for Poem II or VII was received, but the symmetry of correspondences here suggests strongly the presence of a

Chinese Poem I
"Wild Geese Plummeting
to the Flat Sands"

Sho-Sho Scene I
". . . geese line out with
the autumn" — Canto 49

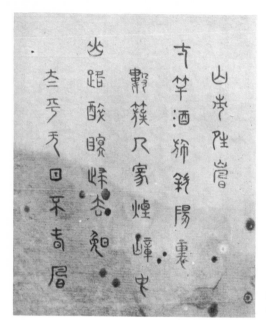

Chinese Poem III
"Mist over a Mountain Town"

Sho-Sho Scene III
"Sparse chimneys smoke in
the cross light" — Canto 49

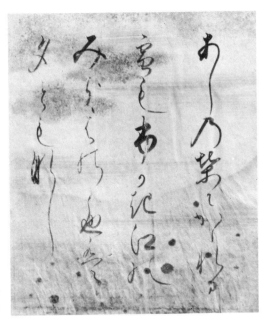

Japanese Poem IV
"Evening Snow over the River"

Sho-Sho Scene IV
"Comes then snow scur on
the river. And a world is
covered with jade" — Canto 49

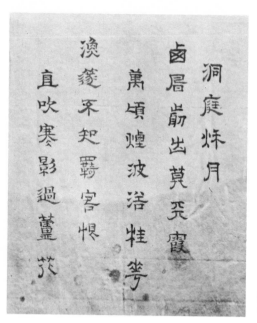

Chinese Poem V
"Autumn Moon on Lake Dōtei"

Sho-Sho Scene V
"Autumn Moon; hills rise about
lakes against sunset" — Canto 49

Chinese Poem VII ("Evening Bell of Misty Temple") in the manuscript. I can also state that there definitely exists a painting for Poem II, a scene showing sailboats viewed from high above. (I saw it and made a note of it when I first saw the photographs of the manuscript at Brunnenburg.) By some mistake, it was not included among the photographs received.

If we remember that the manuscript folds like a screen, we can now deduce its exact structure, page by page. Imagine each fold of the manuscript as the capital letter V, and the whole as a series of connected V's, thus: VVVVV, etc. Each V represents a pair of facing pages, and there must be, or must have been, twelve such pairs in the manuscript, as we can see if we attempt to reconstruct the order of paintings and poems from the evidence of the above list of facing pairs. The following scheme, inferred from the list given above, represents the only possible order of pages in the manuscript:

V_1 = Chinese Poem I (Left-hand p.) facing Scene I (Right-hand p.)

V_2 = Japanese Poem I (L) facing Chinese Poem II (R)

V_3 = Scene II (L) facing Japanese Poem II (R)

V_4 = Chinese Poem III (L) facing Scene III (R)

V_5 = Japanese Poem III (L) facing Chinese Poem IV (R)

V_6 = Scene IV (L) facing Japanese Poem IV (R)

V_7 = Chinese Poem V (L) facing Scene V (R)

V_8 = Japanese Poem V (L) facing Chinese Poem VI (R)

V_9 = Scene VI (L) facing Japanese Poem VI (R)

V_{10} = Chinese Poem VII (L) facing Scene VII (R)

V_{11} = Japanese Poem VII (L) facing Chinese Poem VIII (R)

V_{12} = Scene VIII (L) facing Japanese Poem VIII

(This scheme assumes, of course, that the manuscript is intact.) Thus, each painted scene in the manuscript is set between a pair of poems, Chinese to the left, Japanese to the right, and it becomes clear that the poems are intended to embellish the central scene rather than vice-versa. The manuscript paintings, therefore, ought certainly to be considered as important a source for Canto 49 as the manuscript poems. Accordingly, several of the paintings have been reproduced in the inset.

Index

Acoetes, 48, 49
Acrisius, 55, 56, 60, 65, 67
Actaeon, 277
Adams, John, 138-40, 146, 147, 149-52, 212, 213, 232-34, 289n.
Adams, John Quincy, 138, 140, 141, 152, 153, 160
Adonis, 163, 173, 175, 177-79, 182, 189-91
Aeschylus, 31, 70, 71, 75
Aesop, 152
Agamemnon, 66, 71, 72, 75, 101, 267
Albigensian Crusade, the, 106
Alvarez, A., 7, 33n.
Analects, 202
Analyst, The, 37n, 48, 61, 77n.
Anchises, 279
Annotated Index, The, 54n., 127, 225
Antheil, George, 204, 205
Aphrodite, 41, 43-45, 47, 50, 58, 61, 63, 70, 72-74, 78, 79, 86, 120, 124, 128, 175n., 182, 191, Chapter X *passim*, 296
Apis, 60
Apollo, 48, 291
Apollonius of Tyana, 145
Aquinas, St. Thomas, 32, 161, 255
Ares (Mars), 72-74, 79, 120, 124, 128, 155
Aristotle, 95, 121, 161, 250, 251, 255, 256
Artemis, 115-21, 123, 124, 127, 128, 268, 273, 276-79, 281; *see also* Delia, Diana
Astyages, 56, 59, 60, 65, 67
atasal, 263, 280n., 289

Atreus, House of, 75, 101, 267; *see also Agamemnon*
Atti, Isotta degli, 92, 142, 261, 271
Avicenna, 156n.

Bacchus, 200; *see also* Dionysus, Zagreus
Baha'ism, 170
Bank of England, 170
Bank of the United States, 137, 139
bank war, American, 139, 140, 160
Barabello, 76
"Battle Hymn of the Republic," 275
Baudelaire, 259
Baumann, Walter, 56n.
Beardsley, Aubrey, 257
Beckett, Samuel, 5
Bede, the Venerable, 297
Biddle's Bank (Second Bank of the United States), 139
Bion, 175, 182
Blake, William, 56n.
Book of Rites, The, see *Li Ki*
Borgia, Alessandro, 129, 131
Borgia, Cesare, 60, 65, 130, 131
Borgia, Giovanni, 60, 65, 66, 69, 74, 75, 125, 258
Borgia, Lucrezia, 126-29
Born, Bertran de, 74
Botticelli, Sandro, 254, 279, 281n.
Briffault, Robert S., 106n.
Brooke-Rose, Christine, 47n.
Browning, Robert, 19, 52, 84, 258; *see also Sordello*
Buddhism, 225

Maensac, Pieire de, 64, 65, 70, 105
Maia, 272, 273
major form
definition of, 3
in the *Cantos*, 27ff.
Malatesta, Lucrezia, 257
Malatesta, Sigismundo, 40, 85, 92,
93, 98, 102, 113, 141, 142,
168, 207, 226, 257n.; *see also*
Tempio Malatestiano
Mandane, 56, 58
Manicheans, 106
Mars, *see* Ares
Marx, Karl, 135
Matter, 111, 112, 128, 129
Matthiessen, F. O., 140, 289n.
Maupassant, Guy de, 76
Maximilian I, 220
Mayo, Robert, 37n.
McLuhan, Marshall, 130
Medes, the, 55
Medici, Alessandro de', 65-69, 88,
89
Medici, Lorenzo de', 65-68, 89
Mencius, 198
metamorphosis, theme of, 47, 100
Meyerhoff, Hans, 21, 46n.
Middle Ages, 52, 73
Milton, John, 32, 80
Moby Dick, 31
Montaigne, Michel de, 31
Monte dei Paschi, 140, 166, 167
Montfort, Simon de, 106, 106n.
Mozarello, 66, 76
Mussolini, Benito, 40, 140, 141,
160, 161, 166, 243

Napoleon, 140, 152, 153, 216
nature, concept of, 28, 30, 43, 123
Nekuia, 37, 39, 40, 173, 174, 177,
182, 187, 257, 295
Nemesis, 50, 56, 129
Neoplatonism, 57, 60, 76, 88, 95,
96, 109, 121, 128, 156, 197,
207, 256
Nilsson, Martin P., 181n., 183n.

Odysseus, 4, 16, 37-42, 44, 47, 92,
141, 162-64, 173ff., 193, 195,
196, 244, 247n., 249, 253, 255,
275, 281, 295

Odyssey, the, 37, 41, 162, 174,
195n.
Ovid, 47n., 48, 71, 72, 74, 121

Paphos, 107, 116, 124
Pearson, Norman Holmes, 151n.
Penelope, 163, 180
Pentheus, 48
periplum, 239
Persephone, *see* Proserpine
Perseus, 55, 56
Philostratus, Flavius, 145
Phraortes, 56
Plarr, Victor, 247, 247n.
Plato, 57, 58, 96, 122, 256, 271
Pleiades, 181-83, 186, 190, 273
Plethon, Gemistus, 57, 95, 98, 104,
273
Plotinus, 57, 60, 155, 156
Poicebot, 64
Pope Alexander VI, 126, 129, 131
Pope Innocent III, 106, 106n.
Pope Julius II, 220
Pope Pius II, 93, 102, 226
Porphyry, 104
Pound, Ezra, Works of
ABC of Reading, 105n., 113,
116n.
A *Lume Spento*, 264
Antheil, 204
"Blandula, Tenulla, Vagula," 61
Cantos 1-30 (A *Draft of XXX
Cantos*), 15
Canto 1: 37-45, 70, 164, 176,
191, 247n.
Canto 2: 47, 48-50, 70, 159, 207
Canto 3: 51-53, 100, 108
Canto 4: 53-57, 63, 69, 70, 169
Canto 5: 47, 52, 57-67, 68-70,
74, 75, 86, 88, 89, 95, 101,
105, 114, 120, 122, 125, 206,
258
Canto 6: 70
Canto 7: 67, 68-90, 99, 101,
108, 111, 114, 120, 122, 125,
127n., 256, 266
Cantos 8-11 (The Malatesta
Cantos), 92
Canto 8: 94, 95, 101, 272
Canto 11: 28
Canto 12: 47, 99, 129